THE DIVINE ONE

Andrea Comer

Copyright © 2021 by Andrea Comer.

All rights reserved. No part of this publication may be reproduced, distributed or transmitted in any form or by any means, including photocopying, recording, or other electronic or mechanical methods, without the prior written permission of the publisher, except in the case of brief quotations embodied in critical reviews and certain other noncommercial uses permitted by copyright law.

Book Layout ©2013 BookDesignTemplates.com

The Divine One / Andrea Comer. -- 1st ed.
ISBN: 978-0-9953904-5-4

This book is dedicated to all mine Aunties and Uncles. I lubs you all- The Divine One.

CONTENTS

Introduction   1

Chapter one
Tongue Pug   9

Chapter two
Peanut In A Baseball Mitt   25

Chapter three
Just The Way You Are   45

Chapter four
Settling In   67

Chapter five
First Vet Visit   93

Chapter six
Altering The Walk   115

Chapter seven
The Divine One   139

Chapter eight
Brenda   157

Chapter nine
Glue   183

Chapter ten
No Sight No Worries   203

Chapter eleven
Blueberries, Strawberries and Carrot
Juice Oh My   217

Chapter twelve
Coats   247

Chapter thirteen
Sounds Of A Happy Home   271

Chapter fourteen
Delicate Little Flower   293

Chapter fifteen
Bunnings   319

Chapter sixteen
Ho Ho Nooooo   341

Chapter seventeen
Feisty Pink Princess   365

Chapter eighteen
Strokes					395

Chapter nineteen
Changing With The Times		425

Chapter twenty
This Is Not The End			455

Chapter twenty-one
A Glimpse Of Heaven			479

INTRODUCTION

To be honest it does seem a bit strange to start writing this book without my littlest writing buddy beside me. Amber was right here next to me while I wrote the first three books and I loved having her nearby. She would sleep on my leg, her tiny grey face using my knee for a chin rest, eyes shut tight, little tongue peeping out, velvety ears twitching occasionally. If she wasn't resting on my leg then she'd be in a little nest beside me. She would often bring her paw up to rest underneath her chin, looked a bit like she was sucking her thumb at these times, Grace used to do that same thing and both of them looked adorable doing it. Amber also used to curl up in a certain way when she was in her nest and at those times she really reminded me of a field mouse. Like those pictures I'd seen in storybooks as a child, cute little field mice curled up in balls in peaceful slumber, well ok Amber couldn't quite curl herself up into a perfect ball shape due to how her back was, but the angle of her body, the look on her face, that little paw brought up to her chin certainly sent my mind back to those pictures I'd seen. There were days when I spent just as much time watching The Divine One sleeping as I did writing, she looked so beautiful huffing and puffing away in a contented sleep, watching Amber sleep always brought me a huge amount of happiness.

And I guess you'd be thinking that I'd be full of sadness now embarking on this book, her book, without her. But the honest truth is that I am not. Of course I miss her with all my heart and wish she was still here but The Divine One lived a good and very long life and I am going to really enjoy telling you her story because the story I am about to tell you is one of a tiny pug that to me was a hero. A little battler who beat the odds and went on to live to an age many didn't expect her to reach and how can I be anything but proud and overjoyed about that. So this is what will be echoed throughout these pages because anything less would be doing The Divine One a huge dishonour. I am going to smile as I write her book and you would be doing Amber proud if you were smiling too because that would be a great legacy for one so dear to leave. Also if at any moment you want to put this book down and applaud The Divine One, well I think that would be a very fitting thing to do. I know this because it's exactly what I found myself doing quite a few times while writing my little love's story. I clapped for Amber a real lot when she was here on the farm so it just seemed very natural to me to be clapping for her now when reliving these memories. And did I ever feel silly pausing mid-sentence and clapping, no I did not, not even for one second. Yes I did disturb a few of the pugs that were sleeping by my side but they quickly settled down to sleep once they'd looked around to see who it was I was clapping for. They realised it wasn't them I was looking at but the screen in front of me so heads would go down just as quickly as they had sprung up and I would finish clapping and carry on typing. You will notice that there are a real lot of photos in this book, more photos then I have ever put in a book before and that's because I wanted The Divine One's gorgeous little face sprinkled all throughout these pages. Also there are some photos that I call a series of photos and they are the ones I took one after the other, I've put them in the order I took them because by doing this I felt it would be like you were actually here watching what I was watching, seeing what I was seeing, witnessing this lovely photogenic blessing in action. I've started the book with one of the photo series because really what better way to start her book then by glimpsing her perfect face. You'll notice that I have ended the book with a series of photos too, a series of photos that are especially close to my heart. And so without further ado allow me to proudly present to you my little Divine One.

CHAPTER ONE

Tongue Pug

Amber's pound photo

It was April 2011 and I was browsing a pound web page when a photo caught my eye. I was not really looking for another dog, I think I was just mainly trying to get myself through another day and playing around on the internet was a good way of distracting myself from my thoughts. My life was very upside down at that point. I was in bad shape emotionally, totally heartbroken and in many ways disconnected, my days were really not my days anymore. Of course my structure and routine was very much the same as it had always been because it had to be for the pugs, but me, myself, well I was very much out of sorts. All I was doing at that point was trying as best I could to hold myself together and look after the pugs I had left. I was only twelve weeks or so out from the heartbreaking loss of Ruby, Grace and Horton and I was still a bit of a mess. I was having a lot of trouble coping with the loss, adjusting to the emptiness, dealing with the sadness that had now become my life and not really doing a very good job of it. Things were pretty hard for me back then, the loss of Horton was especially difficult, I was the worst I've ever been when losing a pug. I was still heavily grieving, my heart was in so much pain. The days passed in a haze of sadness, tears and much mind torment. There were not very many hours that I felt happiness or even smiled. The only things that did bring any joy to me were the pugs and their antics, they were coping with the aftermath a lot better than I was, they were the little lights in my darkest saddest hours, the things that kept me going. They were very much the reasons I got up in the morning because they needed to be walked, fed and looked after, so it was for them that I pushed forward. But a lot of the time I was still not really knowing what to do with myself and as for continuing rescuing well I hadn't made up my mind what I was going to do about that yet. I had days where I knew that I was going to keep doing that which my heart had always been drawn to and then there'd be days when I thought "No, no, I'm done it hurts too much to lose them I just cannot do this anymore". I suppose I was dealing with a lot at the time. So much had gone on. My life had changed very fast and very painfully. It was hard to cope with that and make a decision about rescuing. Some days I would be saying to David that I'll see these pugs through then that'll be it for me, I'm out of the recuing game. And he'd nod his head and say whatever I wanted to do he would support me in it. He has always been really good like that, leaving the choice entirely up to me. Because I am the main care giver, the bulk of the work is done by me so I suppose that's another reason why he didn't say anything. I guess in his mind he had a way he wanted things to go but never told me, never tried to sway me, or maybe he too was having the same thoughts I was having going through his head. Maybe he too was wanting to give it all up one day then the very next day be still intending to carry on. I truly don't think either one of us was in the right place emotionally to make a choice about our future because we were both still reeling from all the loss.

 At that point in time my days were spent in pretty much the same way. I would do whatever I needed to do for the pugs then sit and stare into space, not really knowing what else to do with myself. Two of the pugs I had lost were in need of a lot of looking after, constant monitoring. Ruby needed a lot of extra care towards the end of her life and then there was little Horton, he needed twenty four hour looking after and watching and observing. You could never not have your mind on Horton, you always had to be well aware of where he was and what he needed. Grace well, she was the oldest but she was very agile, very healthy, very little needed to be done for her, she had no special needs, no illness, just an all-round healthy active old darling really but Horton and Ruby were different, they needed me for a lot things and then all of a sudden in the course of twenty four hours they were both gone. Everything came to an abrupt stop. The level of care, the happiness in looking after Horton and being around him, the tinkle trousers, one in the wash, one on him, one ready to go on him and one drying. It all ended and that was very hard to live through. I knew Horton was gone, boy did I know he was gone and yet I'd still be looking at the clock for when I had to next check his nappy, then I'd realize I didn't need to keep an eye on the clock all the time anymore. There was no reason to do so and yet I kept doing it for a few more months until it finally sunk in. And so now I had all this free time, too much time on my hands really and not knowing what to do with all this spare time I had. I guess that's what made me get out the computer on that particular day. I suppose I was just sick of sitting on that porch staring at nothing with my mind going from raging and racing to being numb and a blur. I guess at some point during the morning I had decided that going on the computer would be a good thing to do and really it was a very good thing to have done, a life changing thing to have done but of course I didn't know it at the time. I had thought of going on a real estate site and looking at all the pretty houses. I like looking at beautiful homes that are way beyond our reach, I love looking at great architecture and nice furniture and carpets and curtains that match. I figured a bit of doing that would be a good enough way to whittle away the hours until it was time to give the pugs their midday walk. But when I got online for some reason I went straight to the pound page, probably a force of habit if anything because I had just remembered it was Monday, I always skipped through the pound websites on Monday morning as a lot of dogs get brought into pounds over the weekend.

Back then I was getting calls from people looking for certain breeds of dogs to adopt and so I would take down their details then try and match them with a dog who was sitting in a pound, over the years I had been successful in bringing a lot of dogs and families together and it was always nice to be able to do that. At the time it was a little hobby I had on the side, I don't have nearly anywhere the time I used to have these days but I still dabble in it a little bit because I like doing it. I mean if I can help a dog get out of a pound and into a loving family I am all for it. I'd just finished with one site when I clicked over to the next one. There were three pages of dogs on this particular pound site and Amber being one of the newest arrivals she was on the first page. I saw this beautiful little face, a gorgeous pug with its tongue hanging out. I had an instant reaction to her. It was like my heart instantly leapt up and came softly floating back down again. I felt an enormous surge and I thought to myself "Oh look at you darling, look at you". But that little face did look so terribly frightened and she didn't look well. Pound shots to me are like mug shots. Nobody looks good in them but this little girl looked to be so uncomfortable. I could tell from her eyes that she couldn't see very much with them, she had that dark pigmentation and I'd shared my life with enough blind pugs to know what that meant. The biggest part of me knew in that quick instant that I had just found my new daughter. But I was also a little bit confused and hesitant, me not being my normal self was clouding what I was actually feeling I think, and that's what brought about those emotions. That is what stopped me from jumping right in. In the past after feeling a surge like that I would have already had the phone in my hand and been dialing a number but instead I sat quietly for a little while. Looked out the window, looked at the few pugs gathered by my feet. My body was still but my mind was ticking over.

I turned back around and looked at Amber's photo a bit longer then clicked on the details, found out she was a girl and having always had a soft spot for little old ladies I then went on to look at her age and what her release date was. She was listed as being seven years old. I glanced at her face and thought to myself either they've got the age wrong or this little soul has had seven very hard years on this earth. She looked older than seven to me, not a lot older but she definitely did not have the face of a seven year old pug. Because she had only just arrived in the pound she had to stay there for two weeks, that's the law, it's done in order to give owners time to come and get their dog if that's what they want to do. Not all dogs who end up in the pound are dumped, some go missing, get lost, escape from back gardens and there can be loving owners desperately searching for them and not everybody thinks to contact their local pound right away, they are out there searching the streets and putting up flyers and then and only then do their minds wander to the pound. These days things are a lot easier because of compulsory microchipping, these days lost dogs can be scanned, owners quickly rung and dogs and their families can be reunited within a few hours of going missing, but that law only came into effect a few years ago. At the time I saw Amber's photo not all dogs were being microchipped so pounds would be full of lost souls with no identification.

I remember there was a terrier cross in the same pound as Amber. He was a few photos over from her. Seeing him jogged my mind so I pulled out the exercise book from my desk drawer and began flipping through it. I found the lady who'd contacted me in no time at all. It was easy to do because I would always highlight the breed to make things easier and faster, there were a lot of names in that book and you would have to spend an hour or more trying to fit the dog to the call if you didn't have some kind of system in order. I checked the date the call came through, it was about five weeks back, so I sent off a quick email to the lady who was interested in a terrier. I added a photo to the email as well because although the lady specified she wanted a purebred silky this little dog was just the cutest thing and I thought if she saw a photo she may change her mind about a purebred and give this little soul a home. In the end she didn't take him but another lady I knew did and they went on to have many lovely happy years together.

I went into the kitchen to freshen up the pug's water bowl then walked back into the study and sat and looked at Amber's photo once more. She looked adorable with her little tongue hanging out and well I've always been a sucker for a tongue pug. I enlarged the photo and looked at her face more closely. I looked at her eyes again, the enlarged photo allowed me to see them more clearly, her eyes looked dry to me and yes definitely not much vision there, they never stated the lack of vison in the details, they never do, age, sex and release dates is about all the information they give out. I looked more closely at those old black eyes trying to guess the amount of vision she would have. I guessed about 20 or 30% but that could have been me being generous and of course I would only be able to find out for sure when I met her. A lot of pugs suffer from dry eyes and it's very uncomfortable for them, the corneal pigmentation often comes because their owners don't notice that their eyes are dry so don't think to put drops in and the poor little things start rubbing their eyes to get some relief, rub them with their paws, rub them against walls or furniture. Just doing anything to make the chronic irritation stop and this could have been going on for years with their owners not noticing or if they do notice they have no idea why their dog is acting that way and some don't bother to find out. A quick trip to the vet could solve things and a few drops administered a few times a day will keep the eyes well lubricated and glossy, save vision too. But of course if this doesn't happen and the dog is left to fend for him or herself they end up with pigmentary keratitis and with pigmentation comes loss of vison. Seeing Amber there in a pound in that state was hard. I always wish pound staff would carry lubricating eye drops with them so they can give the dogs in their care a bit of relief but I guess they are too overrun to be able to render such things. Sure it'd only take a few moments but I don't believe they have those few moments to spare and that is a very sad state of affairs. I went and made a few phone calls and answered a few emails but my mind wasn't on them, it should have been but it wasn't, it kept reverting back to the tongue pug. I just couldn't get that image of her out of my head. It was as if she was calling out to me. I made another call and as I was talking I once again brought Amber's little face up on the screen in front of me. I pulled it up while listening to the lady I was speaking to prattling on and on. This lady was a good talker, could hold an entire conversation by herself, not much input needed from me ever, so in a way she was the most perfect person I could have called that morning because it gave me lots of time to think about other things. I hung up from that call and looked closely at Amber, leant closer to the screen and really studied her. I was still umming and ahhing, mind whirling wondering what to do "Jump, don't jump" still not 100% certain and then I thought to myself "I'm ringing, I have to ring" so I picked up the phone and rang a friend of mine who lives in the same state the pound was in. I asked her if she could take a look at this little pug for me, being in rescue I knew this friend went to that pound a few times a week. She said "Are you interested in her for yourself Andrea? The question caught me off guard because for the past few months if I had rung her at all it was due to a dog for somebody else. Even if it was a pug it was somebody else I was ringing for, somebody who had told me the age and sex of the pug they wanted to adopt. The last few times I'd talked to this friend of mine she'd never asked me this question and I thought it funny that this time she did. Maybe my voice sounded different today to how it had done of late. Perhaps that's why she'd asked. This lady knew I'd lost Horton, Ruby and Grace and she knew Arthur was just recovering from his recent back surgery. She had walked down those paths with me and had been a great source of love and support throughout it all. She also knew I was still doing therapy exercises with Arthur every day to help with his recovery, to help him be all he could be and she was well aware of how much he was fighting me on this. Him not being cooperative made the sessions all the harder, far harder than they needed to be that's for sure. She had rung me once during one of our sessions and I was telling her all about his disinclination and we were laughing about it, laughing that he had such a huge spirit that he was up to doing such a thing so soon after having major and quite tricky back surgery. It showed what Arthur had inside of him and what he had inside of him was going to make all the difference in the world to his recovery. At this point Arthur still had a long road ahead but I knew he was going to get there due to the incredible amount of willpower and determination he had. Arthur was probably laughing too because I had to release him in order to answer the phone so he got out of the rest of that therapy session because once I'd finished talking I'd gone off to do something else for one of the other pugs and it wasn't until I grabbed him up again for his next session that I realised we hadn't completed his earlier set. I think Arthur battling with me wasn't the worst thing in the world because it gave me something to concentrate on other than how I was feeling. It took me out of myself and I needed to be taken out of myself. I was trying to do better on a daily basis but failing miserably a lot of the time and I was very much aware of that. But I knew I had to put those feelings aside while I was helping Arthur. For his sake I needed to fully concentrate on what I was doing in order to do those exercises properly and not hurt him. I couldn't have my mind on anything else besides how I was positioning his legs and counting down each set of exercises, his recovery was very important so I sort of put those feelings somewhere else while I took care of him but as soon as I finished they quickly came back again. It was like I put them on a shelf as I walked into the room with Arthur tucked under my arm then just as I was about to walk back through the door again I reached up and slapped them back on my shoulders. I was doing those exercise with Arthur six times a day, the surgeon said four would be good six would be better and so I would do them six times even though Arthur wasn't at all impressed with that. The exercise sessions were not lengthy, over and done with in a about five minutes or so, it wasn't about length of time it was more about regularity, keeping him limber, keeping those muscles moving and slowly building up strength. So I did get those few minutes of relief throughout the day and that was a good thing for me to do. But the exercises were quick and so I would be right back where I had been once they were over.

"Are you interested in this girl for yourself are you Andrea? The question was asked again because I guess I must have been taking a while answering, either that or she thought due to the line I'd not herd what she had said the first time. I paused for a moment still thinking about what my answer would be and then I heard myself saying "Yes I most certainly am" and without hesitation she said "Great, ok, let's see what we can do" I knew she was very busy, she is the founder of a large and incredibly well run rescue group here in Australia and yet she didn't let on how busy she was, instead she set about securing Amber for me and I was so grateful to her for doing that. She said she'd ring a friend of hers who lived close to the pound then quickly hung up the phone. From the background noise I could tell she was on the road but pulled over and made the call to secure Amber. When she rang back she said that her friend had put her name down to buy Amber if the owners didn't show up, the way the pound system works is that private buyers get first option over rescue groups. She said "If she doesn't go home we will definitely get her" I smiled and said "Oh thank goodness" I now knew that no matter how many people walked through that pound and gazed upon that sweet little face there was nothing they could do about it, nobody from the general public or any other rescue group could get their hands on Amber now. The only person who would be able to do that would be her legal owners. But you know what, I wasn't worried about that happening at all because I just had this sense from that very first phone call that Amber was mine, that they were not coming for her. I guess I would have had the shock of my life if they had actually turned up, but I had this deep sense that Amber was already my daughter, I just hadn't met her yet.

Me and my rescue friend talked about a few other dogs for a little while. She had named one of her rescue dogs Horton in honour of my boy and she told me that he had just been adopted out. Again I caught myself smiling, I felt happy that this other Horton now had a forever home. It was a good home she told me, pug people they were, she knew them well because they had adopted another dog from her a few years ago. And I guess when they were ready to add to their family they once again contacted her rescue group. Once all the dogs had been talked about we caught up on what was happening in our personal life. Then we were straight back to talking about Amber. I told her I was a sucker for a tongue pug. She asked what a tongue pug was thinking it was a special type of pug, something she hadn't heard of before, but I told her that it was just my terminology. That's what I always call pugs whose tongues hang out of their mouths all the time. She laughed and I was saying to her that I wondered if Amber's tongue hung out permanently or if it was just like that in the photo. Pound photos, well all photos really, are just a quick record of a single moment in time. For all I knew that little girl could have merely been flicking her tongue around and soon as the photo was over it had shot back inside her mouth again where it stayed most of the time. Harpers tongue hung out of her mouth all the time and I loved that about her and when I lost her I really missed having a face like that around the place. When I saw Amber's face and tongue I thought to myself do I dive in and get this little old darling or do I hold back and heal a bit more first, give myself some more time to think about what I really wanted to do as far as keeping on rescuing was concerned. It was like do I jump in with both feet right this instant or do I turn around and walk the other way. Also, did I have the right to bring another little soul into my life when I was still in such a distraught state? Could I rise to the challenge and give Amber the best life possible and love her with all my heart while I was in this much despair. Was I being fair to her, she deserved all of me and could I give that to her right now, to be honest I wasn't totally sure that I could, wasn't sure that my heart was ready. But the thing was Amber was ready, she was there waiting, I had to make a quick decision, if I had waited another month or two months or for however long it was going to take for me to heal then Amber would have been lost to me forever and I knew I couldn't let that happen. There was way too much of a connection there. She was already important to me, I hadn't even met her and yet she was already very important to me, far too important to let slip through my fingers that's for sure. And so I guess I let that lead me. That's why I set things in motion and made the call.

At this point David knew nothing about it. I hadn't even told my husband I was about to contact a friend in rescue about a pug, normally that's exactly what I would have done, he is usually the first person I call before going any further, but not on this occasion. I guess I didn't want to waste any time, I wanted to get a hold put on this little old girl as soon as possible, so I suppose my mind was already very much made up when I picked up the phone, I just didn't 100% know it or feel it. Then again such things were not something new for me since losing Horton. I was like that about a lot of things during that time, muddy minded, not much clarity, mind too much on thinking about so many things and feeling so many emotions, roller coasting my way through life and not being able to put the brakes on and the waves of complete and utter sadness and loss of control washing over me all the time. But even though that's where I was at and how I was feeling I still picked up the phone and made that call, something made me want to do it. Was it her face or was it her tongue, probably a bit of both, with the tongue slightly in the lead because to be honest if she hadn't had her tongue peeping out I may have not started the ball rolling at all. I may have merely shut the computer down and that would have been the end of it. But I believe I was meant get on the computer exactly when I did, I was meant to see the pug with the tongue, I was meant to have this enormous pull towards her, a pull so strong and so powerful that even in my darkest hour I couldn't stop myself from acting on it. I think if I had procrastinated any longer she would have gone to somebody else and on finding that out I would have been completely devastated, filled with regret for the remainder of my days. With Amber I felt I had to be her Mum that was the biggest part of everything going on here, the biggest part of everything I was feeling. I wanted so very badly to be this little girl's mother, I needed to be her mother, I knew she was meant to be part of my life. Of course at the time I had no idea how big of an impact The Divine One was going to have on my life. All I knew back then was that every time I looked at her photo I felt a feeling so strong that it could not be denied and to this day I am very glad I made that call. Before my friend hung up the phone she told me that she was going to the pound in a day or so and would go have a look at the tongue pug then ring me afterwards and tell me all about her. I thanked her once again for her help, honestly I have lost count of the amount of times this lady has helped me, been there for me, looked after me and gone out of her way for me, I owe her an enormous amount of thanks. She says she never needs thanking but the truth of the matter is this, I am incredibly grateful to have her in my life. She isn't just a dog rescue friend she was a true friend when I really needed one the most. When David was going through everything at the hospital and what they did to him in there. She told me what to do to get the help we needed, David was in no position to help himself, he was in a pretty bad way and I, in never having to deal with anything like this before was worried sick but this beautiful friend parted the clouds and advised me on what I needed to do next, told me the path I should take and made a very stressful situation less so with her knowledge and advice and I can't thank her enough for doing that.

After Amber was secured I sat at my desk in my office chair and spun round and round a few times thinking about our new pug. I was picturing her here, picturing her walking around the farm with her little tongue peeping out and I was smiling to myself about it. But on the fifth or sixth spin I realised that I really needed to stop daydreaming and ring my husband right away to tell him exactly how I had spent my morning. So I quickly picked up the phone and rang David at work, he answered on the first ring which told me he had time to talk. "Dave" I said getting really excited now "We are back in the pug rescuing business" he paused for a few seconds, it seemed like a lot longer because I was a bit nervous wondering what his reaction would be, but in reality it was only a second or two of complete silence and then he let out the biggest laugh then listened intently as I told him all about his new daughter.

CHAPTER TWO

Peanut In A Baseball Mitt

Amber at the airport

I heard back from my rescue friend a few days later, she rang in the afternoon saying that she'd been to the pound that morning and had a look at the pug. "She's only little Andrea" and I said "Nice". I had no idea she was small because I couldn't tell that from the photograph, to me this was an added bonus really. "Her eyes were full of pus when she came in" I sat quietly and listened as she spoke. "This little old girl looks to have been quite neglected" my heart felt sad at hearing this but I kind of knew it was the case. I could tell that from her photo. "She is microchipped" I had no reaction to this, I should have done because that would mean the owners details were on record and they would have already been contacted. But I didn't have any response at all, no fear of losing Amber, no worrying about her not coming to me, instead I stood staring out the window at the front paddock in a very peaceful and relaxed manner. "But the details are out of date" I said "Ok" as a way of letting her know I'd heard what she had just told me. "Her eyes look very dry to me" I said "Yes they are" she responded, "Andrea if I lived closer I would take Optimune in and ask them to put it in her eyes twice a day as her eyes are very sore. But they may not have time to do it unfortunately" I said that she'd be fine in that area once she got to me. I was very well used to taking care of sore little eyes. I talked about the microchip details being out of date, said that I thought she was older then the seven years they had put on the internet. She said she felt Amber was older then that as well. She then went on to tell me that she was in regular contact with a lady who worked at the pound and that this lady was watching over Amber and taking care of her. I was glad to hear that because it sounded like Amber really needed to have somebody doing that for her, helping her until she got to me. I honestly think that if Amber had gone into the pound in the middle of winter that she would not have survived, in fact I'm positive of it. Also as fate would have it Amber was in one of the better pounds, the runs were quite good I had been told and also the smaller breeds were kept indoors. And things like this can make all the difference in the world when it comes to little old dogs that have been neglected. It was then mentioned about Amber not being desexed, to be honest I hadn't picked up on that when looking at her details and you would think I would have done as that is a big thing to overlook. "She's never had a litter though, never been bred with" I was pretty happy to hear that news because she was way too small for breeding, the first litter could have possibly killed her.

I think everybody involved with Amber must have felt the same way I did about her owners not coming because we started talking about having her desexed as soon as she was released from the pound. "Andrea I am going to get my own vet to do the operation" I was quite relieved to hear this as I felt it would be a lot better to get a trusted vet to do the job. My mind instantly went back to a dog I had rescued from a pound many years ago, the stitched area became infected, I don't know if it was due to a careless vet or unhygienic conditions. But the image of the swollen weeping wound shot instantly into my head and I didn't want such a thing happening to precious little Amber. "I've been using this vet for many years" said told me. "All my rescued dogs go to him" well that spoke volumes to me, that was all I needed to hear in order to feel secure, it would mean Amber would be in safe hands and I could relax a bit more. Sure I would still have the regular concerns about an older dog having surgery but I would be more concerned if she was being operated on in a pound in time stretched poor conditions. And to be completely honest I felt she had spent enough time in the pound already, getting her out of there was what I most wanted to do. Being operated on by my friend's vet meant she was going to receive the time, care and attention she both needed and deserved. This little pug may have been neglected in her previous life but she sure did have a whole lot of people taking really good care of her now. By the time Amber's release date came around my rescue friend had eight puppies in her home and couldn't risk them coming into contact with a dog that had spent time in a pound. She said she'd have the pound staff put Amber in a crate at their end and the vet nurses take her out at the other. That way she was not going to spread anything to these tiny puppies, much care always has to be taken when you are dealing with dogs that have spent time in the pound system and very young puppies. You have to make sure that babies that are too young to have had all their shots completed don't catch anything from a sick dog that may have been dumped in the pound. Amber could have been an innocent carrier of illness so my friend was taking the proper precautions. It's like you wouldn't take a new born baby into a flu ward at a hospital it's just basic common sense.

Then we got around to discussing costs. She knew we were still paying off Horton's enormous vet bill and she knew a few weeks after losing Horton that Arthur had undergone a hugely expensive back surgery. In a matter of seven weeks we had been hit with over fifteen thousand dollars' worth of vet bills. My friend knew were we struggling so out of the goodness of her heart said that she would pay Amber's pound fee and also cover the cost of desexing and that I could pay her back whenever I was able to do so. She said she didn't mind how long it took either. I guess she knew we were poor but she also knew we were honest, we would never have not paid what we owed. "Andrea do you want me to cover the cost of the flight down as well" she asked. I felt slightly embarrassed but answered that yes it'd be great if she could do that for us. She said "No worriers" and reminded me again that we could take as long as we needed to pay her back. I was incredibly grateful to her for doing that for us because it meant we didn't have to add any more money to the already overstretched credit card. We could just keep ploughing away at our vet bills until they were all sorted out and then we would be able to pay for Amber. It took us many, many months to pay off our debt but during that time Amber was here with us, she was settling in, by the time we fully paid my friend what we owed Amber was very much part of our family. So it all turned out pretty well. Amber was going to have a full dental work done at the time of her desexing. It makes sense to do everything while they are knocked out, saves having to put them under more than once which is always important but especially so when you are dealing with a pug. As it happened Amber did need to have a few teeth pulled. Her operation had to be postponed for a day though due to the vet surgery being busy but the nurses did give Amber a much needed bath and a capstar flea capsule and she was put in a cage in a nice warm room with a lovely soft blanket while she was waiting for her surgery. She'd been given a delicious meal as well I'd been told and gulped it down at lightning speed. Once again this needy little girl was being so beautifully taken care of and I bet after the neglect she had been used to she would have been lapping all this goodness up. She may have been at a vet surgery but to Amber I think it would have been like five star accommodation. The next morning she was desexed and my friend called me as soon as the operation was over. "She's fine Andrea, surgery went well, not sure how many teeth she had pulled but

I think it was quite a few" and that was it as far as that conversation went, being busy she rushed off the phone, but that was fine, those few words about Amber being ok were all I needed to hear, they were what I had been waiting for. I quickly rang David at work and told him the news. Amber stayed with the vet for a few days while she recovered from having the surgery. It was coming up to Easter and as anybody involved in animal rescue knows Easter and Christmas are the busiest times of the year, it's when pounds overflow with dogs being dumped due to owners wanting to go on holidays. Personally I've never quite understood this, I don't know if it's done because they don't want to pay for their dog to be boarded at a kennel while they are away or if they just think to themselves that this is as good a time as any to get rid of the family dog. I seriously do not know how they can dump their dog then get in the car or onto an aero plane and not give what they have done a second thought. They are off having a good time while that poor dog is in a pound pen wondering what the hell just happened. I do believe that some people dump them knowing they have two weeks to go and get them back again and if their holiday is less than two weeks then they can just go and claim their dog before it gets adopted out or put to sleep. No cost of a boarding kennel involved then, just two faced owners turning up saying their dog got out of the yard while the next door neighbour was feeding it. I wonder how many times pound staff have heard such stories.

My friend rang and asked if I would like her to send Amber down to me before Easter, if not she could go and stay with one of her foster carers for a week or so, have her stitches taken out and then be sent down after that. I thought about it for a few moments. Thought about how well Amber had handled the operation, if she went into foster care it would have meant mucking her around a bit, have her settling in there and then being moved on again. I had been getting regular updates on how she was going and she was doing great. During one of the updates I was told that the vet who did the desexing put Amber's age at nine and that seemed about right to me. Later on our own vet would put her at the same age. He looked in her mouth and said "I'd say she'd be about nine, I don't think she's any older than that" And that was good enough for us, two trusted vets put her age at nine so nine it was. I wasn't worried about Amber coming down with stitches because I knew we would deal with having them taken out when it was time. I was just wondering if she would be ok with the flight. So I said "Ask your vet what he thinks, if he clears her for flying then yes I would really love to have her come down before Easter, if not then it'd be best to leave her where she is, give her a bit more time to come good". But I was really hoping to have her arrive before Easter, in my mind that would be perfect because David would be having a few days off work over the Easter break, the whole family could be together while Amber was settling in. He always likes to be home for a few days when we have somebody new joining our family and so whenever possible we always try and work it that way. A phone call came through a little while later saying the vet didn't think there was any reason why Amber couldn't be put on a plane. I was happy to hear this, glad she was doing well, overjoyed that she would be arriving sooner rather than later. My friend said "It'll be hard on her but it will be over in no time" And she was right about that, the plane to Melbourne takes only one hour but the dogs have to be there an hour before the plane leaves in order to get boarded. But we would do everything in our power to make the day as easy as possible for Amber. "I will make sure she goes into the bigger crate and is comfortable" my friend said then paused and added "At least the weather is cooler now" I said yes it was. We were just coming out of a very hot dry summer. I wouldn't have wanted Amber being sent down during that heat, being a snub nosed breed the last thing you want is them being exposed to high temperatures. You worry about them until they are safely in your arms, you worry because of airport staff not realising they are dealing with dogs that cannot tolerate heat very well, you worry about them being left sitting out on tarmacs. Things like that play on my mind whenever I am flying a pug in.

Amber was on both antibiotic tablets and Optimmune but medication cannot be sent down in the crate with them in case they accidently eat it. So Amber was given an antibiotic injection to cover her for a few days and her medication was sent to us through the mail. But being Easter it would mean the medication would take a while to get here, it would have taken a while anyway but due to Good Friday and Easter Monday being public holidays it would mean that it'd take even longer. Not having any Optimmune in the house at the time was fine, we had plenty of lubricating eye drops here that we could keep putting in until the other meds showed up. Amber was the first one of our pugs to be put on Optimmune, we'd never used it before but boy are we used to using it now, at one time we had five pugs that needed to be on it and it is very expensive for such a small tube. But if they need it you get it for them, end of story really, it's called looking after your dog. I was glad she was given an antibiotic injection because the last thing I wanted was for her stitches to become infected.

David was working on the day Amber was flying in. She was to arrive late afternoon. He went straight from work to collect her. He asked me if I wanted to go with him but I said no. And there were two reasons for that, him having to come all the way back to the farm to collect me than double back seemed like an awful lot of extra driving for him to be doing and he already had quite a trip to make as it was. The other reason I said no was because of how I was feeling. At the time I was staying pretty close to home. After losing Horton I hid away from the world, retreated to the farm because that's where I felt safest, it was my healing place. I felt far too broken to go out and be amongst people. Looking back I really wish I had of gone, wish I'd been there to witness that little blessing being unloaded. Been right there to scoop her up in my arms and smother her with kisses. Tell her what a good brave girl she was for getting on a plane. But at the time I couldn't do it. I think in times like this we do our best, you are not in a normal place when you are grieving so you do the best you can do and when you can do better you do better. It's just how it is with grief and trauma and everybody copes differently, copes with it in their own way. I felt a large airport with all those people was far too much for me to deal with back then. The last thing I needed was to have rude self-centered people pushing and shoving because they were rushing to catch their plane, I was hurting so badly on the inside that I didn't want to be touched on the outside. I felt if somebody shoved me I would have broken into a million pieces or if not that collapsed on the floor and sobbed like a baby. I knew what my limits were, I knew the best place for me was to be at the farm so that's where I stayed and David, bless him, kept phoning me regularly so I didn't miss out on the joy of what was going on. He knew everything that I was feeling so he was trying to make me as much a part of Amber's arrival as he possibly could and I was grateful to him for doing that.

David called me when he'd gotten Amber out of the crate. I'd asked him to ring me as soon as she was off the plane because it's only then that I can put my mind at rest and stop worrying. "Is she ok? I asked "Yes she's fine" he reassured me "She's very little" he said and I could tell by his voice that he was really happy. "So I keep hearing" I said but in my mind I was thinking just get her home as fast as you can so I can see how tiny she is for myself. I could hear him talking to her in the background and then his voice came nearer to the phone once again. I could only assume he'd put the phone down while he was tending to Amber and I was right. She had gotten one of her front legs caught in the lead and he was freeing her before she fell over. "She's got her harness on and has just gone for a short walk" was what he started telling me. "Has she had a wee? I asked because I always like them to have a stroll on what little patches of grass there are at the airport, I like them to relieve themselves before the long ride home. They'd be uncomfortable if their bladders were full. And back then there wasn't much grass for you to take the dogs on, now there are more trees and grassy areas because they've overhauled the entire airport and prettied it up a bit, which makes it a lot better for us when picking up a dog. "Yes a big one" was his answer. "She must have been holding on until she reached some grass" I felt sorry for her holding herself all that time, a lot of dogs hold their bladders during the flight because there is so much going on and they are a little confused. Then again some wee all over themselves and the crate because they are terrified, as yet we've not had one of them, but towels are always taken just in case. David told me that Amber had sniffed the grass, relaxed and let loose. So much wee for such a little dog was what he told me. He was smiling as he spoke I could tell, he seemed both amazed and proud all at the same time. We always take water and food when picking up a dog, they are not allowed to have water with them in the crate because it will get spilt. So they arrive quite thirsty. He had Amber by the car now, I heard him opening the door, he put the phone down while he got the bowl and bottle of water out. I heard a clink on the floor and a little bit of lapping. Then sounds that I couldn't quite make out and it wasn't for lack of trying either because I had my ear pressed real hard to the phone. I heard David laughing, when he got back on the phone he said he was laughing at the speed in which Amber ate the chicken he was hand feeding her. "She absolutely loves this stuff, can't get it down fast enough" She was more interested in the food than the drink. He took a photo of her and sent it to my computer but with being busy with the pugs nightly routine I didn't have time to get the computer out, I would have to wait until the next day to see that photo. These days he would have been sending it to my phone but back then the phone I had couldn't receive photos. I heard the car door close so knew they were about to leave. I glanced over my shoulder at the clock, made note of the time so I knew when to expect them home, I was so looking forward to meeting her. He told me she had a bit of a cough but wasn't coughing nonstop or anything like that. We guessed it must have been the air on the flight down or the fact that she'd not had a drink for some time, perhaps her throat was dry. It wasn't stopping her from eating the chicken though, we liked that, liked that she was happy and relaxed enough to want to eat something. Before he hung up I told him to drive safely because he was now carrying some very precious cargo and he laughed when I said that.

About half an hour later Dave rang again and my first thought was that something had happened to Amber but I breathed a sigh of relief when he said he was just letting me know they were stuck in heavy traffic, I said it was probably due to the Easter break, people would be going on holidays, leaving the city and heading down to the coast. When I had thought about Amber being flown in at Easter I had not even considered how bad the traffic gets during the Easter break, if I had of done I would have tried to have her flown down a day or two earlier so they could have avoided the traffic jams altogether. David's voice was no longer light, he said it was the worst possible place to be stuck then asked me to guess where they were. His voice was not his normal impatient irritated at being stuck in traffic voice but more his slightly unnerved voice and knowing him as well as I do and knowing the path they would be taking I realised they were stuck on the Bolte bridge. Well David doesn't like high bridges at the best of times but it was a very windy day so that would have made it all the worse. And he has a real disinclination to be on exposed bridges and the Bolte is extremely exposed and lengthy and being at a complete standstill for as long as they were, well that wasn't doing him any favours. It would be like somebody who is terrified of heights being stuck at the top of a broken down Ferris wheel for over an hour, stuck up there swaying about, no way out. I knew how that would affect him. I asked about Amber and if it was affecting her the same way, "Nah she's just finished off the last of the chicken and is sniffing around for more" I smiled at the thought of her doing that, clearly she was happy and comfortable being with her new Dad, if she was eating and wanting more she was pretty much feeling right at home with him, she had put her trust in him fast and I liked that she'd done that. "How long will you be" I asked knowing that he really couldn't give me an answer. "Well we are going nowhere fast" he said and I said "Then you may as well just enjoy getting to know Amber and concentrate on her" he said he would do that and hung up the phone. I figured if his mind was on her then he would be less inclined to be thinking about his surroundings, I mean it probably didn't work but as I freshened the dogs drinking water I was really hoping that it would. It seemed there was an accident that night too which only added to all the traffic being backed up. I pictured David sitting there with his new daughter next to him wishing he was now driving down our quiet county road instead of being trapped like that. I felt for him because I knew how much he hated being stuck up there. I've been on that bridge a few times myself and felt anxious being up there. You glace to the left and to the right and there is nothing there, nothing close to make you feel secure. I was always very apprehensive when approaching it and so relieved to get off at the other end. It's like you are in a fairy-tale, like you have to pass some sort of test to prove you are worthy of what is on the other side, it's like one of those things you have to cross over in order to receive something special and what we were receiving that night was very, very special. After what seemed like an eternity David called and said he was ten minutes away from home, I asked how Amber was, he said she was fast asleep on the front seat. He said she was sitting up for around half of the journey but had then gone to sleep while he was stroking her head. The day had been a long one for her and being stuck on that bridge hadn't helped, she should have been home hours ago. No wonder she was tired. I guess she must have sensed who David was, realised she was with somebody who loved her very much and that knowledge had allowed her to relax enough to drift off into a deep sleep.

When I walked out of the house I was smiling and feeling incredibly excited but as I made my way down to the gate in the darkness I felt a twinge of sadness enter my heart. I was feeling both excited and numb, a bit of a strange feeling, but then again I had spent a lot of time feeling this way in the last couple of months. The day had been a particularly hard day of missing Horton, one of the most difficult ones I'd had in well over a week. Waves of grief had begun crashing over me from the time I got out of bed that morning. Something must have triggered it so I did what I always do in times like this, I cried it out. I don't believe we are meant to hold things in, god gave us tears for a reason. I believe they allow our hearts and souls to have a release, they are not a sign of weakness they are a sign that you cared, a sign that you loved and that you have lost. That somebody meant so much to you that they are worth grieving over. So that day I made sure to cry it all out. I wanted to get myself sorted because I knew I had a little girl arriving on an aero plane soon, a little girl that I wanted very much. I needed to get myself ready to greet her. I didn't want Amber meeting her new mother in this state. I didn't think that would be fair on her. She needed me to make her feel loved, secure, that everything was going to be alright in her world from now on. And I didn't feel I could do that properly if I was feeling like this. I cried about a few things that day, yes the fact that Horton was gone but I was also crying about the fact that every pug I rescued in the future would be taking me further and further away from the life I had with him and that did upset me a little bit because I didn't want to be taken further away from Horton,

I wanted to be nearer to him, I wanted him back, I wanted him here with me now, sitting beside me waiting to meet his new sister. He should have been here. I was still grieving over the unfairness of it all. Horton was little and Amber was little, they would have been the two smallest pugs in the family, how adorable would it have been seeing the two of them together.

I believe this was just another part of the grieving process, something else I had to face, something I had to go through before I could move on. David had rung me while all these thoughts were going through my head. He asked what was wrong so I started explaining how I was feeling. He said "Are you feeling this way because you don't want to take in another dog? And I said "No, no that's not it at all, I still want Amber desperately, that hasn't changed" He seemed to breathe a sigh of relief when I said this. I guess he knew he was about to pick a pug up from the airport soon so my answering the phone in a flood of tears wasn't an ideal situation. "Dave I still want to be Amber's mother none of that has altered" I told him it had just been a very hard and emotion filled day. I said emotion wise it was probably the worst day possible to be flying a new pug in. When the flight was booked I had no idea I would be having such a hard day and that's how it is with grieving, you have no warning when it is going to hit, so you just do your best to get through it and then carry on living. "Tomorrow will be better" I told him and I could say that with full confidence because I knew it would be. The days after I'd had a release were always happier days. After I hung up the phone I wiped away my tears and took the pugs for a walk. The sun was shining, the wind was light and breezy and my heart felt happy watching the pugs sniffing about. Whenever one of them wandered over to me I would reach down, pat them and whisper in their ears that they had a new sister arriving in a few hours.

When I reached the gate I leant against it gathering my thoughts, I was glad it was dark, the darkness and the stars comforted me. There were so many stars out that night and they were really beautiful. As I looked up at the sky, a quick thought shot into my head, it didn't last for very long but it was there all the same. "Was what I was doing now being disloyal to Horton? And that was quickly followed by the thought of "What would he think of me taking in this little girl" But I didn't even really have to think about it, I already knew the answer to that question. I knew he would be thrilled, be overjoyed that I was about to help somebody else, helping them in the exact same way that I had helped him. I truly believe he would have been extremely disappointed in his Mummy if she hadn't gone where her heart was leading her. I was glad I had those few quiet moments alone to sort this all out. I didn't know I needed it when I walked out the door but I was glad to have them all the same. The reason I'd left the pugs behind and come out alone was because of Amber. I wanted to give her time to have a little walk and a wee in peace, a quiet moment without being rushed. I didn't want her to be brought straight into the house with pugs clambering about, didn't want anybody jostling her. I knew she was tiny, I knew she'd just recently had surgery. I knew she would find it hard after the day she'd had. I wanted to make things as easy for her as possible. We didn't have as many pugs as we had when the year first started out but we probably still had more pugs than Amber was used to dealing with. I'd said to Dave that I'd meet them at the gate then I'd walk Amber slowly up while he went ahead and said hello to the pugs. They always go nuts when he gets home and I wanted to give the hugging, kissing, dancing, squealing, ballistic frenzy time to subside before me and Amber got there.

Because I couldn't see all that well my hearing was heightened. I heard a car in the distance but it wasn't David so I went back to looking at the stars. I have always found star gazing to be very peaceful. I was once again back to feeling happy and looking forward to meeting our new little girl. I shifted positions. I was now standing with my chin resting on the top bar of the gate. Another engine approached and this time it was David so I flung that gate open as fast as I could so that my husband and my new little daughter could drive straight through. David pulled in and stopped the car, he gave me just enough space to close the gate behind him. I walked around to the passenger side of the car with excitement building as I went. Opening the door made the light come on inside the car. I peered in looking for Amber but she was so tiny that I couldn't see her at first. The car was a Celica and the seats dipped down and she was on a tan coloured blanket. I only saw her when David pointed out the area she was in, he sort of waved his hand above her body to indicate to me that she was there. He didn't make contact with her though because she was in a deep sleep. Honestly she looked just like a peanut in a baseball mitt. The sight of one so little and so precious made my eyes well up. But I didn't cry, after the session I'd had earlier I really didn't have any more tears left in me, instead I smiled at the sight of her. My little blessing was home and I was so relieved to finally have her here. The night air was cool, a bit too cool for this time in April, the rush of air coming into the car woke Amber up. She opened her eyes and slightly turned her head, not towards me, towards David, I guess she was more used to somebody being on that side of her. I thought she would have woken up when the car stopped moving and the engine was turned off, they normally do, but not this little soul. I gave her a few moments to come round, didn't want to rush her, let her head come fully up when it was good and ready to. She faced David a little bit longer and she was sniffing at the air as she did so, then sensing somebody was on the other side of her she turned towards me. When she did I spoke to her and reached down to softly stroke her head, she was quite happy to allow me to do that so I gently lifted her out of the car. As I held her in my arms I started telling her that I was her new Mummy. I did feel sorry for Amber that night because she wasn't meeting the same Mummy Horton had met when he first arrived and I felt quite bad about that I really did because she deserved to have that same person greeting her and I couldn't give it to her yet. With Amber in my arms I stood and watched David's taillights disappearing up the driveway. Then I whispered in her little ear "You are not getting me at my best sweetheart and I am so very, very sorry about that but I am still going to be a wonderful mother to you and I will love you with all my heart" I told her that I would give her everything I had in me at this time and I asked her if she could do the same thing with me. I knew she had been through a lot too, I told her that we could both heal together. I said we will have good days and bad days but whatever each new day brought that we would now be facing them together. I walked halfway up the driveway and put Amber on the ground by my feet. I turned my torch on so I could always see where she was. The way she was moving I could tell she couldn't see very much and it had nothing to do with the time of night. I shone the torch on the area beside her, didn't want to shine it in her eyes so I always made sure to hit the spot next to her. Gee she was little, what everybody told me about her was true. So very tiny and quiet, still coming to terms with all she had been through, she'd had an incredibly huge ordeal happen to her of late and was probably wondering if this was the end of it, it was, but she didn't know it at the time, yet she was such a brave little thing and my heart went out to her right away. When I lost Horton Amber was still living in her family home and then for some reason, a reason I'll never truly have an answer to, she was discarded from it.

I lingered near the trees for a little while in order to give Amber something to sniff at, hoping a bit of a sniff around would encourage her to wee, it didn't though because I think she was too scared to. I mean I may have been wrong she could have snuck one out while I had my back turned but I don't think she did because every time I looked there she was with her little head down no doubt concentrating on the sound of my feet so she didn't lose me. I would never have allowed that to happen but she didn't know that, she was in a strange place with a strange person and there were plenty of strange smells around, she had stitches in her tummy and she couldn't see very well, she was as out of sorts as you could get. I kept talking to her so she knew I was there. Every time the wind changed I could hear the commotion up at the house. I reached down and gently stroked Amber's teeny tiny head. And as I did so I thought to myself that her life was about to get a whole lot better, but what I didn't know at the time was that my life was about to get a whole lot better and a whole lot happier too. In that moment I had no idea the enormous impact this little pug was going to have on my life. I turned and trudged slowly back up to the house in the darkness. And as for one of the best decisions I'd ever made in my entire life, well, she was following on a step or two behind me, keeping close so she always knew where I was.

Steffy, Amber and Casey

CHAPTER THREE

Just The Way You Are

When I started telling people that we were taking in another pug we received a lot of well wishes, people were really happy for us, people who knew our story and what we had been through were thrilled that we would now be sharing our lives with this dear little girl. It was also mentioned to me that this new pug would make me get over loosing Horton. One even said that Amber would be replacing Horton and I said "You know what, it doesn't quite work like that" and it doesn't. It's not like your kettle breaks so you go out and buy a new one, job done, instant fix. No animal can ever replace another one and nor would I want them to. Amber wasn't going to arrive and suddenly I was going to be ok about losing Horton. She was not a bandage to be put over a gaping wound in order to help stop the bleeding so I shut down those comments pretty quickly because I felt they were being disrespectful to Amber. In my mind it was very clear that Amber was not here to be a substitute for anybody. I wouldn't be so cruel as to expect her to do that. That would have been a real lot to put on this little darling, an unfair state to make her live in, far too big of a burden to be putting on an innocent old pug who was already down on her luck. But even if she was a young vibrant full of health puppy that was just embarking on its life it would still be far too huge a burden. No dog should ever be made to carry the ghost of a past dog on their backs. Nobody should be forced to replace somebody else because not only are you being unfair to who they are, you are also asking the impossible. Would you want to have that kind of pressure put on you if you were entering into a new relationship? In any relationship the best thing you can give somebody is the freedom to be 100% themselves and totally accepted for it. Wouldn't you rather be loved and appreciated for being yourself, for being who you are and what you were born to be instead of somebody trying to turn you into something you are not and nor will you ever be. Well it's the same with our dogs. They don't want to be living under the shadow of your former dog. Although to be totally honest it'd be more like living under a heavy thunderous rain cloud. Imagine the stress and sadness of being made to do that. I have never welcomed a new dog into the family fold and wanted them to be somebody other than who they are. Amber deserved a lot better than to be asked to be another Horton, Ruby or Grace. She was an emotional being, she had feelings and I felt her feelings needed to be taken into consideration at all times. She had a right to be "Just Amber" and 100% loved for it, loved unconditionally, no other expectations then that. Yes I had a void but neither she nor any other being besides Horton himself would be able to fill it. Amber was coming into my life not knowing what I had recently gone through, she had the right to enter my home and be freely herself, beautifully herself that was all this loving mother's heart ever wanted for her. As her new mother I knew it was up to me to look for things about Amber that were going to fill my heart with joy. And I knew she'd be doing this over and over again, all I had to do was give her the chance to do it. I loved Horton for everything he was and I would now be loving Amber for everything she was, but she'd only just gotten here, her characteristics hadn't been revealed to me yet but once they were I knew I would be loving each and every one of them. Amber wouldn't be patching up my life she would be adding to it, writing her own special chapter. That's what every relationship in our lives is, regardless of who it's with, it is them and us writing our story together, letting things unfold naturally, letting them become what they are going to become and that can be a very exciting thing. What I had with Horton had been incredibly precious and beautiful, a truly joyful experience and I was grateful to have had it, it was a life altering experience for me. But I knew I would now go on to have a beautiful relationship with Amber, it would be totally different to what I had with Horton, I was well aware of that fact, but it would be equally as lovely. In life all our relationships are different whether it is with a human being or an animal, they are all different because you are interacting with completely different souls and their individual personalities. But you still enjoy those relationships, and if you are wise you will cherish and treasure each one for what they are, for the gifts they bring, and that really is what a relationship is, a connection of souls and each connection is unlike any other, that's what makes it special.

Also, I truly believe that our pugs in heaven are watching over me and David and every other being living here at Grace Farm and that a lot of the time they have a hand in the new dog entering our life. They play a part in guiding them to us. And they do this for two reasons. One because there is a little soul out there that desperately needs a whole lot of love, care and understanding. And they know Dave and I can give it to them because they have lived here with us, they've felt loved and safe and well cared for, they know we are good at making little old souls feel incredibly special, they know we can be trusted. I also think they send us another soul to share our lives because they don't want us to be sad or alone when they have gone, I believe such images break their little hearts. I imagine them in heaven, in this beautiful happy place looking down on us and wanting that state of happiness for us too. They want us to feel what they are feeling and so we open up our hearts and we let a new dog in. Of course we never forget the dog we've recently lost for such a thing is impossible to do. It always makes me sad when I hear people saying they'll never get another dog because losing them is too hard to go through because I guarantee there is a heartbroken dog sitting in a pound or with a rescue group with your name on it. All these beautiful warm loving homes are empty because people are afraid to take a step. But I ask you this, if the roles were reversed would you want your dog to be alone when you are gone or would you be happy to have them sharing their lives with a loving companion. Well your dog thinks exactly the same way. They don't want you to be alone, living in a dog free home. I believe they would want you to help their fellow brethren, you can do no more for the little soul you've just lost but you can do something to make the life of another dog better and in doing so make your life better too. No replacements ever, certainly not, only a new loving and rewarding relationship.

When the lady who made the replacement comment finally came over and met Amber she still had it in her mind about her replacing Horton. I thought we'd sorted it out over the phone but clearly we hadn't because she was here now saying it again, only this time it was worse because she was now saying it in front of Amber. Amber was a few feet away from where we were standing, she had taken herself off on a sniffing expedition near the veggie patch, but she had limited vision and so those little ears of hers were extra good at picking things up. I didn't want her to be burdened with this so I thought I'd get it sorted out in this ladies head and in Amber's head all at the same time. This lady didn't know why I suddenly walked off in the direction of Amber, I guess she thought I was going to check on her, she was used to me darting off if I saw one of the pugs needing a bit of help so I suppose she just figured I was doing that and followed along like she usually does. The two of us were positioned directly above Amber when I began speaking again. I went over all my personal thoughts on the matter and as I spoke Amber was busily sniffing around the edge of the veggie patch. She had her head down and her little tongue was peeping out and she looked to be very interested in what she was doing. Most of the time she was just swaying and sniffing in the one spot, but then she'd move off and if she got more than a few steps away I would once again go and position myself directly above her little old head making sure she wouldn't miss a word of what was being said. And just in case I still hadn't properly gotten the message through to this lady I made it more personal to her situation because I knew then that she would get it. And I wanted her to get it so I didn't have to be going over it all the time. I said "How would you feel if you were being constantly compared to Sharon? Her face instantly changed when I said Sharon's name because Sharon is a sore spot for her and I knew it. She quickly spat out that even on her worst days she was still a million times better than Sharon. And I said "Ok, but what if Rob didn't know that? "What if Rob was expecting you to be another Sharon? Again her face changed but this time it was for a different reason, this time I could tell that she finally understood.

Amber spent her first night sleeping peacefully in a little pen on her own. A pen with walls around it, the pen Horton had used when he first arrived. It was a secure pen with lots of soft bedding and it was right beside David's side of the bed so he would be able to keep an eye on her during the night. I wanted her to be next to me but there were so many dog beds on my side of the bed and if we moved them around it would have upset the dogs that were used to sleeping down there so we left things as they were. Also, you can't go moving things around when you have blind pugs in the house, it confuses them and you can't have that so the best thing to do was move nothing and just have Amber next to David. I put her in that pen as soon as I walked into the house with her. We felt sectioning her off was the right thing to do for now. She'd had a huge day and we knew she was worn out, she also had stitches and endured a rough couple of weeks. Life for Amber had changed in so many ways and now it had just changed again. We felt this little girl needed some rest and privacy. Our house as loved filled and happy as it is can take a bit of getting used to and we always take that into account when a new little soul joins the family. Amber was probably an only dog, she wouldn't have been used to other dogs being around, we didn't want her freaking out if our pack encircled her. We were looking at things from her point of view we always do that because it's important. You need to stop and think about how they will be feeling and each case is different. We felt putting this teeny tiny vision impaired girl on the floor and letting the others gather round for a sniff could well have been quite terrifying for her. And add the fact that she was recovering from surgery into the mix. Both David and I were very protective of Amber so she went into a pen and she didn't mind that at all. She settled down to sleep very quickly and didn't stir once during the night. Amber's first full day on the farm was spent pretty much the same way, in her little sectioned off pen with either mine or Dave's face peering over the top checking she was alright, she was fine just very tired, spent almost all day sleeping. But every time she woke up one of us would bring her out on her own for a toilet break, we kept her to the decking area only and she'd do what she needed to do very quickly, wasn't at all interested in walking around.

I placed a bowl of clean fresh water outside the door so Amber could have a drink before coming back inside. We also fed her a few mini meals while she was out there. We wanted her to be able to wee in peace and have something to eat and drink in peace too so that's how Amber's first day in her new home was spent and the other pugs watched on from the windows with great interest as we were doing this. Sure they would have loved to meet their new sister, they probably couldn't wait, but the timing wasn't right yet. Little blind Arthur would have been fine he always is he'd just be pottering around like he does and would stop and give Amber a good sniffing over when he eventually came across her. And as for Steffy, well, being full to the brim of sensitivity she would have started mothering Amber right away. Emily could be a bit on the rough side and she was very mischievous too so you didn't want her racing around frightening Amber, Sarah was the boss she was top dog, but we knew she would see no threat in little old Amber. And as for Tommy, he was so big in comparison to his new sister, a soft gentle giant but Amber wouldn't have known that then. She would do in time but not today. Each pug on their own would have been fine for an introduction but all of them together gathering around this poor little soul well, we wanted to give her a bit of time to rest up before that happened.

 The next morning I was already out walking the pugs when I saw David carrying Amber out of the house. I smiled watching him doing his big long strides while tenderly holding our new little blessing in his arms. I watched him looking around for a special spot to place her. Like he was trying to decide if she'd like to be put down near a tree or by the fence, he knew Amber was lacking in vision and I guess he was trying to think of the best spot for her. Clearly she had just woken up and he was bringing her outside to do her business and because we didn't know her personality yet he didn't know what she would prefer. It was like his mind was ticking over saying "Fence or tree, fence or tree". I had checked on Amber before leaving the house, glanced into the pen saw she was still sound asleep so crept out of the room letting her rest, trying to keep the other pugs as quiet as I possibly could do. David said he would stay behind in case Amber woke up, neither one of us wanted her to wake up alone. We both felt it best if she had somebody there with her when she opened up her eyes so Dave sat beside Amber's pen and I took off with the pugs. I was down by the front fence and stood watching David turning round and round. He was looking this way than that, eyes searching the ground, but Amber had held her bladder all night long and I thought to myself if he doesn't put her down real soon she may go in his arms. In the end he put her near the base of a tree and really that was the most perfect thing to have done because over time it was revealed to us that Amber really did love weeing on trees. In fact later in life she would only go to the toilet near the base of one particular tree and that tree became known as Amber's special weeing tree and it still goes by that title today. I'll often use the term as a way of telling David where I'll be or where I am going when I walk out of the house. Or he'll ring from work and I'll be talking to him and he'll say where are you and I'll answer with something like "A few steps from Ambers special weeing tree" he'll get a visual and then we carry on with our conversation.

I watched Amber take a few steps then squat. Being some distance away gave me an opportunity to observe her entire body, it's a thing I like to do with all the pugs because you can learn a lot about them by watching how they move. I do it with the sheep and horses too. With elderly souls, especially elderly souls who can't tell you how they are feeling, it pays to pay attention to the signals they can send you. By taking the time to pause and observe you'll be able to make note of how they are holding themselves, the position of their backs, how their hips, shoulders, heads and legs move. The way they carry themselves reveals how they are feeling both in their bodies and in themselves and it's never so important to watch them as it is when they first arrive. This is the time you really want to get to know them and constant observation tells you a lot, especially if you know what you are looking for. Normally I am looking for areas where there could be pain, say arthritis, inflammation, sore joints, what areas of their bodies they are favouring. A limb could be moving a certain way due to injury and then you try to gage if that injury is old or new. And you don't just watch them on the first day of arrival either, you keep an eye on them for the next few weeks as it's the only way you'll be able to familiarize yourself with the little blessing that is now in your care. But really I am always watching my pugs no matter how long they have been with me. I am always observing everything about them and making a mental note of it. It's my job to look after them and so I watch on as they are ambling about the place. Yes it's fun to see them all meandering around the farm like little free range chickens but I will also be looking for any change in their bodies, you can spot an issue pretty fast then go and investigate further. See if they've hurt themselves, see if they need their doses of glucosamine or flaxseed oil upping or if they now need to go onto something more and so we'll talk to our vet, get him to check them out and see where we stand.

I was meant to be walking the pugs but I now stood completely still and focused all my attention on my tiny new daughter. I held my hand up to my face to shield my eyes against the bright morning sun so I could get a better look at her. Sure I was glad it was a sunny morning, you are always happy to have a warm morning after a cold night but it did make things a bit harder to see. Then again I was a fair distance away too so that wasn't doing me any favours either. But the pugs love their walks, they love their little routines, love the paths we tread and look forward to sniffing. I watched Amber walking around and quickly noticed that she wasn't moving right. I hadn't noticed this before because she hadn't done much walking, yesterday on the deck only a step or two had been taken, but now she was in motion I could clearly see that something wasn't right with her gait. The line of her back wasn't sitting properly to me it looked like it was out of alignment. Not the walk of a normal pug, although to be completely honest in this household very few of them walk like a normal pug. That's why most of them end up with us in the first place. But with Amber she had the walk of a dog that definitely had something going on with its back, could it be made right with chiropractic care, well at that point I had absolutely no idea, we would have to get our vet to take a look at her and see what he thought. Amber wandered around a little bit then went and stood beside her new Dad's legs. Seeing as the rest of us were some distance away Dave picked her up and strode over to us. When David and Amber reached my side I told him what I'd seen. "I think Amber has something wrong with her back" David looked at me and said "No she walks ok" and I said "No she actually doesn't" He couldn't see it because he was looking at her from an aerial view. The pugs I had with me had grown impatient because I was standing still for so long, they had taken themselves off for a little wander around and were now milling about near the trees on the other side of the paddock. I glanced over and saw they were happily enjoying their sniffing session which worked out pretty well because we now had an area where we could put Amber down on her own. David gently lowered her to the ground and as soon as he did she plodded off for a sniff and he was going to go after her to make sure she was ok but I told him to hang back a bit, give her a moment to get ahead so he could see what I'd seen. David watched Amber for a few minutes then turned to me and said "Yeah I see it now but it's nothing too bad" and I said "Oh I know it's nothing too bad" I mean after Horton seeing Amber walk, well, she looked like a normal dog in comparison, but there was definitely something not quite right there and I wanted to know what it was. I told Dave that I'd be really happy once our vet had a chance to look at Amber. David must have seen the look of concern on my face because he asked if I wanted to take Amber in to see him straight away, like that very day and I said "No, she'll be needing her stitches out soon, we'll get her looked at then". For now she was happily settling in, I didn't want to disturb that flow, I thought it would be nice to leave her to get her bearings. It would have been a very different story if she was showing signs of obvious pain, I would have been at the vets at lightning speed if that was the case but it wasn't so I let her be. Also they can sometimes get knocked about on the flight, turbulence can set them off balance, set them off their feet, we've had a few that have flown down and walked a bit funny for a day or so afterwards then come good. Sometimes you have to give them time to get over having been on an aeroplane and I was quite happy for The Divine One to do this.

We didn't want Amber doing a lot of walking while she was recovering from surgery so David went and picked her up, she was a determined little thing though, really wanted to walk, she tried to scurry off when she heard him approaching. And she wasn't too happy about being carried but you have to do what's best for them. There would be plenty of time for walking when her stitches came out. But for now I wasn't about to let her do too much, common sense needed to be used here, of course it did. Sarah must have had her fair share of sniffing because she began heading back to us so David knelt down and let the two siblings meet one another. At first Sarah was unaware that Amber was nestled in Dad's arms, she was just really happy to have David out there and her little tail kept going faster and faster the closer she got to him. He stroked Sarah's old grey ears and talked to her a little bit and her tail was wagging away happily, when she realised he was holding another dog she jumped up, put her front paws on David's leg and came in close. At this point in Sarah's life she didn't have much more vision than Amber did, neither one could see each other very well but they both leant in and gave each other's face a good sniffing over, familiarized themselves that way, Sarah wagged her tail the entire time she was sniffing, the introduction went smoothly.

I could tell the other pugs were going to be a while so sat down on the ground next to my husband and I could do that without getting a wet bottom because the sun had taken care of the dew a few hours ago. I thought we could sit together and chat while we waited for the others to come over and meet their new sister. The day was neither too hot nor too cold and there wasn't much of a wind about, it was the most perfect day weather wise. I leant back and looked at the sky, it was a lovely shade of blue and there were a few fluffy clouds floating around, the only sounds to be heard were the birds in the trees talking to one another and the cows across the road having an occasional moo. I glanced across at Amber, she seemed to be really enjoying being outside. And why wouldn't she be it was so calm and peaceful out there. The next one to meet The Divine One was Steffy, she had picked up on the scent and quickly stopped what she was doing to come over and investigate. She was so overjoyed at meeting her new sister that she started screaming and Amber wasn't at all bothered by it. I guess after spending two weeks in the pound and a week in a vet surgery Steffy's noise was nothing to be concerned about. Also, the way Ambers head shot round when Steffy first started hollering told me that our new little girl had perfect hearing. Amber realised the sound was coming from Steffy and leant in to sniff the side of her deaf sisters face and of course Steffy was ecstatic about that.

Steffy and Amber

When Tommy first left my side he had begun doing laps, out of the corner of my eye I saw a fawn blur approaching, no need to look up, I knew it was him due to the size and unique movement. He was just about to give us a look of acknowledgment and keep going but paused and decided to wander over for a better look. I guess he saw that a fuss was being made of something and wanted to know what that something was. By this time Amber was sitting on the grass with Steffy by her side. Tommy had the kind of face that always looked like he was smiling. I watched him come sauntering up the embankment grinning from ear to ear. He stopped and stared directly at Amber and his tail gave one of those long slow windscreen wiper types of wags then he was off doing his laps again. Arthur had been moseying about by the fence, seemed pretty occupied with sniffing around the base of a fence post, he was a few months out from having back surgery and on the walks I was still carrying him a fair bit, it all depended on the kind of day he was having, but he was still not up to walking all the way. I'd put him on the ground when I paused to watch Amber and he'd slowly ambled off doing his own thing. I was always monitoring him, always aware of where he was and what he was doing, I saw that he was now standing still, his head was moving about like he was trying to figure out where I was. He couldn't see and he couldn't hear so his sense of smell was everything. I got up and brought him over to where Amber was sitting and put him down a few feet away from her then went and sat down again. I knew this would be a beautiful meeting, I knew how much Arthur had grieved when we lost Horton, Ruby and Grace and then his back had collapsed. He'd been through a real lot these past few months, but he was a trooper, Arthur was a glass half full kind of a dude. Dave was looking down and stroking Sarah who had recently climbed up onto his knee and I said to him "You must watch this because I think Arthur is going to be so happy when he finds out he's got a new sister". When I put Arthur down I made sure he was directly in front of Amber because I wanted to make things easier for him. He stood still for a few moments, nose in the air, figuring out where everybody was and when he'd gotten that information he decided to take a few steps forward, another pause then another slow step was taken, he was now inches away from Amber's face, and I knew the exact moment he realised she was there because his little corkscrew tail went from hanging down limp to rotating around like crazy, he was silent, didn't scream like Steffy had done, no Arthur didn't say a word the only way we knew he was aware of Amber was because his little tail was going absolutely ballistic. He leant in and sniffed her face, gave her nose a bit of lick and all the while that little corkscrew tail of his was in overdrive. When all the excitement was out of him he sniffed the air some more then came over and found me and I lifted him onto my knee. Tommy had come back and joined us by this time too, he was sprawled out on the grass in front of Steffy and Amber, mouth open, panting a bit, but smiling, always smiling, he was surrounded by yellow flowers, yes they are common weeds but beautiful just the same. Emily eventually came over and stood back observing us all, she gave our little group the once over, her ears altered a bit when her eyes came to rest on Amber, it was like "Oh I see you there and yes you are new and yes you are very tiny, but I have important things to do" and she turned and ran off again. I guess she was thinking there would be plenty of time to get acquainted when we were all back inside the house and there was. Emily having spent so much of her life with no access to the outside world was now making up for lost time. In fact most of her life with us I felt she was making up for lost time. She didn't let anybody interfere with her outside agenda, but that was fine Amber had met enough folks for now and was happily sitting on the grass enjoying herself. The sun was no doubt nice and warm on her petite body. She would have been able to hear the birds and smell the fresh air. Every time a fly landed on her face she'd straighten up, shake it off then go back to sitting slightly slumped over again, but content, very content. I'd lean over and rub her little back as way of letting her know I was nearby and I'd talk to her as well and she'd half turn in my direction, then go back to facing the other way, nose in the air sniffing again. And so that is how The Divine One met her new family, in the middle of the front paddock with one sibling after another trotting over at certain intervals and although it wasn't planed I thought it was a perfect way to introduce everybody.

After a while Amber stood up and walked around in a bit of a circle. Steffy got to her feet quick smart and went with her, she was not letting that little soul out of her sight. She walked alongside her new sister like she'd just appointed herself Amber's bodyguard.

Tommy watched them go but made no attempt to go after them. David and I sat there talking a while longer, Sarah still on his knee Arthur still on mine, there was no rush, the scene in front of us was a beautiful one so we decided to sit and enjoy it. We both love these times of contented bliss. Watching those we love enjoying themselves really does fill your heart to over flowing and now we had a gorgeous new little girl to watch. Amber was taking her time walking and she walked with a slight swaying motion, she was doing tiny slow steps, only a few at a time, then she'd pause and sniff the ground around her feet before another few short slow swaying steps were taken and the sniffing would be repeated once again. She was doing what all vision impaired dogs do, sussing everything out, familiarizing herself with the place, and all the while there was Steffy right by Amber's side watching on. And not with a face crumpled with concern either, more a face of delight and curiosity. Steffy's face was alive with excitement she was in love with Amber already I could tell. When Amber walked she was always hugging the ground, cautiously walking, she was close to the ground anyway being so small and all and blind dogs do hug the ground when they are walking in areas that are new to them. They do it until they know the layout of the land and they'll deeply sniff at everything as way of finding marks which help to guide them around the place. At times Amber was walking slightly sideways. The ground hugging didn't bother me because I knew our little girl had limited vision. I was glad she was taking her time, those slow steps wouldn't disturb her stitches if she was walking fast then I would have had to rein her in. But what she was doing wasn't hurting her and it was giving her a bit of time doing something fun, something other than being in a pound pen. No wonder she wanted to be out and about discovering, she was now doing what dogs were born to do, what they love to do, she was sniffing new territory. The sideways walking wasn't normal though and your mind then goes to why she could be doing that, was it due to her back or was it more neurological. Then again it could have been simply because she was walking on uneven ground, the embankment was sloping and this could have just been Amber's way of dealing with it. David and I watched her taking her slow steps and when Amber moved away a little bit further we started discussing her and we were leaning in close, whispering because we didn't want her to hear what we were talking about, we didn't want to upset her. You don't know exactly how much they understand but I think every animal in this world understands a heck of a lot more than most people give them credit for. We both thought Amber was not a very well-bred pug, I didn't think any from her line would have met the pug standards which made me feel even sorrier for her. But of course she would never know about these thoughts, when whispering into those little velvety ears of hers I knew I would always be telling her that she was cut from superior cloth. David and I wondered if Arthur's physiotherapist would be able to do anything for Amber. She had been really good in aiding Arthur with his recovery so maybe she could help our new little girl too. Arthur was due for another session soon and we thought it'd be a good idea to take Amber along with him. I watched Amber some more, made a mental note of the calluses on her back legs, thought I'd start rubbing cream into them. I didn't think I'd be able to get the hair to grow back but I could at least soften them for her. In very hushed tones we started talking about why Amber may have ended up in the pound system in the first place. I believe some people dump their old sick dogs in pounds because they think they are dying or that they need to be put to sleep and they themselves don't want to be the ones to do it. It's sad and it's completely heartless and horrible but I know it happens. Perhaps that was the case with Amber, nine isn't old but maybe to them it was, people see things differently to the way we see things. We've often had pugs come to live with us at nine or ten years old and been able to have them with us until they were fifteen, sixteen and even seventeen. And I've often wondered if their previous owners ever thought about them or if they had all been quickly forgotten about, did their old families just assume they'd never made it out of the pound.

Emily and Amber

David and I sat there heads together but eyes glued on Amber watching every move she made and summing her up. It's what we do with all the newies, observe, assess and then work out a routine of care. We started talking about what would come next for Amber. Yes the first thing would be getting her stitches out but we were more thinking long term, thinking about how we could help her with her back. Our vet would be able to guide us in that area so we would wait until we'd seen him before doing anything ourselves, you can't go rogue with things like this, no matter how long you have been dealing with dogs with back issues you still can't go rogue, every case is different so you need to get an experts opinion, know exactly what you are dealing with otherwise you could end up doing more damage to the dog and you don't want that. David mentioned that he'd heard Amber coughing a few times during the night and had peeped over the bed to see if she was ok. If the cough got any worse we said we'd take her to see our vet earlier then planed. But for now what Amber needed was rest. I glanced over at my new daughter, she was about as far away from us as I wanted her to get and I also felt she'd had enough walking for one day so David went and scooped the little blessing up and we all walked back to the house together. Amber slept most of the afternoon away, came out of her pen to eat her dinner and be offered a drink, then back in the pen again and back to sleep as soon as she was put down. By this time Tommy had taken a lot more interest in Amber, whenever she was put in the pen he'd go over and jump up, place his chin on top of the pen and peep in at her. She was too tired to notice him and he was the only one who did this, then again he was the only one big enough to be able to see inside the pen and he had to be standing on his hind legs to do so. He did the same thing when we were about to go to sleep, got lifted up on the bed and quickly shot over to stand on David's pillow because that was his best view of Amber. Sometimes if we were taking a while with the other pugs he would lay peering over the side of the bed, huge smiley face watching Amber sleep. Then when Dave got into bed he'd move Tommy over and that was it, lights out, a chorus of snoring until morning.

CHAPTER FOUR

Settling In

When Amber was outside she was good, fine, confident, no problems at all, sure she had limited vision and an unusual gait but she didn't let such things stop her from enjoying the little trips outside she was having throughout the day. At this stage she was still only being taken outside for wee breaks but each time we went out I let her have a leisurely stroll and a sniff about. She was a good little sniffer too, loved being out there, and it was a way of her familiarizing herself with the farm. All the other pugs were now coming out with us too, they'd already met Amber and the meeting had been a calm peaceful one so there was no longer any reason to keep them separated, they'd all just wander around together usually weeing on the exact same spot everybody else had just wee'd on. At night Amber was still sleeping in the pen because we couldn't have one of the bigger pugs getting in bed with her and squashing her and of course neither David nor I could keep an eye on her if we were fast asleep. During the day everything was different because I was always there watching what was going on. Amber was carried out and placed in the same area of the farm each time we went outside because I felt that was best. By the time her stitches came out she would at least know one part of the farm very well and then could go on to investigate the rest of the place when she was more up to doing it. So down she would go and I, with a heart overflowing with love and admiration would stand by watching every move she made. I loved seeing her pottering about, just the size of her in amongst the others was a beautiful thing to see. She was so tiny and yet so determined and positive, like she had absolutely no idea how little she was compared to everybody else or if she did she simply did not care. And she wasn't following the pack either like a lot of our new pugs tend to do, limited vision or not she was happy enough to go off on her own and if the others followed so be it and if they didn't she was fine with that too. I felt that Amber had spent a lot of time on her own so was used to doing her own thing. She had definitely been an only dog. Dogs who live together tend to move around in a pack but Amber never did this, well at the start she didn't anyway, she would make up her mind to do something, go a certain way and off she'd go, no turning her head to see if anybody else was coming, just happy to be doing exactly what she wanted to do. Steffy, like me, was constantly aware of where Amber was and what she was getting up to. Sometimes she'd shadow her, other times she'd stand by my side and we would both watch Amber from a distance. And when I felt she'd done enough back inside the house we'd all go until it was time for the next toilet break.

The outside Amber and the inside Amber were two very different dogs. When in the house she seemed unsure of things, a bit nervy and I was trying to work out why that was. We have wooden floorboards and they do make a bit of a noise, noisy when the pugs are walking on them, even noisier if they are running. I guess with being so open underneath everything echoes and everything sounds so much louder too. It was probably a noise Amber had not heard before. I observed her and the other pugs barking didn't bother her, me playing music didn't worry her, loud cattle or milk trucks rolling past the front of the property didn't bother her, tractors in the distance didn't worry her either, so I started trying to think of what was troubling her and because she was only troubled inside the house the only thing I could think of was our bare floorboards. Really it's all about guesswork and reading your dog and then some more guesswork. If carpeted the noise would have been softened. I myself had been aware of the floorboard noise when we first moved in. I'd be out walking the pugs and hear somebody waking up inside the house, even from some distance away I could hear them running around looking for us and then they would shoot out the back door and come find us. But I always knew they were coming because I'd heard them. I had long ago gotten used to the noise and Amber would too in time but for now it seemed to be bothersome to her. This told me two things, either the floorboard thudding was reminding her of something in her past life that had frightened her, maybe not even floorboards but something that was similar sounding or that she was just not used to being inside a house. And if it was the latter well that was truly heartbreaking. I'd look at her and wonder how anybody could leave one so tiny outside. I was quite amazed that she had lasted as long as she had, nine winters outside would have been very hard on a little soul like this, well hard on any dog really, but I felt one so tiny should have had much better care taken of her then she did. It got me to wondering about her past life. Perhaps she was owned by an elderly person and when they became ill or died Amber had gone to live with somebody else, a friend or neighbour of the deceased, maybe or even a family member, an individual who stupidly thought a dogs place was outside. I used to wonder if they thought to put a coat on her or how she coped during thunderstorms and on dark cold nights, surely she would have been given a kennel or maybe she slept underneath the house or in a closed in veranda. Either way I hope she had some form of protection and again I couldn't fathom how anybody would not have the heart to let her sleep inside. I have often thought this with a lot of the dogs I have taken in but with The Divine One, well it seemed to bother me greatly and I think it had everything to do with her size. If she did sleep underneath a house and that house had floorboards and she wasn't treated kindly in that house, well that could be the cause of what was happening now, perhaps she was having flashbacks. I couldn't do anything about the flashbacks but I could keep reassuring her so that's what I set about doing and hoped those flashbacks would lessen and lessen over time. For now all I could do was love this dear little blessing that was now in my care, love her with all my heart day in day out and wait for her to heal. And it didn't take her as long as I thought it would do either which was a good thing.

So we would all come clambering in after our wee breaks and as soon as I put Amber down she would walk straight into our bedroom and hide underneath the bed, each sound making her back further and further against the wall. I popped a blanket in her safe spot to make it more comfortable, she had showed me what she needed to do in order to cope with getting used to her new home so the least I could do was make sure her little hidey spot was nice and comfy. I also started her on a nerve tonic, a natural one from the health shop, just put a drop or two in her food, the dosage depended on the kind of day she was having. I used it for a couple of weeks from memory and it did seem to help her. I've used it on and off throughout the years when I've taken in a dog that is having trouble adjusting and it has always made a difference which is fantastic because you want to make the transitional period as easy as you can for them and if they need extra help, well you just go ahead and give it to them, whatever works right. You wouldn't leave them suffering when there is something you can do to take a bit of the pressure off. Due to her back Amber made a clunking sound as she walked and it was very evident where she was when she was walking around the house and it did sadden me to hear her clunking into the bedroom day after day. I knew one day it wouldn't be like this but for now my heart felt deeply for her it really did.

I was still giving all the other pugs their normal walks around the farm and at those times I would put Amber in her night-time pen then bring her out again when we all got back inside. Sometimes she'd be sitting up waiting for me to lift her out, other times she would be fast asleep so I left her there to rest. As soon as she woke up she would give a little growly woof and I'd be listening for that little growly woof and shoot into the bedroom to lift her out as soon as I heard it. Then I'd carry her to the water bowl to see if she wanted a drink, she didn't, she would never drink any of the water no matter how fresh it was. And I always made sure it was fresh, that was my routine. I'd hear little woofs coming from the bedroom then go quickly freshen up the water so Amber wasn't drinking water that had been lapped at by other dogs. If she had been an only dog then drinking water that somebody else had touched may have been displeasing to her. I thought that was what was putting her off, it wasn't, she for some reason just did not want to drink out of the water bowl. She would stand in front of the bowl, sniff it, then look up at me as if to say "I'm not going to drink this and you can't make me" and she was right I couldn't. So I began adding water to her food as way of keeping her fluids up and that was fine she had no issues with that which was good because you can't have them becoming dehydrated at any cost. I still kept trying to get her to drink from the water bowl though, but it just wasn't happening. She'd stand there sniffing at it in case it was food then give me a little woof and back away and go clunking of into the bedroom. The good thing about Amber was that she began communicating with me very early on, it wasn't the first day but I do believe by the second or third day she was constantly interacting with me when she needed something and I would always stop what I was doing and go see what she wanted. I'd stand above her and say "What do you need sweetheart, how can I help you" I'd always gently stroke her shoulder with one finger so she knew I was there and so she knew it was her that I was talking to. I never touched her head. David and I never do with blind dogs it's always their shoulder, a gentle shoulder stroke will let them know not only that you are there but which side of them you are standing on. It's like "Hey I'm here standing on your right" or "Hey I am standing on the left side of you and there's a chance that something is about to happen" it could be that we are going to put their eye drops in, or that they are about to be picked up and you need to let them know these things so they can be prepared for it. Although we do run our hands over their bodies to let them know when we are about to pick them up, the running over of hands is the pickup signal in our house. It's what we do with all the blind pugs, first it's a gentle shoulder massage with one finger to let them know we are there then we'll softly run our hands over them to indicate that they are about to be lifted off the ground. You simply cannot go racing across a room and scoop a blind dog up without giving them some warning, that'd scare the hell out of them. Also the shoulder rubbing thing comes in handy with blind dogs at treat time, especially when you have pugs with perfect vision standing right next to them. So it'll be a shoulder stoke and then their heads will turn either left or right and you can get that treat into their mouths pretty quickly. Amber was especially adorable at treat time, I'd rub her shoulder and her head would turn and her beautiful little teeny tiny mouth would begin to open. She knew what was going on, what I was stroking her shoulder for and she was ready.

The shoulder rubbing thing starts on day one with our vision impaired pugs. So Amber would bark and I'd go over and stoke her shoulder and she would turn her head and I'd talk to her, then try and figure out what she wanted. I was thankful to Amber for her communication. It's really helpful when they start letting you know they want something. And because I was responding to her she kept on communicating. I guess if I'd been one of those people who ignored their dogs because they aren't aware why the dog is barking then Amber's voice would have eventually fallen silent, being ignored will do that and it does make me sad knowing there are dogs out there trying to communicate with their people and being disregarded. Imagine being blind and old and trying to settle into a new home and you are trying to tell this person you are now living with that you need something and they just don't care enough to listen to your voice and investigate. Me, I'll respond straight away, well as long as I'm not already helping one of the other pugs I'll respond straight away, if not I'll call over to them to let them know I've heard and am coming as quickly as I can. I'll also start to learn to read the different barks. The settling in period is for both me and my newest family member, it's a case of not just them getting used to me but me getting used to them, so I watch, I listen and I learn.

But you do have to familiarise yourself with both the bark and the dog. Because I have lived with some that just bark their heads off because you are not getting dinner ready fast enough and at those times I don't encourage communication and after a few days of that happening they come to realise that barking in a demanding manner is not going to get them anywhere and so they stop. But communicating woofs from a blind, old or special needs dog are never ignored because there is a reason they are doing it. And it's your job as their guardian to learn what each different bark means and go help them out. Amber wasn't the type of dog to bark for no reason, I've found that a lot of the dogs who come to live with us don't bark unless there's a reason for it, they bark to let you know they need you, bored dogs are the only dogs I've found who bark for the sake of it and I think that's because they are trying to amuse themselves somehow. I have lived next door to a lot of barkers when I lived in suburbia and I knew it was because they never got taken for a walk, that one small boring backyard was their only source of entertainment and that can be a pretty sad way to live especially when a daily walk could cure it. So they are not really barking for nothing are they, they are barking because they are bored out of their brains and want to go for a walk or to get a bit of attention from somebody. I've found that contented dogs are generally silent. Yes they'll woof with excitement for the usual things like when a visitor arrives, a paddock sibling walks by or a bowl of food is placed down in front of them, or they'll give little woofs as they dance around your feet when you are in the kitchen and they'll give excitable woofs when you are about to go for a walk and those woofs are fine but the demanding yap, yap, yap well that'll be nipped in the bud quite quickly here because you can't live like that. Don't get me wrong, I've been living with dogs long enough to know the difference between a talker and a demander. I'm not an airhead clapping my hands with glee while a pile of dogs bark madly at me in a deafening way. I'm not standing there all simple minded and encouraging because I think I've got a houseful of brilliant little communicators, no definitely not, what I'd have then would be a houseful of misbehavers who were making life unbearable for everybody who lives on or near the farm and nobody wants that. There is a huge difference between a talker and a barker and it is up to us to know what that difference is. Although I have to add here that some dogs, just like some humans, do have different volumes of voices, you could have a dog that has been born with a very high pitched voice and you can't be constantly telling them off for it, that'd be no life for them. They can't help how they've been born so you just have to work around it, work out a way to live in harmony with them. I've got one here now who isn't bored and isn't being naughty but his communicating voice is just naturally high and it can be really annoying sometimes, yet all he's doing is happily woofing along with his siblings having absolutely no idea that he's about ten times louder than everybody else. At those times you just have to more or less grin and bear it. There's not a lot else you can do. You merely have to accept him for who he is.

I was very glad Amber was talking. I'd hear her little rumbling pug voice and think to myself "Lucky, lucky me". Her voice was pleasing to my ears and helping her was pleasing to my heart and soul. I'd reach down and stroke her shoulder after I'd gotten her what she wanted, I'd lean in and tell her how grateful I was that she had let me know she needed help and that next time she needed me she must once again give a little woof and I'd be right there. When Amber was in the bedroom nervous and hiding she didn't woof for me, I think at those time she really needed to have a break from everybody and everything and that included me. And I was fine with that. I didn't interfere. Amber wasn't the first dog to have done this and I doubt she'll be the last, you just have to look at everything from their point of view and if a dog is so scared that they feel their only option is to run and hide, well you need to be understanding of that. When Amber clunked into the bedroom she always went and sat beside her night time pen because I guess that was familiar to her, she couldn't get in but she would have been able to smell her bedding in that area and such a thing would have been comforting. And if that bed hadn't been enclosed she would have been able to get in it, and more importantly out of it when she wasn't feeling so afraid. But the night-time pen is enclosed for a reason so that's why I went and placed a new blanket down for her, at first I put it right beside the night-time pen but when I saw her backing further underneath the bed I began moving it with her so that she always had a nice place to lay. All the dogs we've taken in who felt the need to hide under our bed have always chosen David's side, never mine and that's because David's side of the bed faces the bedroom door. That side allows them to know when somebody is entering the room and such a thing is very important to them, it's also the best place to hear what everybody else in the house is getting up to, all throughout the day those sounds would have been being picked up by little greying ears. Amber's hearing was perfect and her sense of smell divine, she knew who was coming her way without having to see them. She would have been able to tell who was who out of the pugs due to the way they walked and them all having their own unique smell. She would have been able to tell the difference between me and David too, our different sounding shoes, our different ways of moving, his stride, my sway, his masculine aftershave, my vanilla body spray. Heck she would have even known what flavour lip gloss I had put on that day. Probably knew when I was standing in front of the mirror with a different flavour in each hand trying to decide if I should go with bubble gum or pineapple. From her little nest underneath the bed I bet she was thinking to herself "For the love of god woman will you just pick one, life is short, it really doesn't matter in the long run". I have no doubt at all that Amber was very much aware of even the tiniest incident that happened throughout the day, the routine of our daily life was constantly being made note of and stored and gaining all this knowledge was making her feel more secure. From her safety zone she could listen to everything until she felt confident enough to want to join in. I even had one dog who was so terrified that I gave them their meals in the bedroom, I didn't like that they were eating in that room but we take in a lot of dogs that have been through hell, they come to us deeply traumatized and I would never ever drag a dog out to eat if they are petrified and trembling. I'd rather feed them on a towel and then go clean the area up when they've finished eating. As soon as they are happy enough to walk around the house though, well that's when I start to feed them with everybody else. When they enter your house they are doing the very best they can do at the time and when they can do better they will do it, you just have to give them some time and a whole lot of understanding and really it's not a big deal to change the feeding rules for a few weeks until they've settled in. Also when I'm sliding myself under the bed to retrieve the bowl and clean up any dropped food it gives me a chance to give them a gentle stroke of reassurance and whisper a few kind words into their little ears so they know everything is going to be ok. The thing you always need to have in the back of your mind is this, once they are no longer full of fear, once they trust you enough, once they have given you their heart, they won't want to be hiding in the bedroom anymore, they'd rather be wherever you are. Once you become their person they will never want to leave your side.

And that is exactly what happened with Amber. I can very clearly recall the day she decided to put her full trust in me inside the house. I can see it now like it only happened yesterday. It was a beautiful moment and as with all of life's beautiful moments they stay with you. I believe it happened the third or fourth week she was here, I can't remember the length of time exactly but I sure can recall everything about the day. I was sitting at the kitchen table having a bit of a cry because I was missing Horton so much. The dogs and I had all just come in from a toilet break and as was always the case Amber had quickly taken herself off to the bedroom while the other pugs settled down to sleep in one of the lounge room beds. I was sniveling but not all out bawling my eyes out. No need for a handkerchief this time. I just let the tears roll slowly down my cheeks and fall onto my t-shirt. I believe I had been thinking about Horton while I was outside and when I came back in it was very evident that he was not here anymore. And it was around Mother's Day too and I was sitting there thinking this time last year I had a little pug's nappy to change and now I didn't, the entire thing hit me hard. I was pretty much lost in my thoughts, completely absorbed in my own world of memories when I heard that all too familiar clunking sound only it wasn't moving away from me, no this time it was coming towards me. I instantly stopped crying because this was no time for tears. I knew exactly what was happening here and my heart was about to burst open with excitement, my love, my teeny tiny little love was searching me out and it was the first time since she'd arrived that she had done this. I was elated, totally elated but I had to sit calmly and wait. Getting up and moving about would have frightened her, the kitchen chair scraping across the wooden floorboards would have had her scurrying back underneath the bed faster than lightening I knew it would. So I sat very still and listened to the clunking. The island kitchen bench was between me and Amber so she was completely blocked from my view. I heard her clunk to the bedroom door then stop. I guess she must have been sniffing at the air, finding where I was, getting her bearing and also deciding if she was going to come out any further or not. This was a big step for her I knew it was. I also knew this could be far enough for her today, it may well have taken a few attempts before Amber was feeling confident enough to come all the way. I was straining to hear her over the sound of pugs snoring; of course I didn't begrudge them a midday nap but I did wish that just for today they could snore a little less loudly or at least snore in unison so I could hear Amber in-between their contented huffs and puffs. After a period of time the clunking started up again. Amber was now entering the kitchen. There was another pause, not as long this time, I knew she was now standing directly on the other side of the island bench, if she kept moving I would soon be able to see her. I kept my eyes on the floor, waiting, holding my breath and waiting. The clunking sound started again and then suddenly there she was. My eyes focused on the teeny tiny figure, she was sort of creeping along the ground. Amber was still very frightened. I could tell by the way she was moving. The sight of that little soul being so brave changed my mood instantly. I was incredibly proud of Amber in that moment. It was a real breakthrough for her. My little darling was feeling confident enough to come out from underneath the bed and I couldn't have been more excited for her, for me, for both of us. Amber paused again and started to sway a little and I thought to myself well she'll either walk the rest of the way to my chair or she'll turn around and I'll be able to smile as I watch her little bottom shuffling off. Either way I was good with it, she'd taken a huge step and that was more than enough for me to be happy about. But then with all the triumph of an Olympic gold medalist crossing the finish line Amber started clunking towards me.

She was a couple of steps from my chair when she paused again, her little nose went straight into the air and she began sniffing but her legs remained completely still. I spoke to her, said "Hello little love" If I had wanted to I could have easily leant over and gotten her, but that would have meant dragging her across the floor a little and I certainly did not want to be doing that because it would have frightened her and totally ruined everything she had accomplished, so no I had to sit there and wait for her to come all the way to me regardless of how long it took. It had to be Amber's choice and if she turned around and clunked her way back into the bedroom then so be it, she would come to me the next day or the day after that or even next week but at all times the choice was entirely hers. I could tell she was thinking, I hadn't known her all that long but I had come to know in that short time what her thinking face looked like and that was it. I observed her, there was nothing else to be done so I took joy in seeing her standing there, I marveled at my beautiful, brave little daughter. I thought she was smart too because she had come through the kitchen, not walked into the middle of the lounge room which was a more direct path, oh sure she would have still been able to find me if she'd gone the long way round, everything is open plan so she would not have been blocked from me. But she had come through the kitchen because she knew exactly where I was and I thought she was absolutely brilliant for doing that. Clearly she had heard me pull out my kitchen chair, her time hiding underneath the bed had been well spent, she probably knew exactly where I was at all times but until that day hadn't had the confidence or inclination to come and find me. No doubt she had known when I was standing at the kitchen sink or in front of the washing machine unloading. She would have taken note of my footsteps and knew when I was heading out the door to peg the washing out. She would have known I was walking differently to how I normally did if I had a basket of wet towels on my hip, it would have given me a different way of moving and given The Divine One an indication of exactly what was going on. Blind dogs hear absolutely everything.

Amber was right beside my chair now so I rubbed the side of her shoulder with my finger, ran my hands over her body then leant down and picked her up. I held her in my arms and kissed her little old ears and thanked her a million times over for loving and trusting me enough to do what she had just done, I told her I knew it was a big thing for her. I told her how much I appreciated it. How very grateful I was to her for opening up her tender little heart to me, told her I felt blessed. We sat there together quietly for a little while and then I began talking softly to her again, telling her she was beautiful and brave and fantastic and wonderful, that sort of thing. She sat calmly while I stroked her then I began humming to her, nothing loud, just a quiet little tune. She wasn't responding much but she didn't want to get down either, so we just sat there happily together. Because of her back she couldn't sit on my knee the way a normal dog would sit, I kept putting her in that position but she kept letting me know she couldn't do it. So I kept repositioning her until she was comfortable, she was tilting down on an angle and it looked a bit awkward but it must have been what felt good for her. Together we had figured out a way where she could sit quite comfortably for a period of time. Yes it was an unusual way to be, but she was comfortable so she stayed. And really that was the important thing, her comfort, I read the signals she was sending me and positioned her accordingly. Amber had already had the "Always and Forever' talk some time ago but I decided to tell her again anyway. I gently stroked one ear while whispering into the other one that this was her forever home now and that she was loved beyond measure and very much wanted here. I also explained about Ruby, Grace and Horton and that if she ever heard me crying it had nothing whatsoever to do with her, I didn't want my little mouse feeling rejected, so I explained that I was just missing my babies and left it at that. What else was there to tell her but the truth and I knew she understood the missing thing because she would have been missing her old family too.

Well this little routine of ours went on for about a week or so. We'd all go for a short stroll and Amber enjoyed every single second of meandering about, real keen on investigating, loved pottering around, always very interested in the new smells she encountered each day and never in any hurry to come back inside again. But once we were inside she would instantly take herself straight off into the bedroom and my heart always sank a little bit when I saw that tiny frame shuffling off, sad that she still felt unsafe in the house, sad that she was still feeling unsettled, still fearful. But the joy was that after the first time of sitting on my knee she would now always venture back out again. Sometimes she'd have a bit of a sleep underneath the bed and come out when she woke up, other times she'd walk into the bedroom and come clunking out about five or ten minutes later when she realised that she didn't need to be in there anymore. Entire days were no longer spent hiding underneath the bed. She'd be in the bedroom clearly listening to what I was doing. I would finish doing the dishes, dry my hands and then there'd be the sound of the kettle boiling. She would have heard that I was making myself a cup of tea. And when I have a cup of tea I generally sit for a bit and Amber was well aware of this by now. I'd walk over to the kitchen table, put my cup down, pull my chair out and a few moments later I'd hear Amber clunking out of the bedroom so she could sit on my knee. Just like clockwork she would appear. I guess she must have been sitting in her nest just waiting for that all too familiar sound of the kitchen chair being pulled out. As time went on Amber started coming out of the bedroom when I wasn't sitting down. I could be anywhere in the house but when I heard those little paws clunking I would quickly stop what I was doing and go see if she was ok. I didn't ever disturb her, just watched on from a distance to see where she was moving to. I both wanted and needed to know where she was at all times. She never headed for the kitchen table when she knew I wasn't there, but I did see her scouting around for some safe hidey spots in other parts of the house and when she found them I would go and put a blanket down for her. Amber's nests were all in hard to get at places because that's where she felt safest, her spots were chosen where there was just enough room for a little old girl to squeeze into. She chose the spots I just made sure there was some soft cushioning down for her in each one of them. During the settling in period Amber had a few well-chosen areas and she'd move from one to the other depending on how she was feeling. If I was outside hanging the washing when Amber moved spots the first thing I always did when I came back inside was go check on her and a lot of the time I found she was no longer where she had been when I left the house so it was a game of hide and seek until I located her. And I'd find her but act like I hadn't because in doing so I felt she would feel more safe and secure. A lot of the time she'd actually wait until we were all outside before moving positions, I think she waited for when the house was the quietest, the safest. Sometimes if I was on the deck and heard her clunking I'd go to the windows and press my face against the glass to see what she was doing. If we were in the house when she moved occasionally one of the other pugs would sniff at her as she clunked along and I noticed that she wasn't too fazed by that, wasn't too happy the first few times it happened but she soon got used to them checking her out. And it was funny because she got used to them around the same time they got used to her way of moving and so less and less pugs got up to check on her, it was like "Ok that's just what our new sister does so we'll leave her to it". Well apart from Steffy, Steffy almost always checked on Amber, sometimes just with her eyes, like she'd look up and watch her go then put her head back down and carry on sleeping.

Eventually Amber started only using the one hidey spot in the lounge room. I watched on for a couple of days and when she no longer went to her other nests I packed those blankets up. I also packed up the blanket she had underneath our bed because that too was no longer being used. Clearly Amber had found her preferred position and was now spending all her time there, if she wasn't out on a walk she was in the area between the side of the couch and the coffee table. It was only a tiny area, not even enough room to turn around in, but it was a through and through so she could enter and exit from either side which was a good thing because due to her back she wasn't all that good at walking backwards, a lot of dogs with spinal conditions can't back up. This bed was smack in the middle of the room. I think that's why it was chosen. I believe she wanted to know everything that was going on, she may not have wanted to be in the thick of it all yet but she was at least wanting to be nearer to the action and her coffee table spot was closer to it than underneath the bed was, she was more part of our family activities now and yet still would have felt safe. I loved seeing her little face there, as I moved around the house I'd bend down, glance in and there she'd be as happy as a clam. So I'd spend a few moments watching my little field mouse sleeping then carry on my way. We were all doing our normal things, going about our business and from a comfy nest in the middle of the room a beautiful little blessing with it's tongue peeping out was taking it all in. The sound of the dishes being washed, dried and put away, the sound of the fridge opening and closing, the beep of the microwave, the sound of the phone ringing and me answering. She would have heard the washing machine stop spinning; it makes a sound that reminds me of fairy music. I've always liked that about it and I wondered if Amber did too.

Clearly the noise from the floorboards weren't bothering her as much now either. From her central nest she would have also been listening to the sound of the outside doors being opened and closed, she would have been able to tell which door we were using from the slightly different sounds that came floating in. Two doors open onto the front deck and one leads out onto the small back deck and down the ramp. If she heard a door opening and the sound of cows she would have known it was one of the front decking doors I was using. Amber was picking up on all these little clues I knew she was. I knew she knew when we were using the back door because that's when she would make a move. Amber knew that if there was a bit of pug tap dancing being done by the back door then we were probably about to go for a walk and there was no way she was going to miss that so out she would clunk. The other doors well, we would more often than not be constantly traipsing in and out of them so she didn't always bother getting up. If she heard me making a cup of tea then heading outside she would have known I'd be going out to sit on the deck and enjoy the view while I sipped. And at those times she did quite often make a move, not as fast of a move as she did when we were at the back door. I guess she was making sure that I was staying put for a while before venturing out from her comfortable position. So off I'd go with my five little blessings and find a nice spot in the sun and the door was always left open for my new daughter to join me. I'd hear her clunking, see her little shape go right past the door, she was on a mission to find us and she'd do a lap of the lounge room then come back to the open door again and stand there so I'd go pick her up and carry her out and she would lay in the sun with us. It was lovely looking down at those peaceful slumbering bodies scattered all around me. The ones I was well used to and my new little blessing who was tinier than all the rest.

After a while Amber began trying out every single one of the regular lounge room beds, but only if they were unoccupied. I'd see her approaching one of them and I'd see a pug in there even though she hadn't discovered them yet. I always hoped she would get in the bed with them, have a bit of company, but for those first few months she wasn't ready to, such things would come in time. So she'd clunk over, find a sleeping snoring body there and simply turn and clunk off to one of the other beds and if she was ever unlucky enough to have all of them taken then she'd give up and go back to her coffee table couch nest. I think she was chasing the sun when she was moving to the other beds because being central to the room her coffee table couch nest didn't get any sun. And I do think that's what made her eventually climb in beside a slumbering sibling. I think she thought to herself "Bugger this, I'm getting in, why the hell should you have all the warmth". Incidentally Steffy was the very first pug Amber chose to climb in with and it was nice to see her snuggling up with somebody else, for a while there I thought it was never going to happen. To the point where I once for a split second on seeing where Amber was heading thought about racing ahead and lifting a half asleep pug out and putting them in bed with somebody else just so Amber could have a bit of sun. But I don't like disturbing sleeping dogs it's not good for them, and besides Amber really had to make the decision on her own. Sure I could have very easily picked her up and put her in a bed that was already occupied but that would have made things worse. Sometimes as much as we want to help and think we are helping we just have to sit back and allow them to do what they want when they want to do it. When Amber decided she no longer needed her middle of the room nest I picked the blanket up and placed it in one of the dog beds so she could claim that as her own. I put it in the end bed, the one nearest the kitchen table and sink so she could be nearer to me. She knew it was her bed, recognised its smell, walked over and clunked right in. Then as time drifted on she'd just get in any bed she liked with whoever she pleased, she blended in nicely with the pack, never bossy and never timid, just her being herself, content living within the family fold. I was glad Tommy had his own special chair that he liked to sleep on because he was so huge against The Divine One's frame, he rarely slept in the dog beds on the floor and after a while Amber started to figure this fact out. I guess she wondered why he had special privileges and she didn't. One day she got out of her bed and walked over and stood in front of Thomas's chair, I'd seen her do it a few times when Tommy was on the couch with Steffy and Emily and thought she was merely pausing for a moment or two as she was passing by. But when she went and stood in front of his chair and there was nobody else on the chair but him I realised it was her way of asking to be up there with him, so I lifted her up and placed her behind her big brother. Amber seemed too really like Tommy. Sure she liked the others as well but she did especially love being around Thomas. I thought it funny our smallest had chosen our biggest to be her friend. I believe she was drawn to his quiet, docile, peaceful nature, that's why she gravitated. I think Tommy's overall calmness was soothing to Amber at a point in her life when calmness was exactly what she needed and he seemed to like that she'd latched onto him. Outside she didn't need him as much because that was her domain, I never saw them walking around together, well sure they walked together sometimes but I never saw the same clinginess that I witnessed inside the house. And Steffy wasn't in any way put out by Amber and Tommy's new found closeness. She was on the couch next to Emily when Amber first made a move towards Thomas's chair and she merely lifted her head, watched what her little sister was doing, saw me lift her up, stared at Amber, stared at Tommy, then quickly went back to sleep. I guess she knew that Tommy was helping the new one out so there was no need for her to worry.

My only concern with Amber being up with Tommy was Amber's lack of vision, I didn't want this limited visioned soul falling off and hurting herself so I used Tommy's body as a shield. There was plenty of room on that chair for both of them so each time Amber asked to be with her brother I would reposition Tommy to protect her. Slightly move his big body over so that he was always between her and the edge of the chair. And Amber being the kind of sensible pug that she was made the situation easier, she realised she was up high, she knew there was a drop, she had just enough vision to know that and I knew if she was behind him that I could go to the other side of the room and she would be ok. With Tommy being there I knew I didn't have to sit beside the two of them all the time, I could walk off and do what I needed to do and again the open plan lounge room allowed me to be able to keep an eye on the two of them. So I would place Amber behind her brother and wait until she had settled down to sleep then off I'd go vacuuming or folding the laundry, always with the two of them in view and even though I trusted them I was never silly enough to go outside leaving them there like that. I always waited until Amber woke up before venturing out the door. Tommy didn't mind Amber being up there. Tommy was a friend to everybody, he was more than happy to share. I thought their friendship was nice for both of them. Amber was the same size as Lilly so he was back to being around one so small again, maybe they brought comfort to each other but for very different reasons. From the other side of the room I'd watch them together, she'd be there with her little tongue peeping out, eyes closed but flickering around in sleep. She'd use his neck or tummy as a chin rest. I often worried if in a violent dream she may have bit her tongue but she never did and I was so glad because it was such a lovely little tongue she had. I wouldn't have liked to see her hurt herself by doing something as natural as falling asleep. Amber always seemed to sleep more soundly when she was with Tommy and I could fully understand why. Tommy was such a teddy bear. A big snuggly teddy bear that got into these real deep sleeps, half the time I don't think he realised Amber was there. If he was in a deep sleep he didn't always wake up when I placed her behind him. Even when she was moving about to get comfortable he still wouldn't wake up. So she'd settle down and be there with her little face leaning against his stomach or chest, when his snoring was the loudest her head would be bobbing about each time he took in his huge breaths and if that got too much she'd simply move herself over. Place her head on his neck for a less disruptive slumber and again her moving around didn't always wake him. The times Tommy did stir he'd simply turn round, sniff Amber's little face in acknowledgement then go straight back to sleep. And all the while from the other side of the room a pair of hazel eyes was watching every move they made.

Tommy and Amber

CHAPTER FIVE

First Vet Visit

When Amber met our vet for the very first time she was going to see him for a number of reasons. Yes to have her stitches taken out but also to see about her cough, the medicine we had her on would give her a respite but then she'd once again be back to coughing and was pretty exhausted due to it. Also, in the last twenty four hours or so she had begun showing signs of sinus trouble, mucus discharge, sneezing, sounding a bit wheezy, could her sinus passages be inflamed, maybe, so I wanted her to be checked out in that area too because if you leave these things an infection can occur and I didn't want that happening. That would have been painful for her. It wasn't the biggest time of year for allergies but this little one had just moved onto a farm hadn't she, who knew what kind of things could be setting her off. Amber had quite a bit going on with her at the time, is it any wonder she was exhausted. And then there was her back. Today was the day I was finally going to find out where things stood with that. I was more than happy for The Divine One to be seeing our vet that morning. Looking at her I began wondering if an infection had already started to occur somewhere and because Amber was already on antibiotics it did concern me that she'd still gotten sick. The vet who desexed Amber put her on antibiotics as is generally the case after an operation but those antibiotics weren't helping her with her other issues. David and I both felt she would probably need to be put on a different type of antibiotics to help clear those things up. As we sat in the car park waiting for the vet to open, I looked down at the snuffly little princess sitting on a funny angle on my knee. I was glad that Amber was about to have her back assessed because that situation had been playing on my mind since she first arrived. But I felt peaceful about it because I knew I would be leaving the car park with some answers, and knowing exactly what it is that you are dealing with is half of the problem solved because you can then go on to find out all you can to help the little soul out. I stroked Amber's ears and told her that she would be leaving the car park feeling a whole lot better than she was feeling right now. She didn't look up though, didn't acknowledge me in any way at all, simply sat there coughing and spluttering because at that point it was all she could do.

When Amber was carried into the surgery she was looking and sounding quite worse for wear. To say she was a bit of a mess is probably being polite. We got a few sympathetic looks from people in the waiting room which told me they felt as sorry for The Divine One as her new parents did. David placed Amber on the table while I fished a list out of my pocket. I glanced across at the two of them. Dave had his big hands around Amber softly massaging her shoulders. She looked so tiny sitting there hunched over, the area around her eyes was swollen and she was now coughing loudly again too. Our vet began talking to Amber saying he'd not heard such a big noise coming out of somebody so little. He was bent down level with her head and she was responding to him, she was ill but she could still feel his kindness. Amber hadn't coughed much when we were sitting in the waiting room but she began having a huge coughing fit now and I was glad he got to hear the sound she was making so he could tell what kind of cough it was. Of course I wasn't happy that she was ill but I was glad he was getting to hear the type of sound coming from within her. Sure I could have described it and may have even resorted to actually trying to imitate it. I've been known to do that type of thing over the years and no doubt looked and sounded quite the twit while doing so, but in trying to help him help my dogs I've done it regardless of how stupid I've looked and felt. But this time I didn't need to undertake such actions because Amber was doing a pretty good job of it herself. Listening to her would have given our vet some kind of indication as to what was going on. He had no doubt heard every type of cough there was and was an expert at picking up on all the different sounds. Sometimes you can take a dog in and say this and that is going on with them and then they'll sit there on the table looking and sounding perfectly fine. Or you'll take a dog in that isn't walking too well and they'll march into the surgery with a spring in their step because they remember being there last time and getting a tasty treat but then they'll start limping again on the way back to the car. It hasn't happened too often but it has happened on occasion and you just have to laugh about it because what else is there to do.

I stood back watching our vet gently checking Amber out. He is more then used to us bringing in little old blessings that are in need of a whole lot of tender loving care. We have presented him with some real sights over the years and as wretched as Amber was looking that morning he didn't blink an eye, just got on with the job at hand, started giving our coughing spluttering swollen eyed stooped over ball of illness the once over, the way he does when meeting all of our newest family members. And he never ever rushes, which I love, much care is always taken to see what is actually wrong with them. In all the years we've been going to see him he's always been so beautiful with our oldies and he has a special place in his heart for rescues. We have a country vet for the sheep and horses and on the rarest of occasions one of the pugs will see them too and we have a suburban vet. Our suburban vet is our main vet, our pug vet, he is one of the best vets I've ever met, that's why we travel the distance to see him. Once as we were heading there we started counting how many other vet surgeries we were passing along the way, I believe there were eight that were closer to us, but you can't choose your vet due to location, our pugs are far too precious to us for that. I remember the first time our vet met Horton. Ruby and Grace were going to see him that day and because we couldn't leave Horton on his own he had accompanied his siblings on this vet visit. Grace had an ear infection and Ruby was there for one of her niggly things. Ruby did go to see the vet quite often. Horton was just a baby and the rest of the pugs were elderly but fairly robust, but Ruby struggled in a few areas, struggled when she first came to live with us and as she aged things got a little bit harder for her still. So we walked in and he was about to start checking Grace out and David had Horton in his arms and he looked over at him with the biggest smile on his face and said "Oh don't tell me you've got yourself a puppy? He knew this was unusual for us. Up until that point he'd only seen us with elderly dogs. He knew where our hearts lay, so to see us with this little bright eyed excitable baby, well that was something new, something worth making a fuss over. He couldn't tell at that point that Horton had hemivertebra, yes he had his tinkle trousers on, he always had his tinkle trousers on when we were out and about because he had to, and nappy free time was for the farm only. But the tinkle trousers could look like a normal dog harness, that's all some people thought they were, at least on first glance they did anyway, once Horton was on the floor you could tell there was more to them but only if you had the mind to look and a lot of people didn't because they were now more looking at the way he was dragging his back legs. That was what gave the game away about Horton's spinal issues. But our vet hadn't seen him down yet, so I told him that Horton had hemivertebra and then stupidly started explaining to him in great detail exactly what hemivertebra was. And he just nodded his head politely. And I say stupidly because of course a vet would know all about hemivertebra but I think I had been so used to having to explain the condition to people that I just went on auto mode and started yapping away without giving it a second thought. Horton had been sharing my life for quite a while by this time so I had the explanation well-rehearsed in my head but boy did I feel silly when carrying Horton back out to the car.

After giving Amber a good examination it was time for her stitches to come out, he said he was happy with how nicely she had healed and I was too, the vet who did the desexing had done a neat clean job. While he listened to her lungs I mentioned the name of the antibiotics she was on, he made note of them then prescribed a different kind. Actually the entire time we were in there I was telling him everything I had observed about Amber since she first arrived in her new home. The more you can tell your vet about your dog the better idea they will have about what's going on with them. Me, well, I mention everything I have noticed and I mean every single little thing because I feel you need to. I don't leave anything out not even the smallest or seemingly unimportant detail because sometimes it's the littlest things that give the biggest clue. What everybody wants here is a proper diagnosis and your vet isn't with your dog all the time like you are so it's vital that you are observant and pass all of this important information on. Tell him exactly what you've seen, write it down if you need to so that you'll remember. I often go in with a long list because I don't want to be driving home and remember something that I forgot to mention during the examination. When you have a sick dog everything is important, everything needs stating, everything they are showing you through their behaviour well, it's vital that your vet gets to know these things. He will know what means something and what means nothing. It's up to you to help in every way you can. I started talking to our vet about Amber's back, telling him what I'd witnessed. I also mentioned that I didn't think our new little girl was a very well-bred pug but that it wasn't just her breeding I'd noticed, I thought there was something else going on with her, although when I said she wasn't well bred I mouthed the words to him because I didn't want Amber hearing this. And he smiled about the not well bred thing. I imagined him thinking as he glanced down upon our little slumped over darling that "You don't have to tell me she's not a well-bred pug". Our vet got Amber up on her feet then tenderly began checking out her spine. She wasn't happy about being made to stand up but she was very good while he tested her reflexes then slumped back down again as soon as he took his hands away. He said he felt Amber had suffered an injury to her back in her previous life, happened quite some time ago he said and that the injury was not addressed at the time it occurred. He said if it had been looked at when it first happened maybe there could have been something done to help her, but as it was now and due to her age and condition, he felt it best to leave things as they were. Her back had been made to heal the way it had. He said she wasn't in pain, just looked funny and walked funny. He stroked her little old head, said she'd never be much of a walker so not to expect much from her in that area. David and I both nodded to indicate we understood. He looked at her scuffed up feet. I told him they weren't as bad as that when she first came, that walking around the farm had done most of it but that she was now wearing socks when outdoors. I then started thinking to myself that Amber mustn't have had a big yard in her previous home or had perhaps even been kept inside a small dog run because if the injury to her back was a number of years old and her paws weren't scuffed up when she first arrived then she'd not done a whole lot of moving around before coming to live with us. And, I thought that would have been upsetting to her because in the short time she'd been living on the farm Amber had revealed to me just how much she liked pottering around and having a sniff. Then again maybe the reason she was such a little investigator now was because she'd not been given much of a chance to be one before. Or perhaps she didn't walk much before coming to live with us because she simply couldn't do it, maybe the injury to her back had prevented her from taking more than a few steps. You are thinking of every scenario because you just don't know in these cases. It's all a load of guessing really and you'll never be able to know the whole truth. Her previous owners may have penned her off after the accident occurred hoping that by doing so her back would heal. Maybe they figured rest and restriction would be enough to do it, if the injury was years old they must have given it some considerable time to heal and when time made little difference well I'm guessing that's when she would have been dropped off at the pound. And again it's all guesswork because Amber couldn't talk so she couldn't tell me what had actually taken place. For my part though I was glad to finally have an answer to why Amber walked the way she did. But I was also pretty upset that she hadn't received the care she needed when the accident first happened. I couldn't understand how anybody could leave this little darling in that condition. Even if they hadn't seen the accident occur they would have been able to tell that their pug was now walking differently to how she used to walk and yet they didn't care enough to take her to a vet to see what the problem was, if they had done maybe Amber would be able to walk normally now. So they didn't take proper care of her dry eyes and she'd lost vision due to it and they didn't look after her properly when she'd first gotten hurt and now she walked abnormally. It made me wonder why they had bought Amber in the first place. And it's something I think about a lot with the pugs I take in. Pugs are not cheap, pug puppies are going for incredibly high prices these days and they keep climbing higher and higher every year. You'd think if somebody had spent that much money on a dog they would at least look after it properly.

When our vet had finished the examination he smiled down at Amber and once again stroked her head. It's times like this when you are grateful for having such a wonderful vet, a good vet is a must and I have always been thankful to have found the one we did. He is kind and caring and extremely knowledgeable. He's set so many of our pugs right and you need that, you need to have confidence in the person who is taking care of your little old blessings. We have been with our vet for almost two decades and it's a great thing to have somebody you can fully trust. We had changed vets twice in a short period of time before finding the vet we have now. I am always more loyal to my dogs then I am the vet and the ones we had previously were not taking the best care of our dogs. I was having doubts about their opinions and David was too. And we always go with our gut, because you have to, gut instincts are there for a reason and I have always, always followed mine. I trust my intuition, I've always had a strong one, no matter what the situation or who it is I am dealing with I have always gone with my instinct and I think it's even more important to do that when we are dealing with people who have our dogs lives in their hands. And don't just go with your own instincts see where your dog stands too. Dogs, well all animals really, have very powerful intuitions, they have to, it's what helps them survive in the wild and also because they can't talk they use their intuitions a lot more than we do, they instantly pick up on things. I have often thought to myself what if the dog on the table is getting very bad vibes from the vet and yet I allowed them to go ahead and treat them. How horrible would it be for that dog sitting there knowing things were not right and yet having no control over what is about to happen to them. So when a feeling arises in me I have to go with it, I can't not, and I will also be looking at my dog to see where they sit with things. I'll be observing their reactions and I allow them to guide me. And yes you have to know what is "Just nerves" at being at the vet and what is "Out and out signifying that something isn't right". And again it is all about knowing the dog in your care. I talk about this a lot in my books because it is so very important. Being in tune with our four legged family members is vital for so many things, it's vital for their health, it's vital for their happiness, it's vital for their everyday life. I more trust my dogs, sheep or horses then I do most people. I could site many cases here about handymen on the farm that my dogs just didn't like and later finding out why or shearers who my sheep reacted badly to and farriers and vets who came near my horses. But because the list of incidents is lengthy I'll just have to say please be in tune with all the animals in your care.

Amber was given an anti-inflammatory injection and we were sent home with a strong course of antibiotics, ones more suited to what she was dealing with now. We were told to stop the other antibiotics and just give her this new two week course. When we were walking to the car I said to David that he should drive because I had some serious snuggling to do with our newest little blessing. As we drove along I started talking about how much I loved Amber, I said "I know she's only been with us nine days but she's already brought so much happiness to me" David said he felt exactly the same way. I was looking down at The Divine One and began thinking out loud. I started saying how I wanted to get her to 14, 15 and maybe even 16 years old because she's very precious. David looked over at the two of us and smiled. I guess he was happy to see me engaging again, happy that I had a special little soul that I was wanting a big future for. Amber was sitting on my knee still coughing and spluttering, she really did look like hell, but sick or not her little ears must have picked up on my words that morning because that's exactly what The Divine One went on to give us and we were both incredibly grateful to her for doing that.

Amber responded well to the new medication which was a good thing because we were fast coming up to winter and I didn't want her taking that illness with her into our coldest months. You don't want them ill at any time of the year really but during winter its always worse I think, but the way she was going we both felt that we'd be able to get her over her illnesses before winter hit and we did, it took a few more visits to the vet and a few more courses of antibiotics had to be taken but The Divine One was feeling a whole lot better by the time the weather turned cold. And Amber wasn't one of these pugs to linger making a big issues out of things, no as soon as she was feeling even the slightest bit better that was it, she was off, there was no holding her back and she'd improve more and more every day as the drugs took effect. Due to the personality she had dwelling within it was hard to keep her quiet, harder still to make her take a few more days to rest, she was such a little firecracker. She'd be up clunking about seeing what was going on around the place. So I'd let her do what she most wanted to do, at times I would have liked her to maybe lay in bed a little bit longer but she wasn't having any of it and it's not like you can force them to lay down and stay till so I'd just keep an extra close eye on her, follow her everywhere she went making sure she was ok. And the most usual noises would come out of her sometimes. She'd be coughing and trying to bark at the same time. She particularly liked being out on the front veranda in the afternoon sun. One day she ran across the veranda woofing and coughing and the other pugs went nuts because they'd never heard a sound quite like that before. Emily even shot down the driveway to the front gate maybe she thought there was something strange down there trying to get in. I'd hear Amber coughing in her nest and try and tiptoe outside with the other pugs leaving her to rest and sometimes it worked but more often than not it didn't. She'd hear what was going on and be by our sides in no time. But if the sun was out I didn't mind her being on the deck with the rest of us because I felt a bit of sunshine was doing her the world of good. At times I did Arthur's sets of exercises out there too, figured he may as well be out in the sunshine while doing them, didn't make him like them more or make him any more cooperative so my job wasn't any easier but it did at least let everybody have a bit of sunshine on their backs. Amber seemed to like being around when I was doing Arthur's sets. With what little eye sight she had she'd stand nearby watching, well I guess she was more listening really because she could hear better then she could see. I suppose she was listening to all the commotion going on, and thinking to herself "I don't know what's happening up there new brother but fank goodness it's happening to you not me" maybe she liked knowing something was going on and it not be her who was involved in it. She'd had a few vet visits, a few goes being up on the table getting examined and so no doubt was more than happy to not be the one needing attention this time. I recall the first time I noticed Amber's interest had been sparked. I didn't know she was in the bedroom with us until I heard that all too familiar cough. Normally I would have heard her clunking in but with battling with Arthur I hadn't heard or seen her entering the room just heard a little cough and glanced down to see this sweet tiny face looking up at us with it's little tongue hanging out. She seemed to be quite interested in what was going on or maybe she just liked knowing that Arthur was kicking my ass.

Although we didn't know it at the time that first vet visit would be just one in a very long line of vet visits that Amber had throughout her life. But that's just how it goes with rescuing, some dogs are going to be much needier than others so you take them as they come and love them through it. You'll have some join the family who will rarely have to see a vet the entire time they are with you and others who are at the vets a real lot and that's ok, we are used to it, you just have to take real good care of them, give them what they need in order to live happier, healthier and hopefully longer lives with you. To date Amber is the pug that has had the most vet visits out of anybody, although I have to say that Ruby ran a close second. But I reckon if you printed out a record of every single one of Amber's vet visits it'd look like a roll of toilet paper, well like an entire roll of toilet paper had been unraveled on the floor with dates, times, totals and paid in full stamped at the bottom of each visit. But boy was she worth it. And Amber was a very good patient, always quiet at the vets, no matter what was being done she was quiet, she may not have liked it but would just let them do what they needed to do without saying a word. Steffy on the other hand wasn't like that at all, she'd scream the entire place down, they'd often ring and say we could pick her up earlier than expected just to get her out of there. But Amber was cooperative and quiet and the vet nurses liked doting on her, she was tiny and blind and her tongue stuck out, that combination tugged on their heartstrings, I knew it because it did the same thing with me, they loved having her there and giving her lots of special attention. The Divine One was only little but she had this incredibly enormous spirit and I'd look at her and be thinking to myself "Yes I have witnessed that same spirit before and not too long ago either and he too had a teeny tiny body" a tiny little body that was filled to the brim with so much courage and determination and here was this little old girl behaving exactly like him. I believe the fact that Amber was a fighter helped her overcome some of her ailments. Well not so much overcome the niggly things she had but not let them get her down. She wasn't always feeling 100% and yet she carried on regardless and I watched on, watched her very closely, always making sure she wasn't overdoing it. And at times it was a judgement call, well a lot of the time it was a judgment call, especially as she aged, but I wasn't about to rein her in unless it was absolutely necessary. I didn't want to dampen that incredible spirit she had because I felt it was that which was keeping her going especially when she reached her teenage years. I believe what Amber had dwelling within kept her going when at times we thought she may have been nearing the end.

We had some funny vet visits with Amber throughout the years and she was always so popular with everybody she met. People in the waiting room always seemed to want to come over and talk about her and when they found out she was blind and knew how old she was you could tell their hearts softened towards her that little bit more. She had this face that would instantly draw strangers to her. I think people thought her size was cute too and the way her little tongue always hung out of her mouth, well that certainly didn't hurt either, and if it happened to be a cool day and she was wearing one of her pink coats, of course that drew people to her all the more. They'd move seats to come and be closer to Amber, children and adults alike moved seats to make her acquaintance. Sometimes it'd be the biggest toughest looking bloke in the room who'd come over to say hello and of course as is often the case his dog was almost as big as he was. But they were always respectful and always kept their dog on the other side of them and Amber was never down on the floor, she was always sitting on either mine or David's knee. We were protective of her because you had to be, she wasn't afraid of anything and if let down would have trundled off and been in the face of every dog in the surgery and as we all know not all dogs are friendly and it has nothing to do with size. Sometimes the biggest dogs can have the gentlest souls while the smaller ones can be full of attitude. Also you are in a vet surgery after all and dogs that aren't feeling well can sometimes be snappy. Then of course there is the not wanting your own precious little bundle of joy to pick up anything from a dog that is ill. Amber was always fine sitting on our knee she was never scrambling to get down. She was happy to sit and meet her admirers from the safety of either Dad or Mum's knee. Sometimes Amber wasn't the only pug we had sitting in the surgery waiting but she was the one who always got the most attention from people. She'd go on her own or she'd accompany somebody else who wasn't feeling too well and because she was there an awful lot people started to remember having met her before so would come over and ask how she was doing. With The Divine One you'd have periods of months on end where she'd not need to see the vet at all then other times she'd be there every two or three weeks, it all depended what was going on with her at the time. So something would flare up and she'd look so ill with it and off we'd go to see the vet again and because we wanted to make the experience as happy for her as we possibly could we always stopped for something to eat on the way home. Perhaps that's why she didn't really mind going to the vet. Because she knew there would always be a nice treat coming her way as soon as we got back in the car. Amber got super excited as soon as that engine started up. She'd be woofing her little old head off as we were going through the drive through. Some of the girls who took the order would lean out the window trying to see into the car, trying to see who it was that was making all the fuss. And if the order didn't come her way fast enough Amber would be up on her hind legs sniffing the air woofing even harder than she had been when the order was being placed.

I think I could write an entire book about Amber's vet visits. About the people we met, the dogs we met and the trips there and back. I remember one time being quite late for an appointment due to fussing about with the pugs we were leaving at home. I always like to give them a good walk before we set off that way I know they'll all settle down to sleep while we are gone. And also you want the pug who is seeing the vet to have been able to relieve themselves fully otherwise the examination can be uncomfortable for them. Nobody wants to be pushed and prodded if they have a full bladder or need to have a poo, so we try and make sure such things have been taken care of before setting off. And because we had been late leaving I hadn't checked Amber's face, even in the car I hadn't checked it because she had fallen asleep as soon as our car pulled out the driveway, I guess she was used to these long trips and figured she may as well sleep until we got there. It wasn't unusual for her to sleep all the way up and even on the way home too but only once a treat had been gotten, before that she'd be sitting there all bug eyed with excitement, even when she wasn't feeling crash-hot she'd be there bug eyed and delirious and once her tummy had been filled she'd get herself comfortable on my knee and go to sleep. Also it was a night time appointment and the sky had grown dark not long after we'd left the farm so I couldn't see her face properly anyway. David and I drove along in the darkness chatting away and were still chatting when we carried Amber across the dimly lit carpark. Then as soon as we walked into the bright surgery our vet was standing there ready to see us. There was nobody else in the waiting room which didn't happen very often. I actually think we were their last appointment, after us they were shutting up shop, which made me feel even guiltier than I already did for being late. I only fully concentrated on Amber's little face when I put her on the examination table and there she was in all her glory with a big carrot juice stain above one of her eyes. And the more I looked at her the more stains I saw. Her entire forehead had tiny splatters of orange stains all over it, no doubt her tongue had flicked the juice upwards while she was drinking and I had forgotten to wipe her down, she also had a bit of spinach stuck to the top of her nose, that was from breakfast, that I was very much aware of. I remember seeing it that morning and The Divine One really hated her nose being touched and because she was ill I didn't want to upset her, also it wasn't blocking either one of her nostrils, still plenty of airflow, so I just left it to fall off all by itself. I was hoping it'd happen sometime during the day but clearly it hadn't and so Amber was sitting there proudly having no idea what she looked like. In one way I was a tad embarrassed because the stains did make her look a little unkempt but I also thought her forehead looked like a fancy bit of artwork and I was smiling down at her lovingly when I heard David clearing his throat, trying to get my attention. No doubt he had just noticed the state Amber was in. I chose not to look over because I didn't have to look at my husband to know what he was thinking. The vet must have noticed the stains to, he had to of didn't he, but politely he said nothing, I guess he'd seen far worse. David however didn't follow suit he mentioned the face and forehead situation as soon as we were out the door and I hugged Amber close and said to him "Well at least she had a new coat on" which she did, a friend had knitted Amber the most beautiful pastel pink coat with a little white bow on it and it was that coats first outing. Obviously being a very busy day I had not wiped Amber's face down after giving her a lunch time drink and due to that the fur had stained. Still when you have a sick pug a bit of orange fur is the least of your problems and it didn't stop her enjoying her treat on the way home. She sat on my knee eating broken up bits of meat patty and sneezing up a storm, so much so that I ran out of tissues so handed Amber over to David while I dived into my handbag to see if I could find some more. And for those of you who know my handbag you'll be smiling because I have so much stuff stashed in there it's a miracle I can find anything. I've even got favourite toys from pugs that have passed. I've got Sarah's brown plastic dog in there, Horton's little fluffy yellow chicken and Billy's red bull just to name a few. I like to keep them with me always, and sometimes I've gone into my handbag to look for one thing, seen the toys and drifted down memory lane, then totally forgotten what it was I went searching for in the first place. Anyway when I turned back to Amber there was my wonderful husband gently wiping her little snotty nose with his big manly handkerchief and telling her what a good girl she was. And she wasn't exactly making it easy for him either. Amber was voicing her displeasure and madly pulling her face away because she didn't want her nose wiped she wanted more meat patty. There are many, many reasons why I love my husband as much as I do and the scene I saw that day with him tenderly wiping a little old blind pug's nose is just one of them. Oh and by the way he was able to get that bit of spinach off her nose too.

CHAPTER SIX

Altering The Walk

Finally having knowledge about what had gone on with Amber's back was a real asset to me and David because it helped us in caring for her. And although it still angered me greatly that she'd not been treated right at the time the accident occurred I felt I had to let all of that go and get on with the job of helping this beautiful little blessing of mine. What had gone on in the past was no longer important to Amber and me now, how we were going to live our lives together was, and so that's what I chose to concentrate on. If my mind was on those that had wronged her that would have been a waste of good time and energy, time and energy I could have been devoting to Amber and my other pugs. Her previous owners were not standing in front of me now and nor would they ever be. I would never have an opportunity to look them in the eye and say exactly what I thought of them. Who was standing in front of me right this moment was an innocent little pug that needed an enormous amount of love, attention and gentle looking after. Working out how I was going to best care for Amber and help her live the most wonderful life possible was the only thing that mattered now so I set about doing just that.

On day two of her arrival I figured out that Amber had something wrong with her back and as the days went on it became more and more obvious that something wasn't right. Even squatting for a wee was done in a different way to how a female dog normally does it. Amber would go off and find some uneven ground, we had just put a pile of grass clippings around the base of one of the trees and she would climb up on that mound have a little stomp around then wee on a sloping angle. Near the veggie patches was her favourite place to wee when she first arrived because there was some freshly dug mounds of dirt there and she seemed to like them best, where the grass clippings sunk in, the dirt didn't, it held the weight of her little body nicely and made it more comfortable for her to do what she needed to do. If this was the only thing she was doing I may have thought the weeing on an angle thing was merely part of our new daughter's personality, one of her funny little traits, pugs are well known for having quirks and I may have just figured this was Amber's but it soon became obvious that it wasn't. The reason she was doing it was because it made squatting down easier for her, less pressure being put on the back. The first time I saw her doing it I thought to myself "Oh hello, we've got another Gracie here" because Grace had a funny way of weeing too and I thought Amber was merely taking things a step further. But when you combined that with everything else going on you soon realised there was a lot more happening here with this little soul. Amber walked with her back end sitting higher than the front, her shoulders stooped down, she looked like a bloodhound on the hunt, well a miniature bloodhound on the hunt. But she wasn't hunting, that's just how she moved across the ground and due to this a lot of weight was being put on the front part of her body. She had trouble picking her front paws up. The back paws she didn't have quite as much trouble with but because her body was always in a state of lunging forward her front paws were copping the lot and due to this those poor little paws were getting pretty scuffed up. Sometimes she'd be scraping her paws along the ground like an ape does, then at other times she'd be walking on the side of her paws, she was alternating a lot, alternating trying to best manage the stress the front part of her body was being made to cope with. She was carrying a lot of tension in her shoulders too, that wasn't as obvious to the naked eye as the paws were, but I saw how she was holding herself and knew that she would have been feeling very tight in the neck and shoulder area. So we put some of Horton's socks on her and kept to the soft grassy areas. And off she'd go with her little socks on. I actually put two pairs of Horton's sock on her feet because I wanted to give her some added protection. But there would be times when Amber's wrists would completely collapse. She'd be walking along minding her own business then all of a sudden her two front wrists would buckle. Both got tucked under at exactly the same time and she'd simply carry on her way only now she'd be walking on the side of her wrists. She didn't fall completely down, never smacked her face on the ground, she more than likely did at one time when whatever had taken place with her back first happened, but it was like she was now used to righting herself and be off walking again in that slow but very determined little way of hers. I didn't like it when she was walking on her wrists though so I'd quickly pick her up when I saw it happening and she'd tell me off big time, tell me off in no uncertain terms in that growly woofy way of hers. I think she thought I was going to take her back up to the house and put an end to her sniffing. And even though Amber was noisily voicing her disapproval I still had to check her out. So off the double socks would come and I'd check to see if there was any damage done, there wasn't, so back on the socks would go and she'd potter around happily until the next time they buckled. Seeing a pug with weakness in the front legs was new to me. Back leg weaknesses yes I'd borne witness to that often as a lot of dogs have weakening in the hindquarters as they get older. I can only go from my own experiences but I've found that some old pugs get it worse than others, just like human beings really, we don't all age exactly the same way. At one time I was living with a 17 year old pug that didn't show any sign of weakening in her back legs and two 11 year old pugs that did. It has a lot to do with how they've lived their lives just as how we live our lives affects us when we get older. I've also had two 16 year olds living side by side and one was very bad with back end weakness while the other one showed only a slight sign.

With Amber the wrist collapsing thing was happening on every walk, on some walks they'd buckle more than others and after multiple times checking and rechecking I started just going over and picking her up then putting her back down with her wrists straight. No removal of socks. Just made sure all paws were flat to the ground and she'd be on her merry way again, socks on, tongue out, exploring, having the time of her life. But if I didn't go and fix her up she would continue walking on her wrists. If I hadn't already had her checked out by our vet and been told about the accident then I would have started wondering if her doing this was neurological because sometimes these things can be a sign of neurological issues and then of course we would have gone on a discovery mission to find out what the problem was, find out why the signals were being blocked. Seeing Amber walking on her wrists was very hard to watch. But because she didn't ever try to bring her paws back up I could only assume due to her back that she couldn't manage it or that she couldn't feel what she was doing so carried on walking having no idea it was her wrists she was now walking on. Lack of feeling would have been due to her back. Such a thing is quite common with spinal issues. I began wondering if perhaps her back injury was due to a fall and that Amber had tried to brace that fall with her two front legs, it's the natural thing to do isn't it. Maybe she had fallen off somebodies knee or off a piece of furniture. The thought of that happening to Amber really broke my heart, well that happening to her and nobody taking her to see a vet, that was a truly heartbreaking situation for this little pug to have been in. I'd see her doing the blind dog thing, tiptoeing about, getting to know the layout of the land and was very grateful she had come to me, to us, to this farm where she would be well looked after. And part of that looking after would be that we could no longer walk around the farm the way we normally would go, from now on we would have to start doing things differently, sticking to the full grass areas, avoiding the paths. If this was how Amber was always going to be then we had to cater to her. Normally I'd go with the numbers, do what the majority was doing and push the one who couldn't keep pace in a pram. But I knew Amber wasn't the type of pug to want to go in a pram, she'd already let me know this. It wouldn't have bothered me if she was. I would have gladly pushed her around in one of our Horton prams and really enjoyed doing so. But I never tried her in either of them because I knew she wouldn't want that, she didn't even like being carried more than a few steps, she wanted to be down on the ground at all times because that's where all the excitement was. I wouldn't have minded carrying her for half the walk. I absolutely loved that face of hers, I wanted it to be as close to me as possible, but Amber had other ideas and had no trouble letting me know what they were. I couldn't have her up in my arms if doing so was going to make her miserable. I suppose I could have left her milling about near the house while I took everybody else on their regular walk but my heart wouldn't allow me to walk away and leave her behind. I have done this with other dogs, bigger, stronger, sturdier dogs, done it until they were up to coming on the longer walks with the rest of us, but Amber was so needy and so tiny and she looked even smaller when out in the paddocks so no I could never ever leave her, altering the walk was the only thing to do. We only had five pugs left after losing Grace, Ruby and Horton and things were a little bit out of whack anyway so altering the walk wasn't difficult for them to get used to. I guess to them it was just another change that was taking place in their lives and there had been a good many of them of late. Of course I didn't like that I was making yet another change, I wanted to keep things as normal as I could for them, but I had this new little girl needing help and I had to help her. It did take a few days for the new routine to kick in though, at first the pugs would take off in the direction we normally would go and when I didn't follow, when me, Arthur and Amber headed the other way they'd look up, see what we were doing and come flying across to us, they weren't bothered at all by the change, we were out and about, that's all that mattered, they were enjoying themselves regardless. I would carry both Arthur and Amber over the path to the area where we were going to walk. Once on the ground Arthur would be off doing his own thing, always quick to have a wee, then he would either walk around a bit or sit in the sunshine it all depended on how he was feeling on the day. I knew I didn't have to worry about him too much because he could make his way back up to the house so easily. Yes he was blind and yes we were now in a different part of the farm but he knew the layout of the farm, it was well mapped out in his mind, he could find his way home no matter where he was. Naturally I would always be watching him, always aware of his movements. But he'd been living with us for quite a while and was more than capable of wandering back up to the house when he'd had enough. I'd see him waddling off, see him turn the corner of the house, then a little while later I'd be able to hear him walking across the floorboards in the lounge room and knew he'd had a drink and was now looking to get into a bed. On the days he was happy to stay outside in the sunshine I'd simply pick him up and carry him inside once the other pugs had finished walking. And of course each week Arthur was getting stronger and stronger, he was healing more and more from his back surgery and the better he felt the more he would want to walk to the point where he eventually stayed with us throughout the entire walk.

Amber for her part would take off across the paddock like she didn't have a care in the world. She showed me very early on that she was an incredibly independent little darling and that she really did have her own mind. She was so small and the paddocks were so big and yet she didn't care, she wasn't scared in the slightest, regardless of her size and lack of vision she wasn't at all bothered. This was all new territory for her yet off she'd go doing that unusual walk of hers, but determined, always very determined, couldn't care less if me and the other pugs were with her. She was on a discovery mission and her mind was totally absorbed in that. Sometimes the sheep and horses would be calling out but she didn't seem to notice them, never stopped and raised her head trying to figure out what they were or where the noise was coming from. I guess she must have thought to herself that she'd get to them in time, but for now there were more important things to do. Amber revealed to me quite quickly that exploring was in her personality and it was my job to make sure she didn't come to any harm while she was doing it. There was a lot of monitoring being done with this little blessing even though she had no idea that there was. But each and every single step taken was being watched and analysed. I never let her out of my sight, in a way I was like a love sick puppy following her wherever she went. Well actually there were two love sick puppies following Amber around because Steffy was looking upon Amber the exact same way I was. Amber neither liked nor disliked being with us, it was more that she had no real consciousness of us. For quite some time it was like she was in a little world of her own, no real need to know where I or anybody else was or what we were doing. So yes for sure Amber had been an only dog. She was very used to being alone. I think before she came to live with us Amber was left by herself a lot, perhaps her owners worked long hours. She was well accustomed to going about her business without ever having to think about anybody else so when she first arrived she was still doing that because she wasn't used to living any other way. I guess when she was bought as a puppy she would have been looking around for her mother and siblings, mourning the loss of them and looking around for some form of company and companionship and when there wasn't any to be found I guess she just adapted to being all by herself. Only dogs tend to live by their own rules, they do what they want when they want because there is nobody else to think about, nobody there to do things with. It takes a while for them to relearn how to live in a pack. Amber became very familiar with the route we would take and sometimes was ahead of the rest of us. Sometimes if I dropped back to help Arthur Amber got way ahead but never really bothering that she was alone. She'd simply keep plodding along until we caught up to her or if she was lingering back sniffing as was often the case too, then we would pause and wait for her and when she caught up to us she would just plod by like she either wasn't aware of us being there or just did not care. We'd be gathered in a group watching and waiting and she'd just traipse by us all on her way to doing whatever it was she wanted to do. I used to smile watching her, smile at her independence, I liked that she was happily discovering this farm she had suddenly found herself on. I noticed that there was a whole lot of joy in Amber while she was out sniffing and she would never be rushed. I very quickly learnt that this new little blessing of mine was far too grand to be governed by any clock. Sometimes we'd be out there for the longest time while she sniffed, everybody else had well finished up, but not The Divine One, she always wanted more. It seemed like she wasn't done unless she had sniffed every blade of grass and I was always there a few steps behind, but she didn't care, this independent little miss never once looked around for me. And I never tested the theory, definitely not in the early days and never once over the years either, but I did wonder how long Amber would have been out there exploring if I had given her free rein. Well she did have free rein really as it was always me following her not the other way around, in the early days of her arrival it was anyway then after a while she began following me, but I wondered how long she would have been gone if I'd just let her go and whether she would have barked for me to come get her or merely wandered up the ramp when she'd had enough. I've no doubt she would have been able to sniff her way back home because Amber was a pug that really used her nose. But I was never too far away because I couldn't have her stumbling on those front wrists and maybe that was why she was out there without a care in the world, because even though she didn't ever acknowledge me she always knew exactly where I was.

Everybody quickly became accustomed to our new direction of walking. Emily and Tommy took off as soon as we turned the corner of the house. He sauntered while she ran flat out all over the place coming back occasionally to see if we were still about or if we had gone back inside. She didn't care either way, she just wanted to know so she'd pause, take us all in then turn and be off running again. Sarah stayed close to me most of the time but was ok to run off should something catch her eye, then she'd come back again quite quickly. Everybody was getting their exercise their own way and Steffy being the self-appointed caretaker of them all came and went as she saw fit and each walk differed for her. She'd check on me and Amber then go see what Emily was doing, she'd track down Tommy too just to make sure he was alright. Tommy was easier for Steffy to check on because if Emily was thundering around the paddocks then Steffy had a chase on her hands and if she was underneath the trees spying on the neighbours then Steffy had to hunt her down, go from tree to tree until she found the one where Emily was sitting and she'd locate her then sniff her all over before taking off again. I'd watch her come flying back across the paddock to see what Arthur was up to and she'd spot him then race over to make sure he was ok and if she was satisfied that he was she'd once again be back to shadowing Amber. I'd be watching Steffy's face, see her expression change, knew what it meant, knew that in a moment or two she'd be off checking on everybody else again. Steffy was a great girl to watch when we were outside, you knew what she was doing and why but it was still really interesting to see her going about her business, see the wrinkles on her forehead deepen, know what would be going through her mind. I'd have one eye on Amber and one eye on Steffy, the entire walk was interesting because I got to see them all doing what they wanted to do, what was of most interest and importance to them, each little personality came out on the walks. And Amber wanting to linger really wasn't a problem at this point because the weather was still quite mild so there was no need for her to rush. Everything on the walks was pleasant for The Divine One, the temperature, the scents and the sounds of life on a farm. And when Amber was ready we all went back into the house, one or two may have already walked inside, when they saw Amber pausing by the carport having one last lingering sniff they knew she would soon be heading in. So they'd go ahead of us and already be settled in a bed by the time we crossed the threshold. I never let Amber walk over the strip that the glass door slides along. I always lifted her over because with limited vision and not picking up her feet properly I felt tripping over that strip was a given. I'd be close behind, half bent down both hands dangling there ready to scoop her up and lift her over then put her straight back down on the other side. She was rarely lifted more than a few inches off the ground and when I first started doing it I would run my hands over her body first so she knew I was about to pick her up, then after a while she would stand and wait for me to lift her, she must have realised why I was doing it and appreciated the help. A couple of times she did get wafted in with the other pugs, if I was off helping somebody else and didn't get to Amber in time she'd get moved along by the pack, but having a pug at either side seemed to help, she'd still stumble a little but never went all the way down because her siblings helped hold her up.

It was around week six of Amber's arrival that she got to meet Arthur's physiotherapist. Arthur loved being in the pool, loved being in the tank on the treadmill too, and loved going out in the car full stop and especially loved having a treat on the way home. Amber didn't have a clue what was happening the day I lifted her up and carried her out the door. But she did pick up on Arthur's excitement, how could she not, it was hanging so thickly in the air. He had begun woofing and circling as soon as his harness was put on because he knew exactly where we were going. And Arthur wasn't really all that much of a talker, Amber hadn't heard him saying a lot since she arrived, she heard him complaining when I did his back exercises but that was about it, so the fact that he was being so vocal that morning would have told her that whatever was happening was something good. As soon as I opened the car door Arthur had his front paws up ready for me to lift him in. David was locking the back door so I put Amber down while I helped Arthur and she just stood there with her tongue hanging out waiting for me to pick her up again. We hadn't made a special appointment for Amber, we knew they were pretty laid back and flexible so would have no problem taking a quick look at our new daughter after Arthur had finished his session. And really that's all it needed to be, a quick assessment to see if they thought Amber could be helped, they had been in this business a long time, seen many a dog with spinal conditions so would quickly have known if they would be able to make a difference or not. Arthur had been toweled off but was still a little damp as he wandered round giving everybody he came across kisses and nobody minded, the staff are used to wet dogs there. The physiotherapist sat on the floor with Amber as she looked her over, she made note of the weaker parts of her body right away. Said she may be able to help but gave no guarantees, in her opinion she felt it was perhaps worth giving Amber at least a few sessions to see if there would be any change. She started talking about trying to help strengthen Ambers body in the areas it was weakest but never once did she offer any assurances, never promised any miracles, she made that pretty clear to us from the start. And she also agreed with our vet concerning surgery for Amber. She was more focusing on helping Amber with the body she had now. While Arthur worked the room David and I stood above Amber and the physiotherapist, she repeated once again that it may or may not make a whole lot of difference but she did think it was worth giving a try if we wanted her to try. She looked up at David and me questioning and at precisely the same time both of us blurted out "Try" so she kissed Ambers little old head and handed her back to us. I guess without being given a definite guarantee some people may not have bothered, may not have wanted to put the time, money and effort in, but we are not those types of people, we take our roles as guardians of these little angels very seriously. We knew therapy was only a part of it, that there would be work for us to do at home with Amber but we are used to doing that, we've done it many times before. Both David and I felt certain that Amber gaining strength would help her a lot, sure she still wouldn't walk like a normal pug but we felt by building her weak area's up it would at least ease some of the burden being placed on those shoulders and front paws. Really you'd do anything if there is even the slightest chance of being able to make a difference, even if the chance is small you still do it for them, imprinted on both David's and my heart is the word "Try". Sure sometimes you try and you fail but you at least try. On the way home I sat with Amber on my knee, Arthur was on the back seat sprawled out waiting for the chicken he had been promised. I looked down at Amber and began talking to her. I told her what was going on, told her she was about to begin having sessions with the physio. It felt good knowing that we may be able to help. I massaged her little ears and neck until she fell asleep. Arthur had two more sessions to go before he would be finished with his physiotherapy and so to get Amber used to the sounds and the smell of the place we decided to take her along with him then as soon as Arthur was given the all clear Amber slipped right into his regular appointment and we set off on the journey of seeing if we could make life easier and happier for our little girl. And because Arthur loved his physiotherapist and her staff so much he accompanied Amber on every one of her visits and didn't seem at all bothered that he was no longer going in the pool or tank, he was just happy to be wandering around getting pats and snuggles from everyone he knew, happy to have a ride in the car and extremely happy to be getting a treat on the way home. Also I think having Arthur along helped put Amber's mind at ease. If he wasn't bothered by the ordeal then why should she be, Amber had all three of us standing right beside her as she did her sets. I actually felt pretty sorry for The Divine One seeing her in the tank, black sightless eyes, little tongue flicking around every time it came into contact with the water, teeny tiny body being worked, but I knew she was in safe hands and that they knew what they were doing. I had complete trust in everybody who was handling her. But gosh did she look small when swathed in that big fluffy towel at the end of each session. They normally dry them off but I wanted to do it so they handed my precious bundle over to me and I sang to her as I gently patted her dry.

Well those therapy sessions did end up helping Amber, not aiding her to the point that she was now a completely different dog, but the sessions and the exercises they had us doing with her at home all helped strengthen her body where she needed it the most. The home exercises were just as important as her sessions with the physiotherapist we were very aware of that, we couldn't be lax, each step in this process was important, everything being done was working towards strengthening that little body of hers and as she got stronger she could do a lot more than she could when she'd first arrived. Amber was now able to pick up her feet a bit more and over time began lifting them up even higher and once she started doing that everything changed for her. She no longer needed the socks and was more than happy to be rid of them. Amber could also walk faster and for longer periods of time, she was never laid back at the start but now every movement was a lot easier for her and the better she felt in her body the more she wanted to do. She even wandered over to meet the sheep and horses and showed no fear. She had just enough sight to see how big they were against her but they did not faze her in the slightest, she was quite fascinated by them. Stood by the fence sniffing, she knew they were there on the other side and seemed to like being there next to them. Perhaps she liked the horsey smell just as much as I did. Amber would more walk beside us now too. She integrated herself into the pack, wasn't as interested in going off on her own anymore. Her day to day life had altered. Where once she was alone she was now used to folks always being around her and enjoyed our company. She became very attached to me. She would lift her head, put her nose in the air trying to locate me, come out of her sniffing frenzy to see where I was and what I was doing and not just me but her siblings too, she'd come over to us if we'd not gone over to her, where we went she now went also, she started to become a true part of our family. I guess she realised that she was really one of us now, that she was loved by somebody, well loved by a whole lot of somebodies. In her heart we had become "Her People" "Her Family" "Her Loved Ones" now being with us was very important to Amber and for me it was beautiful to witness that shift, see that change in her because I knew exactly what that meant. It meant she had opened up her little heart to us all, she had allowed us in. And that is the greatest gift any dog can give you, that is everything.

"Bath time"

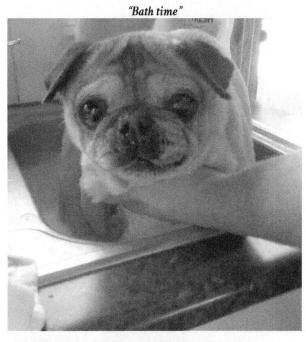

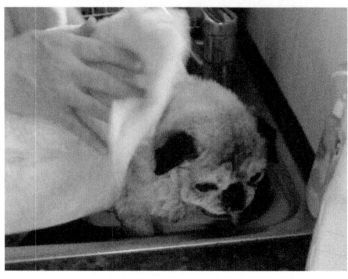

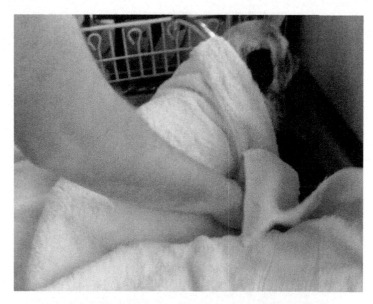
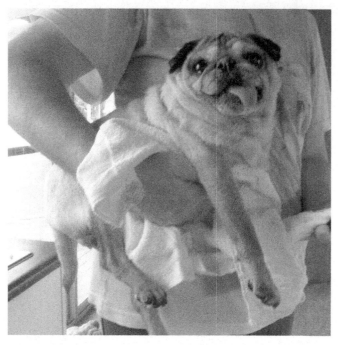

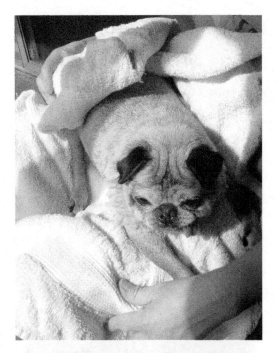

CHAPTER SEVEN

The Divine One

While a little old pug was in a New South Wales vet clinic being desexed here on a small farm in Victoria much discussion was going on about what her name was going to be and her new parents were having trouble seeing eye to eye on it. The one thing we both did agree on was that we wanted our new daughter to have a name that would honour Ruby. David suggested it first, he loved Ruby dearly, she was his special girl, we lost Ruby the same day we lost Horton, it was a double blow to us both and that's putting it lightly. When David first said he thought our new daughter should have the name of a gem I thought it was the most brilliant idea. I was on board right away because I love to honour previous family members, to me it means that they get to live on and at the start when you are using the name you always know exactly why it was chosen and that makes it special and then of course over time the name becomes totally theirs. No other thoughts in your head besides the little dog you are talking to.

I wanted Amber to have the name Pearl. I desperately wanted to call her Pearl because I thought it was a perfect name for a little old lady pug but David had other ideas. He didn't like the name in the slightest, he considered it old fashioned and plain and I said "Old fashioned yes, that's why I like it, but plain, no most definitely not" and I guess I could have tried to push the name I liked best but at the time I didn't really feel up to it. I was still mourning my losses and grieving isn't just a sad state to be in it can be incredibly exhausting and draining. Dave screwed up his face at the name I suggested, well more than screwed it up, he contorted his face so much so that it was like I was now sitting opposite a completely different man. I knew by the level of contortion that I was not going to win this one and I win a lot so that was perfectly fine with me. "Pearl isn't even a real gemstone it's a calcium carbonate deposit" he said all knowledgeably. I was silent for a moment then said "Well Ruby was your special darling so you can choose our new daughters name" I told him that whatever he chose I would be fine with it. Although I knew in my heart that perhaps I wouldn't be fine with it at all, in fact I worried that I'd be far from fine with it. That I may come to regret what I'd just said. But Dave was sitting there smiling so happily and my internal dialogue said "Andrea just let it go" so that's exactly what I did. But I did remind David that our newest family member was very tiny and petite so he should probably keep that in mind when choosing. Dave threw out a few names like Emerald, Sapphire, Amethyst and Moonstone, not really talking to me more talking out loud so I just sat back and listened, after all this was his gig now, I no longer had any say in it, I'd handed over the reins and had no right to take them back again. In my mind I was thinking that Amethyst was beautiful but please, please do not pick Sapphire because Amber was a lot of things but a Sapphire she was not, it didn't fit her face in any shape or form as far as I was concerned, but I didn't have any right to sway him so I kept my mouth shut and massaged Sarah's grey ears instead. I also thought Emerald was no name for a dog and if it was then it more suited a male then a female and I think that was because it was similar to the names Edward, Emmerson and Emmanuel and I made a mental note to put the name Emmerson on my pugs name list because now I'd thought about it I realised I kind of liked it.

David was still going strong. "Diamond and Topaz" were the next few names he threw out then he said the name Amber and I thought to myself oh that's quite nice. And as I was repeating the name over in my head a few times he said "A lot of people think amber is a gemstone but it isn't". I was about to pipe up and say that up until this very second that I was one of those people but decided to stay quiet because I thought I may actually learn something here and I did and I knew I would because David had just put his finger on his chin, the way he does when he has more information stored in his head that he is about to bring fourth. I have always liked that he knows things, knows a good many things that I know nothing about, when we first started going out together I gave him the nickname "The Walking Encyclopedia" because I could ask him anything about any subject and he always knew the answer, it can be pretty handy to have a bloke like that around the place at times. Saves me having to look things up and in writing this I have just realised how lazy that makes me sound but I guess lazy is what I have become with things like this because after thirty years of knowing David I have gotten used to relying on him. "Amber is thought to be a gemstone due to how it looks but it's actually fossilized resin from a tree" I was about to ask if it was the same thing as sap but he was still talking and in time answered my question so I didn't need to ask. I was just hoping that because Amber wasn't a real gemstone that he wasn't about to instantly dismiss it because I was really warming to the name. But I was lucky because David seemed to be leaning towards it also and the more he talked about it the more he seemed to like it and hey it was a name that began with the letter "A" and I've always been fond of those, I mean I have one myself don't I. Also three out of the five members of my original family, you know that little family that came from England to Australia, have names that begin with the letter "A". So Amber was eventually decided upon by David and when he left the room I put Sarah down and ran and got one of my baby name books off the shelf then quickly flipped to the girls section to see what the name meant. I have always been big on the meaning of names because I feel they are very important. It said Amber was an English baby name and I was born in England so that was another tick. It said the name was very popular in the 19th century and that in 1944 a writer called Kathleen Winsor wrote a novel titled Forever Amber and I'm guessing it must have been a pretty good novel because in 1947 it was turned into a movie. That fact interested me a little but what interested me a whole lot more was the meaning of the name. My finger ran underneath a sentence, Amber meant "A Jewel" or "Precious Jewel" and I thought to myself well I can certainly live with that because I think she is. The next time I was on the computer I put the word Amber into a google search because I wanted to see photos of the stone, the colour was the main thing I was looking up but then as is always the case a whole lot of other information came up as well so I started reading. David was at work so he couldn't be looking over my shoulder thinking I was checking up on him, thinking I was having doubts about the name he had chosen. Amber hadn't arrived as yet and I was pretty excited about her coming so this gave me something else to do besides looking at her pound photo, a little way of feeling connected to her I thought until I could meet the real thing. It kept referring to Amber as being a stone as much as it did resin and I thought to myself well I guess a lot of people think like me, I suppose when they see it being used in rings, bracelets and necklaces just like all the other gemstones are then you automatically assume it is one too. But resin or stone what I found out about Amber made me pretty happy. On a gemstone page I read a list of properties attributed to each stone and it said Amber was recognised as being good for all sorts of things. It was thought to symbolize and promote energy, confidence and safety and yes those things were sadly lacking in me of late, I knew for sure that they were and I thought perhaps they may have been lacking in our new little daughter too. It also stated that Amber attracted good luck and I believed that one hundred percent because I already felt lucky and I hadn't even met her yet. Amber was also used as a healing agent in folk medicine. It said bracelets made of Amber were highly effective in controlling pain, rheumatic pain, arthritis, aching muscles and joints those sorts of things. Well to be honest since losing Horton bodily aches and pains were the least of my problems. I hardly thought about things like that, my heart was the main part of my body that was hurting. Apart from the pain there I couldn't feel anything else. Another page started talking about chakras. I didn't read too much about that but my eye did come to rest on a line that said Amber stimulated memory and helped with decision-making. Well my mind was pretty clouded at times, not bad enough that I couldn't make a decision about taking Amber in but I did suffer a bit with making normal everyday choices of late. What to make for dinner for example, silly little things like that had me standing in the kitchen feeling completely overwhelmed. I guess after you lose three pugs in a week such things seem so very unimportant, not worth putting energy into, not worth making an effort with, but I had a husband to feed so I needed to make that choice each night and sometimes I found it impossible to do. Cereal was eaten for dinner a lot of nights in the weeks following Grace, Ruby and Horton's death. The page I was reading also said that Amber was known to bring the energies of romantic love. Romantic love nah I didn't need any help in that area as David is, was and always will be more than enough for me. I did think about buying some Amber jewellery though because most of the pages I looked at had quite a few links to jewellery sites. I think that's what they wanted us to do, read all about these wonderful stones then reach for our credit cards at lightning speed and in a few weeks' time we'd all be doused in gems, adorned in gems, literally dripping with them, barely able to walk under their weight. But I decided not to go that route. I had a daughter arriving soon with the name Amber, I didn't need resin, I was about to become the mother of a living breathing being. She would be a whole lot better than anything I could have hanging around my neck or dangling from my wrist.

At this point I was very much in love with the name Amber. I remember when David rang me from the airport when he'd just picked Amber up, he proudly told me that she really suited the name he had chosen for her. And she did, after a few weeks of calling her Amber I could no longer see her as ever suiting the name Pearl. Although I did hold onto the name I'd chosen for a little while at least because I can clearly remember phoning the vet surgery to book Amber in for her first appointment. I heard the receptionist ask "And who will be coming in to see us?" With having a few dogs they have to ask, if we only had one then they'd know right away. I said it was a new pug that I was making the appointment for. "What's the new dog's name?" she asked and I paused for a moment because I desperately wanted to say Pearl. "Her name is Amber" I said then just like that I was able to completely let it go. I could hear her tapping at the keyboard putting Amber's name in "How old is Amber?" she asked and I said that's what I'd like to find out, another bit of tapping and then she said "Ok Amber is now in our system" then she hung up the phone. I smiled as I walked across the room, smiled at the name David had chosen, smiled because of what it signified.

Amber like a lot of our pugs had a few nicknames which can get really confusing for people, but we know who we are talking about and the pugs know who we are talking to and that's the main thing. A couple of weeks in and I started calling her Amber Blossom Bug, it came to me one day and I liked it so I called her that. And David may have chosen her real name but he more often than not referred to her as "The Bug" or simply "Buglet" he used both names equally as much and sometimes he'd draw the word out saying "Bug-er-let" and

Amber would lift her head and come clunking over to him. And for a while we even started calling her "Yellow Buglet" because the way Dave said "Hello Buglet" when he came home from work sounded like he was in fact saying "Yellow Buglet" so Amber got called "Yellow Bug-er-let" purely for our own amusement and she really couldn't have cared less what we were sniggering about as long as she got her treats and her walks she was happy. And besides she'd been with us a few years at that time so was well used to her idiot parents saying stupid things and laughing like crazy about them. Then once we'd gotten that out of our systems and it was no longer as funny or as cute as it used to be it was back to being just plain "Buglet". David would often walk outside saying me and Bug-er-let are going to do this or me and The Bug are going to do that and he'd stride through the door with Amber tucked underneath his arm and her little uncurled tail and back legs would be dangling down as she went, which by the way was a comfortable way of carrying her due to how her back was, and he'd pop her on the ground and she'd scurry off after him and they'd go check a fence or how much a tree had grown then back inside the two of them would come, and again she'd be back tucked underneath his arm. Once he was just ducking out quickly to pick up a fallen picket, just a fast trip out and back in again but there was no way Amber was going to let him go without her. She did her determined walk across the room like "Wait for me Daddy I want to come" so he carried her outside and I was cooking dinner but from the window I was watching the two of them together. I stood with one hand stirring the pot while leaning as close to the kitchen window as I could get so I didn't miss seeing my little darling trotting after him in her little pink coat. And when they reached the picket I saw him let Amber have a sniff at it so she knew what he was doing, knew what they had gone out there for, well of course she wouldn't have known fully would she, never the less she'd had a bit of a sniff at something new and seemed satisfied with that. As she aged he would carry her more and more because she couldn't walk as fast as she used to and he is over six feet tall so has pretty long legs, far too long for that little darling to ever be able to keep up with. He would still take her with him though, he wasn't going to let her miss out on their little outings together just because she was old. And again I'd see them striding through the house, little old legs swaying as he walked but this time he would only put her on the ground to have a wee then pick her up and carry her all the way to wherever it was they were going then he'd stand there with her in both arms talking to her, telling her what was going on then stride back up to the house with her, putting her down near her favourite tree in case she needed to have another wee before coming back indoors, which more often than not she did, so he'd wait for her to do what she had to do then scoop her up and in the door they would come. It was always really beautiful for me seeing them together and yes I took plenty of photos because it warmed my heart so much.

When you take in a dog you never know what you are going to get character wise and it can be very exciting seeing who they are. Getting to know the new little blessing in my presence has always been a beautiful experience for me, I enjoy it greatly. The Divine One may have only been small in stature but she sure had a whole lot of personality dwelling within. A personally so big that at times I wondered how that tiny frame of hers was able to contain it, but she seemed to managed it ok. And of course she would do wouldn't she, she had after all been doing it for nine years before our paths crossed. I thought everything about her was truly marvellous, she was an all-round glorious darling. From the word go my new daughter was impressive, it didn't take me very long at all to figure out I was standing in the midst of a very special little being. Amber had a lot going on with her health wise but built deep down inside of her was this "Never give up, never give in" attitude. Horton too had that same kind of attitude and I believe both of them benefited from it greatly. I'd look down at Amber and be constantly thinking to myself "What a gift, what a find, how incredibly lucky am I to be your mother" and I'd tell her this too, told her quite often, at the start she didn't respond, but over time she became accustomed to being spoken to and when I talked to her she would start giving the side of my hand or face tiny licks because she knew it was her who I was speaking to. The core of Amber's nature was sweet and serene, she had this wonderful no fuss attitude, she'd be more than happy to go along with most things no questions asked. Amber was great when it came time for me to do the exercises with her, she'd let me do them no worries at all which was lovely for me after battling with Arthur. He really didn't want to be doing his excises at home, he was an angel for the physiotherapist and all her staff but played up like mad for me whereas Amber was a dream. Simply stood there with her little tongue out doing what needed to be done, doing whatever you asked of her no resistance there whatsoever, no matter how long it took she'd cooperate and enjoyed the treat she always received afterwards.

I guess after being left on her own for so long having attention in any form from anybody was pretty awesome as far as she was concerned. It was lovely to have this peaceful interaction with her as I was helping strengthen her body and because building up her strength was not a fast fix I appreciated her sweet nature even more. And for a dog that we weren't meant to expect anything from as far as walking went The Divine One was moving around like a champ, Amber had no idea she wasn't meant to be much of a walker, she just got on with walking. I guess nobody could have predicted the amount of inner determination this little girl had. So tiny, so beautiful and so unwavering there in amongst the others, tongue dangling, legs going like the clappers, she would even start moving her legs a few inches from the ground as if not knowing exactly when contact would be made but she was making sure she was fully ready when it did. And the moment she felt grass beneath her feet she shot off like a little rocket. Her body was still in a slightly slanted down positon but not quite as much as it had been when she first arrived, the strength she gained caused her to be able to bring her shoulders up and that really helped her with being able to lift up her front paws. She didn't look quite so much like a bloodhound anymore, more just like an old pug with an old back. I think gaining strength didn't only help Amber in her body it helped her mind as well. She was stronger than she had been in quite some time, stronger in all areas, I actually felt this was the strongest she had been since the accident with her back first happened and that would have made a lot of difference to Amber. With each step taken being easier she wanted to do more and more and in time she would be running, I didn't know that then, I was applauding her willpower in walking, both in movement and distance, the thought of her actually being able to run would have blown my mind back then but it was coming, Amber probably knew it but I certainly didn't. Over time Amber developed a beautiful way of skimming across the paddocks, she was able to glide along quite effortlessly and quite fast too, still moving in her own unique way but these days she reminded me of a tiny hovercraft. No more buckling, knuckling or dragging, no more collapsing ankles, now it was as if she was walking on air. And I would applaud her progress. Made a huge fuss out of every achievement she made, big or small, the exact same amount of praise poured out of me with an enormous surge of enthusiasm and this is how Amber got the name The Divine One. Every time she had an accomplishment I would cup her little face in my hands, tell her how divine I thought what she had done was and how divine I thought she was for doing it. The reason I cupped her face was because of her lack of vision. I wanted to make sure Amber knew I was talking to her, that she was the one I was praising otherwise it would have just been a pile of enthusiastic words floating above her head. How could this little blessing possibly have known the words of praise were being directed towards her unless they came with some form of action, sure she would have been happy to hear my voice, hear that my pitch was highly excitable, known I was talking to somebody, but I wanted her to know in no uncertain terms that that somebody was her. And the cupping of her little face with both hands or her little chin with one hand was a perfect way of doing it. I'd do this a lot with her and she was so happy when she was being gushed over, at times I'd even go back again, cup her face and gush some more. Over time I just started calling her The Divine One because to me she was divine in every way possible.

One day my sister asked why I was cupping the new pug's face, so I explained and she just smiled. Smiled out of politeness more than anything because I believe she thought I was overreacting but I had taken a lot more notice of Amber then she had, taken notice of her from the start. I saw how she was back then and how much better she was doing now. I thought Amber's accomplishments were the greatest things in the world. My sister I don't think would have noticed the differences unless I was constantly pointing them out. And for her part that was ok because some of the accomplishments were only slight but I would point them out all the same, pointed them out so very proudly to everybody I knew because that's how proud I was of The Divine One. Some friends got right on board with it, others not so much, but that was ok Amber and I knew exactly what she had accomplished, we knew that she was improving and that's what mattered most. So I'd tell her the exact level of her divineness and she'd love all the attention and I loved giving it to her. But I didn't always say "Divine" sometimes I would say "Deee-Bine" instead just cutseyfying it up a bit I guess. Sometimes her face would already be in the air waiting to be cupped. She'd hear me saying her name and knew I was coming over so I'd cup that little upturned face and say "You is Deee-Bine, you is Deee-Bine" then I'd ask "Who is Deee-Bine? And cup her little face again while answering "You is" and then I'd kiss the top of her head twice or cover her little ears in tiny kisses.

In the house The Divine One still walked with a slight clunk but the sound was now lighter, not half as noticeable, sometimes you wouldn't be able to hear it at all if the other pugs where pitter-pattering. But walking around the house on her own, yes I always knew it was The Divine One, never any mistaking it was her. Then again there is rarely any mistaking anybody for me because I am so in tune with each one of my children. So I'd hear Amber coming and call out a greeting without having to look up from what I was doing. Just a cheery hello, unless she came and stood beside me then I would bend down and stroke her or ask her if she wanted something then try and figure out what that something was. Sometimes if I heard her on the move I'd be secretly hoping she was going over to the water bowl to have a drink. And of course that was something I'd want to be witnessing so I'd stop what I was doing and move over to get a closer look. But time after time she went right by the water bowl and so my next thought was that she was going to her hop in one of the beds and I was happy because I knew I would be able to watch her getting in, see her settling down, getting herself comfortable. I loved watching her climbing into bed. Those little old back legs of hers were so beautiful. I liked how cute they looked when she was lifting them. So again I moved position so as not to miss seeing it. Then one day I heard the clunking and began watching on. She walked right by the water bowl, nothing unusual there The Divine One normally did, but she wasn't heading to a bed either and now I was really curious so I slowly and quietly followed her. I was wondering if she may have gotten herself confused, had she made a wrong turn and now had no idea where she was, would the little sight she had be enough to guide her to where she needed to be. Would she need me to help her, would she let me help her or would she simply continue clunking on her way as fast as she could go. I looked down at her for guidance, trying to gauge the best thing for me to do. I was trying to get any signal I could get from her, all the other pugs were in their beds asleep and I was glad about that because I felt if they were walking in front of her, even for something as simple as getting themselves a drink, then it could have made her even more confused. She was near the back door now and stood there silent and still for a few moments as if she was figuring out what to do next. It was at this point that I became fully aware that The Divine One was a ponderer and not only that but that her expressions changed when she was pondering something. I was smiling down at her now thinking she was the cutest thing ever. Her teeny tiny head was facing upwards in my direction so I was having a real good look at her face and feeling this huge overwhelming amount of love for her, my heart was filling up more and more with love as I watched her standing there. Then just like that she turned and marched out the back door, stepped right over the strip I normally lifted her over, this time she managed it all by herself. I watched as she very steadily and very carefully lifted each one of those little legs of hers up, she didn't make contact with the strip once, no stumbling at all. She stood on the doormat for a second or two then tilted her head slightly sideways and she gave a little woof as if you say "Well new Mummy are we going for a walk together or not". The way she was standing there all determined like told me she may have been going regardless. So I stepped out the door fast because there was no way I was not going to accompany her, Amber must have felt me side stepping her because she took a step or two forwards. By this time some of the other pugs had come outside to join us and we all stood gathered together a few feet from the back door. As soon as Amber heard us all behind her she began marching confidently down the back ramp and we, her new family, followed on behind. My smile grew wider and wider with each step those delicate little legs took, when she reached the bottom of the ramp she paused and I rubbed her shoulder with my finger to let her know

I was with her and that what she was doing was ok. Well it was more than ok it was brilliant I thought, absolutely brilliant but there was no way of conveying that to her. I hadn't invented a finger stroke to signify brilliant but that was fine, The Divine One didn't care, she could feel how wonderful I thought she was, so I cupped her little face and told her how "Deee-Bine" I thought what she had just done was and we all set off down the paddock together.

CHAPTER EIGHT

Brenda

Before I start this chapter I must tell you that I contacted my friend Brenda and told her that I was going to put this story in The Divine One's book because I thought it was too funny not to. And I explained to her that because I was looking at this from Amber's point of view that it would not always show her in a very good light. I asked her if she'd prefer it if I changed her name and if so would she like to choose what she wanted to be called. We laughed about it as she came out with all these glamorous sounding names, movie star type names, some of the names were very long too and she said "You know like rich people have", other names were ones that she had wanted to be called all her life and there were also a few names with double meanings and we laughed even harder when she rattled off those. But in the end she said "No, keep it as me" she then added "That pint sized princess shunned me for years I think the least I deserve is a chapter named after me" so I hung up the phone and began typing. And later when this chapter was finished I rang Brenda again and read the entire thing to her and in between sentences I could hear that old familiar laughter coming down the phone. I asked her if there was anything she wanted changed or added and she paused for a few moments and I could almost hear her mind ticking over, then she broke the silence with "Geez that little bugger hated me didn't she" and I was going to say "With a passion" but instead I said "Pretty much" and we both roared laughing. Then Brenda said "No that's exactly how I remember it, you've captured it as well as any camera lens could" and I said "So it's a wrap then? And she laughed and said "Yeah it's a wrap".

Brenda was a friend I met not long after moving to the country, it was my sheep that brought us together. She had come up the driveway wanting to know what breed they were as she'd not seen any others like them. I was inside the house with the door open when I heard footsteps on the deck. The pugs outside were tap dancing around a little bit faster than they normally would so I walked outside to see what the cause of all the commotion was. I was baking so had my pinny on and a tea towel slung over my shoulder. It was a warm sunny day and the sheep and Gerald were grazing in the front paddock. As I stepped out the door I came face to face with a lady in a very unglamorous and unfeminine sunhat. She was puffing and red faced, looking a little worse for wear. I am one of these people who sums folks up pretty quickly. I'll have decided if I like them or not on one glance sometimes, they don't even need to speak, but when they do then I'll be guided by that too. I liked this little woman instantly. She was shorter then I was and older too, shorter by at least a foot and older by at least a decade, but her smile was warm and she was bending down patting the pugs and not at all bothered by the fact that they were jumping all over her. Her hair was cropped and she had a purple streak through it. Not a pale old lady purple rinse or anything like that but a deep striking purple, a purple that would be hard to miss even if she was standing in the shade, a teenager purple, a bold purple, a purple that I thought belonged to a person who didn't give a damn what other people thought of them. I liked that about her so after a few moments of conversation I invited her in for a cup of tea and she smiled and accepted right away. She was the first person who had readily accepted such an invitation, I'd met a few people already but they weren't for being friendly. I came to the country thinking it was all about scones and endless cups of tea but the first few people I met quickly let me know it wasn't. That the notion was from a long time ago, that people in the country were now too busy for these types of things. But what I realised was that only some country people were too busy for such things and I would go on to meet a whole lot of people that were quite happy to keep these traditions alive and Brenda was one of them. She took her shoes off at the door and strode across the lounge room in bright pink socks. I motioned to the kitchen table and she pulled out a chair. I would have told her to take a seat but she hadn't stopped talking since she first said hello. Not even to draw breath. She'd be shooting questions at me without giving me time to answer. And that was fine by me because I found her quite comical, a true country gem. "What type of sheep are those? "Kinda funny looking aren't they" she paused here but only long enough to laugh. "Look like goats, are they goats, no they are definitely sheep aren't they" "Did you breed them yourself? Then she was bending down patting the pugs again, "Like pugs do you? "You must be a breeder, do you show them as well? And once inside the house "Oh you are cooking are you? "Smells great" "What ya cookin" then her hand shot into the air "No, no don't tell me, let me guess" and while she was guessing I put the kettle on. "Its biscuits isn't it, you are baking biscuits, no cake. Cake, you are baking a cake? "Yes it's definitely a cake" she was staring at my face now for answers so I nodded my head. "What type is it? I went to answer but her hand was up in the air again, "No don't tell me, let me guess, I'm a good guesser" so while she was guessing I put some biscuits on a plate and carried them over. I took her a glass of water as well because she looked like she needed one and she gulped it down fast. When I finally brought our cups of tea over and sat down she was still guessing. And getting further and further away from the truth, not quite the good guesser she thought she was I thought to myself before putting her out of her misery. "Passionfruit" I said and her hand flew up to her head. "Ooooh I should have said that first, I saw the vine as I came up the driveway that should have given it away". We did have a fantastic passionfruit vine when we first moved here, such wonderful tasting fruit it grew too, but then the sheep ate it so David cut it down and built a wall and that was the end of the tasty passionfruit.

Amber, Ruben, Tommy and Casey

And so that was how Brenda entered my world. That cup of tea and a biscuit turned into three cups of tea, a slice of passionfruit cake and a friend for life. Our conversations changed over the years, they deepened and expanded. My hair stayed the same, hers didn't, that purple streak changed colour a good many times and once her entire head resembled a rainbow and I clapped and cheered when I saw her walking up the driveway that day. I didn't have Amber when Brenda and I first met but I did have Horton, he wasn't one of the pugs on the deck that greeted her, he was in the kitchen with me and followed only as far as the middle of the lounge room. Brenda was loud and Horton was not fond of loud noises, when she came inside he went and played with his toys by the window, when we started eating he scooted over to see what we had and it was only then that Brenda really took any notice of him. I think when she first walked in she was too busy with the others. She spotted Horton and squealed, and then of course the normal Horton questions started. "Who is the little black one? "Can't he walk? "What's wrong with him? "Birth defect or did he have an accident? And "What's that thing he's wearing" Horton and the others shared a plain biscuit between them while I told her what she wanted to know. To save time I answered her in the way she talked. "Horton" "No" "Hemivertebra" "Born like that" "Tinkle Trousers" "Has to wear a nappy" "And if you lower your voice he may actually come closer to you" I said this because she was reaching out her hand trying to get Horton to come over and he wasn't interested in doing that at all. But over time he did and over time she got to know all the names of the pugs and the names of the horses and sheep too. And I in turn got to know all about her children, her sick husband and the mother in law who used to live with them. She never said "My mother in law" it was always "The mother in law" then she would start with a rather long but totally interesting story. It was a nice friendship and I looked forward to our get-togethers. I even took Horton with me to her house, pushed him round there in his pram, she had an old boxer that she'd rescued. He was a lovely old soul and Horton wasn't the least bit worried about him, not intimidated in the slightest even though Horton's entire body was smaller than Bruce's head, he still wasn't afraid because he could sense there was nothing to be afraid of. Bruce had come bounding off the deck running flat out towards Horton's pram as I unlatched the gate. And Horton just sat there doing little woofs at him. I went and sat on the deck with Horton on my knee and Bruce's big head came over my shoulder to sniff the little guy and Horton just sat there sniffing Bruce back. I remember crying with Brenda when Bruce died of cancer and I remember Brenda crying with me each time I lost one of my pugs. Our friendship was mainly based on laughter but we were also there for each another in times of tears. And then The Divine One arrived on the scene.

I remember how excited Brenda was to meet Amber. I think she was one of the people who thought that after losing Horton I would not be carrying on rescuing. I think that was part of the overall excitement, she told me I was brave to be carrying on. I said bravery had nothing to do with it, that I'd simply fallen in love and that she would too when she saw Amber's photo, which she did on her next visit. I had the computer ready with Amber's pound shot front and centre. I told her to close her eyes and when she opened them there was little old dry eyed Amber with her tongue peeping out. Brenda put her hand on her heart at the sight of her face, she hadn't taken in another dog since losing Bruce but she was happy that I was about to. She'd ring me countless times throughout the day when she knew Amber was being desexed and ask if I'd heard anything yet. Brenda was part of the entire process of Amber coming down to us and she was the first one of my friends to meet her face to face but as much as she loved Amber my little Divine One wouldn't have a bar of her. It was a love hate relationship that I thought may turn into a love love relationship over time but it never did, the love that gushed out of Brenda seemed to not affect Amber in the slightest, oh she could feel it I know she could, everybody in the house could but it made no difference to Amber, she just couldn't of cared less. And it wasn't for Brenda's lack of trying either because poor Brenda tried everything to coax Amber round but nothing would change her mind. She'd summed Brenda up almost as fast as I did and she just did not like her. But The Divine One was like that, she seemed to pick and choose who she liked, made her mind up very fast she did and once she had decided they couldn't win her over no matter how many treats they had in their hand.

Billy and Amber

It was a bit hard to watch at times, totally cringe worthy, there would be Brenda crouching on the floor. "I'll get down to her level" she'd say. "It'll help her to feel less afraid of me" she'd say but I knew it wouldn't and I was right. Normally doing such a thing is a good way to connect with a dog that's feeling threatened, it lessens how imposing you are, they are no longer looking up at you seeing you towering over them, they are now looking across at you and that can go a long way in calming a little ones nerves. And it wasn't exactly easy for Brenda to get down on the floor, not with her arthritic knees but she did it each visit anyway, such was her love for The Divine One. And Amber would sniff at her hand and back away. Walk off leaving my poor friend crouching there and I'd have to go over and help her up. And once she was up she'd straighten her clothing and vow never to get down on the floor again but the next visit would find her in exactly the same position. I'd be over tending to a pug and hear Brenda shouting out for help and knew exactly why she needed it. "Come and help me up will you, my knees are a bit dodgy today" and I tell her that her knees were a bit dodgy every day and that it may be a whole lot better if she didn't get down on the ground so much "But that face" she'd say pointing at Amber and I knew exactly what she meant because there wasn't anything I wouldn't do for The Divine One either. Once you looked at that lovely little face of hers you were instantly under her spell. I think Brenda was so taken with Amber because she was the smallest pug on the farm. With Amber it wasn't just one thing that drew you in. It was the face and the tongue and the teeny tiny body and those eyes, those wonderful beautiful eyes. They would linger on your face, total pools of love they were, she'd be lingering due to her lack of vision, she was trying to see as much of you as she could, but for us looking on you couldn't help but fall in love. Brenda's second favourite pug was Casey and that was fine because Casey I am pleased to say loved Brenda right back. And I was very happy about that because I think it would have been real sad for Brenda if both of her favourite pugs had rejected her. But Casey would charge at my friend as soon as she came in the door, she was all over Aunty Brenda, danced in circles by her feet and sat on her knee like a little grey faced Queen. Wouldn't even get off if Brenda wanted to go to the toilet, Aunty Brenda had to carry Casey with her and neither one of us minded because it was wonderful for my friend to be loved by this little clinger. I think Brenda just had a real soft spot for the ones who she thought needed that extra bit of loving so would try and shower them with love. There were times though when Casey was a bit more interested in what was on the plate in front of Brenda then she was in Aunty Brenda herself, but as long as she was being hospitable I was happy. I'd see my friend sneaking little bits of food into Casey's old mouth and thought it was nice for both of them.

I don't exactly know what it was about Brenda that Amber didn't like, she wasn't petrified of her, I observed her and I saw that there wasn't total fear in her just an enormously huge amount of dislike. I suppose it's like us and why we are drawn to some people and repel others even though they have done nothing wrong. It's just a feeling you get I guess. But still I did try and figure out what made Amber dislike Brenda so much, was it the loudness of her voice or perhaps the perfume she would wear. Her perfume was pretty strong I have to admit that, it would come up the driveway way before Brenda did. She learnt to lower her voice by a few decibels whenever she was inside the house but then she'd get overly excited about something and be off shouting again and she did arrive perfume free a few times too to see if that was the cause but it made no difference at all to The Divine One. So we'd sit there and try and think of what else it could be. Did Brenda perhaps remind Amber of somebody in her old life, a person who had not treated her very well? Is that what Amber was picking up on, did my friend Brenda talk, walk or smell exactly like the person who had done her wrong. I personally had the feeling it had everything to do with smell and that maybe it wasn't even perfume. It could well have been that Brenda used the same washing powder or shampoo, or maybe it was something else in Brenda's home that Amber was picking up on. And it may not even have been Brenda herself, it could have been her husband, Brenda could have given her husband a hug as she walked out the door and been innocently bringing the smell of his aftershave here with her. Also Brenda's husband wasn't well, maybe it was the medication he was on, maybe that was what Amber could smell. Due to her lack of vision Amber's hearing and sense of smell was heightened, she would have been picking things up on Brenda that I with my limited human nose wasn't even aware of. Either way something about my friend was triggering a memory, and sadly that memory never faded for Amber.

And as much as my friend wanted me to I wasn't ever going to pick Amber up and place her in Brenda's arms, if The Divine One was going to have a connection it had to be entirely her own choice. I loved Brenda but I always put my dogs first, I always have and I always will. A dog's home is their haven just like a person's home is their haven, why do you think they fight so hard to protect it, they have a right to feel safe in their own home just like we have a right to feel safe in our own home. I used to hope, and Brenda used to think, that over time Amber's heart would warm to our frequent visitor but it never did. The first visit Amber was still hiding under the bed and Brenda went and crouched down in the doorway of the bedroom to get a look at my new daughter in the flesh. I was standing next to Brenda and she was giving a running commentary on what Amber was doing. The rest of the pugs were circling their aunty Brenda and giving kisses and she'd be saying things like "Amber is sniffing at the air now" and I'd say "Yes she's very good at telling when there is somebody new here". Or "Her heads gone down now maybe she's going to sleep" and I'd be thinking to myself no, not while you are in the house she won't but I never said anything. I just knew Amber enough to know that she would never relax and fall asleep when she was on guard and she was on guard a lot of the time in the first few months she was with us and even more so when there was a strange voice in the house. Then everything would be quiet for a while, but we'd all still be in our positions in the doorway, me standing, Brenda crouching, pugs circling. Then she'd be shouting out once more "Oh her heads up again now, maybe she's thinking about coming out" and I'd still say nothing just be thinking no not while you are here she won't be doing that. But Brenda was so hopeful and I wasn't going to be the one to burst her bubble. Amber was already making Brenda feel unloved I wasn't about to destroy her hope. I'd just be there looking down at the top of her head, counting colours and wondering how long it'd be before she got sick of waiting for Amber to come out. The bedroom was bright so Brenda was able to get a pretty good look at Amber and she seemed happy about that. Happy because I believe she thought this was only going to be a temporary thing. That soon she would be out mingling and circling with the rest of the pugs. But time went by and Amber started feeling comfortable enough in the rest of the house but she was still never comfortable around Brenda. Sometimes The Divine One would be asleep in one of the lounge room beds when Brenda walked into the house and in a fit of excitement she'd go over and stand beside Amber watching her sleep, she got joy from that and I knew she would because the sight of that old tiny body doing slumbering huffs and puffs was a beautiful sight to see. But Brenda's presence was soon sensed, Amber slowly came around, it did take her a while to come fully awake as is often the case with old dogs, but as soon as she did she would climb out of the bed and take herself off into the bedroom. I started giving Brenda treats to feed Amber as a way of connecting with her. Amber sure did love her treats and I thought this was a perfect way of bonding the two of them. I didn't just give Brenda a treat for Amber I gave her a treat to feed everybody. At the start Amber wouldn't take anything from Brenda, she would only take it from me, but after a few weeks she allowed Brenda to feed her and it was a joyous occasion for all involved because Amber wasn't confused, she knew it was Brenda who was feeding her yet she took it off her all the same. And of course Brenda was in raptures about it, she thought it was the start of a budding friendship and to be honest I did too. I mean she had paid her dues, week after week she had stood by watching me feeding Amber and was ok doing that, she was happy enough to watch on as The Divine One ate because she, like me, loved the way she chewed. Amber had a way of scrunching up her little face whenever she was gnawing on something and so each visit Brenda would be eagerly watching out for Amber to start doing that.

Amber, Steffy, Ruben and Baby

It was around this time that Brenda decided she would start bringing special treats for the pugs, mainly Amber, in order to gain favour. She thought it just may do the trick. Bringing something Amber didn't have on a daily basis surely had to draw her interest. So Brenda would arrive with a bag of treats and they were good treats too, the real expensive super tasty ones and it did hold Amber's attention. Her full attention was on Brenda for all of about thirty seconds, for just as long as it took her to finish eating her special treat and then once again The Divine One would turn and with her saggy little ass and uncurled tail she shuffled off into the bedroom and that's the last anybody would see of her until Brenda had gone home. Sometimes Brenda would be struggling trying to open the pack of treats and we were kind of hopeful on many occasions because Amber would stay in the lounge room during those times, she'd stand and wait in amongst the other pugs while Brenda battled with ripping open the seal. I don't know why they seal them up like that, normally it'll take a pair of scissors to gain access, there is always a tear arrow but you'll try with all your might to rip the pack open and all you'll do is wrinkle the packaging. But the sound of that happening was enough for Amber to stay put because she knew what was coming. And she'd have her treat, sometimes she'd have two or three and she'd happily take each one out of Brenda's hand. She'd even let Brenda give her little old ears a soft gentle stroke but then she'd smell that the treats were all gone and move away from the gentle stroking hand, like she was thinking "I'm having no more of this" and off to the bedroom she would go. I used to be a tad embarrassed that Amber wouldn't even stay in the same room as Brenda, it's like when one of your children plays up in front of a visitor and all you can do is watch. But I knew Amber wasn't really playing up, that she was feeling uncomfortable and this was her house, she needed to feel safe here so Brenda was never allowed to go into the bedroom after her, no matter how many treats Brenda brought with her nothing would gain her access to the bedroom because The Divine One needed to know that she had a safe spot, an area to feel at ease in when the main part of the house felt like an invasion and our bedroom once again became her safe haven just like it had been in the early part of her stay. This was her home after all. She had priority here. It's how it always was, how it always had to be, no matter what dog I have at the time or what their needs are they always come first. Sure I felt a little sorry for Brenda because she went to an awful lot of trouble with the treats but I am here to protect my pugs not somebody else's feelings and Brenda being a friend understood this. So again she'd have to be content with kneeling on the floor in the bedroom doorway, sometimes she'd even lay flat out in order to watch Amber and I had to deter the other pugs from jumping all over her back. Sometimes Casey would sit in the middle of aunty

Brenda's back and refuse to get off and I would go over to lift her off because it's not polite to let your pugs go jumping all over a visitor. But Brenda would sense it was Casey and tell me to leave her there. So I'd make all the other pugs behave and we'd stand close by listening to Brenda talk. It was kind of funny seeing this tiny woman sprawled out on the floor, ultra-colourful hair, old black pug with a greying face sitting in the small of her back like a statue. And all the while she'd be telling me what she could see. If Amber had a new blanket Brenda would comment on that and a conversation would be had about it. Brenda liked the hot pink blankets best so I'd make sure to try and have one of them washed and dried for Amber to sleep on whenever I knew Brenda was coming over. She also liked the jade green one I had as that seemed to make Ambers face easier to see. And if Brenda had forgotten to put her glasses on before getting down on the ground she'd yell for me to bring them to her and I'd end up having to dig around in her handbag which I felt a bit uncomfortable doing. I used to offer to bring her handbag over so she could find them herself but she'd just say "Nah it's all good just grab them for me will you" so I did but it always seemed kind of rude to be looking in somebodies handbag. I think ladies handbags are such personal things. And I also think you can tell an awful lot about a person by what they choose to carry around with them. If I am being honest I reckon I could write a page or two about what Brenda chose to cart around with her, her handbag was just about as colourful and crazy as she was. It was like entering another world when you looked in there.

I was pretty happy The Divine One had somewhere safe to hide and Brenda didn't even have to enter the house for Amber to start walking out of the lounge room either. Amber would hear Brenda coming up the driveway bellowing hello to Gerald and the sheep. Due to having old pugs that are quite slow moving I always get people to leave their cars at the gate and walk up to the house. I never want anybody running my little old blessings over, this is their farm after all and I make sure they are always safe, that they can wander around at their leisure and no harm is ever going to come to them. So Brenda would get out of her car and all the way up the driveway she'd be calling out greetings and no doubt Amber could hear her getting closer and closer. One moment she'd be by my side, the next moment she'd be gone and I always knew where she was. I'd hear her doing her clunky walk all the way into the bedroom then you'd hear it stop and know she was safely in her nest. I'd wait until I heard that then I'd go out and greet Brenda. If it was a warm day when Brenda came to visit I would go and put the air conditioner on in the bedroom so it was nice and cool for Amber when she chose to make her escape. I put it on an hour or so before Brenda was supposed to arrive, always ensuring Amber would be comfortable and happy. In winter it was the heater that went on an hour before the arrival and when I saw that little figure in the pink coat disappearing into the bedroom I didn't have to worry, I knew she would be escaping into a lovely pre-warmed room. A few of the others occasionally followed Amber into the bedroom, but they'd all wait around for a little while to see if they were going to be given a treat or a bit of biscuit first, when they weren't they'd file off one by one and hop into one of the beds in there. Some stayed with me, just lay by my feet or walked off and put themselves into a nearby bed, they didn't seem to mind Brenda at all. They even slept through our many fits of hysterical laughter, didn't even open up their eyes, just slept right the way through no matter how loud we got or how many times we broke out laughing, and there were many, many times when we did that. Sometimes I'd be aching from laughing when Brenda left but it was well worth it.

Making sure Brenda has gone

On the days when The Divine One wasn't quite fast enough making her escape Brenda was always so lovely to her, she kept trying and trying to win my little mouse over. Once again getting down to her level and be saying things like "I'm your Aunty Brenda" or "Aunty Brenda loves you so much" and there wouldn't be any kind of a response. So then Brenda would say "You don't like me do you Amber" and Amber would sneeze, turn and walk off leaving my poor friend kneeling on the floor. She'd just bared her soul and been shunned but The Divine One wasn't for caring and her walk was very determined. She walked like she was saying to herself "You are not mine aunty", "You are not mine anything". And both Brenda and I would watch on until we couldn't see that little uncurled tail any more. Amber wasn't rushing away, just doing that slow clunking along that was completely her own but there was a whole lot of determination in her stance and she wasn't turning back for anybody. I think Amber always preferred it when she made it all the way to her safety zone before Brenda stepped foot on the deck. I'd watch her dear little body gently step over the run of the sliding door and a second or two later be hearing the clank of the front gate and be thinking to myself that it was lucky The Divine One had decided to go when she did. "Good for you sweetheart, you timed that well" I'd call out to her as she shuffled away. But it was never a coincidence, it happened far too many times for it to be, I knew there was more to this than meets the eye. So I began watching Amber more closely because I was fascinated to know how she knew when Brenda was due. It wasn't like she could read the hands on the clock, even if she had full vision she still wouldn't have known what the hands meant and also Brenda wasn't always on time, in fact she was often late because she'd gotten caught talking to somebody and couldn't get away. But Amber had still disappeared well before Brenda's voice echoed up the driveway. If it only happened once or twice I would more than likely have brushed it off as being a fluke but it kept on happening. Nine times out of ten it'd happen. So on the mornings Brenda was coming over my eyes would be forever watching Amber looking to see exactly when she'd turn and walk away and at times she was doing it even before Brenda had her hand on the gate so it wasn't the chain being rattled that was alerting her like I thought it may have been and even if she did hear the gate how could The Divine One have possibly known it was Brenda who was down there. It could have been anybody, maybe even somebody Amber liked. At times Amber would turn even before Brenda's car came into view.

I'd be watching and off she'd go and then a few seconds later Brenda's car would come up the road. I knew Amber was special but I also knew she didn't have superpowers and I knew for sure that I didn't have a clairvoyant pug on my hands because she would have let me know this about her a long time ago. So I kept trying to work it out and sometimes she'd be gone the second Brenda's car pulled up to our gate and other times she'd leave and I'd have my eyes on the road because I knew I'd soon be seeing Brenda's car and sure enough that's exactly what happened. It took a while but in the end I figured it out, it was the sound of Brenda's car brakes that set Amber off. If she heard the car brake before it came into view she'd head off, but if Brenda only hit the brakes to turn into our driveway, well that's the precise moment Amber would take her leave. The reason Amber knew it was Brenda was because Brenda had a really old car, it was her father's, she kept it for sentimental value really because it wasn't much to look at and it wasn't always reliable either. But it was unique in the sound it made when slowing down or coming to a complete stop and it was that that Amber was responding to. I guess if it wasn't for Amber I would never have picked up on it, not being all that car minded I don't tend to notice such things, to a mechanic or a car enthusiast it would have been instantly noticeable and it was instantly noticeable to Amber too but for a very different reason. That odd sound was a dead giveaway to The Divine One, she knew exactly who that noise belonged to, she knew it would be soon followed by bellowing greetings, overpowering perfume and sometimes treats, well there were always treats but Amber didn't always feel they were worth waiting around for, she was well gone before they got dished out but Brenda would always leave one or two in the bag for her and I'd feed them to Amber the next time I saw her face.

One time Brenda was using her husband's car for the day and that really did confuse Amber. She was lying in the sun quite happily when all of a sudden she heard Brenda's voice. She couldn't have been fully asleep though, not with the speed she was up on her feet and she would have been able to make her escape faster but some of her siblings were standing in the way and Brenda had already made it onto the deck before a path had been cleared for Amber to walk through. Brenda had treats but Amber wasn't interested in them, I guess she had been completely satisfied with breakfast that day. Brenda's eyes lit up at the sight of her little darling still being there in amongst the others. But The Divine One didn't even turn her head towards our visitor she was more concentrating on trying to find a path to the door but with everybody being lulled into dopiness by the morning sun they weren't for getting out of the way. It didn't put Amber off though she just decided to go around them all instead, found the door in no time, shuffled inside, cleared the threshold to our bedroom and we didn't see her again until Brenda had gone home.

Ruben, Emily and Amber

There were short visits, there were long visits and there were really long visits but as soon as Brenda left the house everything would fall silent again and a little while later Amber's tiny frame would appear at the bedroom doorway. She'd sniff the air and listen for a while, trying to figure out if Brenda had really gone or not and if she felt the coast was clear she'd come slowly clunking out. If not she'd pause there a little while longer sniffing and listening just to be sure. I'd be in the kitchen putting the dishes in the sink and be watching all of this, just waiting for her to feel safe and when she did she'd clunk over and stand by my legs until I took her outside for a wee. Then I'd bring her inside again and feed her the treats Aunty Brenda had left for her. Sometimes it took Amber quite a while to come out and I'd use that time to clean up the house a bit. I think on those days Amber must have been in a real deep sleep and I'd wait and wait for that little flat face to appear in the doorway and when it did we'd all go for a nice wander around in the sunshine. Sometimes I'd walk my friend to the gate and the other pugs would come with me and we'd chat for a while, sometimes for quite a while, then she'd get in her car and wave as she was pulling away. And me and the pugs would slowly make our way back up to the house again, I'd let the pugs have a good sniff while I walked along with my hands in my pockets thinking about all the things Brenda and I had talked about. Then we'd re-enter the house and there would be Amber standing in the middle of the lounge room sniffing at the air, wondering where we were. Sometimes I'd hear her woofing for us as we approached the house and she was so happy when we finally walked in, happy enough to start smothering me with kisses as soon as I picked her up, but I think she was even happier knowing that the house was once again her own.

I did find it funny that Amber would wander around after workmen who ignored her half the time due to getting on with the job at hand and yet she wouldn't have a bar of somebody whose heart was close to bursting with love for her, somebody who tried everything in their power to win her over. But dogs, unlike us, see no reason why they should be polite, if they don't like you you'll know it and if they love you you'll know it, they go entirely with their feelings, no social graces getting in the way, no manners, no etiquette, just feelings and acting purely on them. I kind of envy that about dogs. I wish I didn't have to be nice to people I have no interest in being nice to, like the bitchy nurse I encountered when I was in hospital, really wish I could have told her exactly what I thought of her, told her she had no right being in a profession that was meant to help people if helping people was the last thing she wanted to be doing. But I couldn't air my views. I had to keep quiet or I think she would have left me hanging when I needed some help, well left me until last anyway and gone off to help the people who perhaps hadn't given her a piece of their mind. It's times like this that you have to choose what's worth saying and what's best keeping to yourself. The Divine One though, well she didn't have to worry about such things, she just went with how she was feeling and sometimes Brenda would be here for a while and you could hear Amber clunking around in the bedroom. Only a tiny frame but she'd make quite a lot of noise and that wasn't all to do with The Divine One but more our wooden floorboards. You really shouldn't have been able to hear her as loudly as you could. Yeah sure she was stomping due to being impatient because Brenda was still here and she probably thought she should have gone home a long time ago, but still you should not have been able to hear her as well as we could hear her. And I'd see the look in Brenda's eyes, see the elation spread across her face and she'd stop talking mid-sentence. Poor Brenda was beside herself at these times. She'd hear the clunky walk and sit up straight in her chair ready to receive her darling. She thought Amber was coming out but I'd heard those noises before and knew exactly what was going on. Amber was simply moving from one bed to another, obviously getting herself more comfortable on these extra-long stays. So Brenda's hand would slowly push the bag of treats back into the centre of the kitchen table and her eyes would lose a little bit of their sparkle and she'd be silent for a few moments until another conversation was started and off we'd go again.

I remember the exact day Brenda told me she was moving interstate. Her husband had died a few years back so she'd decided to go live closer to her youngest daughter. "To help with the grandkids" she leant back in her chair as she told me. "Three under five" she said but I already knew that because she'd called me as soon as they were born. "That's too much for anybody to cope with" she said in a matter of fact way "At least I had the sense to spread my lot out, that way the oldest could help with the youngest" and I knew this too because she'd told me of her good planning many times over the years. I was upset at the thought of Brenda leaving but I think there would have been a little old pug sitting in a soft comfy nest in the other room air punching when she heard the news. Until she moved away Brenda would drop by the farm on a week day morning just like she had been doing for a good many years, if life was still she'd come once a week but when there was a lot going on in either of our lives she would come by once a fortnight and we'd sit at my kitchen table trading news. After she moved we had to make do with trading our news by phone and again once a week or once a fortnight depending what was going on in our lives. This was a friendship that distance couldn't affect, a great friendship too and to think if she'd not walked up the driveway that day asking about my sheep we would never have met. Or if I had been inhospitable and not asked her in, merely answered her questions and sent her on her way then we would never have gotten to experience the many years of laughter that we have. It's funny how people enter our lives, at times it's as if the wind seems to just blow them in and sometimes they settle and at other times the wind blows them out of your life again just as fast. It's like they stay as long as they are supposed to and then they are gone. I suppose in normal circumstances we'd not have struck up a friendship because we are two very different people but we both have a similar sense of humour. That's our link, the bond that kept us together and has kept us talking and laughing all these years. There were never ever any uncomfortable silences when Brenda was around. She used to keep me entertained for hours with her stories and she had so many stories to tell. And the best part of her tales was when she got up from her chair to act things out, it was like I was now looking at the people she was pretending to be, she had a talent for things like that. Brenda is unique. Brenda oozes self-confidence. But I had a feeling that self-confidence didn't come with age for Brenda as it does for most people. I thought she would have had that same amount of self-confidence even as a teenager. Brenda's hair, clothing and style are as loud as she is. But she never tried to tame any of that down and I totally admire her for that and for everything else in her life she set free. She's a wonderful person and I tell her that often. After we lost Amber I rang Brenda but she didn't pick up and I didn't want to leave such news in a message so just said that I'd ring her back. In the end she beat me to it and her voice was light and airy when I answered the phone. But when she heard what I had to say Brenda cried like a baby. She was totally heartbroken by the news. Between sobs she kept saying "I don't know why I am crying so hard, after all Amber didn't even like me". And over the coming months we would laugh often about that fact, about her visits and about how The Divine One shunned her every time. Even today we still talk about Amber and laugh a lot about her too and really I think it's a nice thing for us to be doing, a lovely way of remembering this special little blessing.

Casey, Baby, Amber and Brian

CHAPTER NINE

Glue

Amber and Steffy

For the first few months The Divine One was living with us she spent every night sleeping in a closed off pen beside David's side of the bed, it was to keep her from getting squashed by the pugs in the house who were so much bigger then she was, it was a safe place, somewhere David and I knew she would be protected so could close our eyes and go to sleep knowing all was well. That bed was nice and warm but we would also give her a wheat heat bag for extra warmth, the rest of the pugs were all curled up together but The Divine One was sleeping alone, the wheat bag was doing the job that one of her siblings would have been doing if they had access to the bed. I always like seeing the blessings snugged up together, that lovely sight makes me smile but in winter it makes me happier even more because I know they are gaining warmth from one another. But at this point in time Amber couldn't have that so we gave her the next best thing. Each night we'd pop the wheat bag in the microwave to heat up before putting Amber in bed. Once the microwaved dinged The Divine One knew it was bed time and also the wheat bags smell a little bit like porridge when they were being heated up so that too was a dead giveaway that it was time for bed. We have used the wheat bags off and on for a number of years now, used them for pugs that aren't well and for old pugs that need an extra bit of warmth and care, and Amber being the delicate little flower that she was really needed some special looking after. And she loved that wheat bag. Sat in her bed each night waiting for one of us to bring it over to her and when we did she would get herself comfortable beside it, close her eyes and go to sleep and it was hard because I just loved looking at her, but I didn't want to disturb her so I would only allow myself to hover for a little while. I seriously reckon I could have stood watching her sleep all night long but I knew my presence would have been disturbing to her, I knew she needed to rest, so I'd get my fill then reluctantly move away. And as I did I'd hear her snoring and be really wanting to race back over for just one more look at her little face before lights out but I'd stop myself short because I knew if I did I wouldn't be able to walk away.

We have four wheat bags here, two medium size and two small ones, but you can't put them directly beside your dog, they have to be wrapped in something, it's just like you wouldn't put a hot water bottle right beside your own leg, it'd burn, that's why hot water bottle covers have been invented. And you can get some real pretty ones too, big fluffy ones that would be great for keeping old bones warm throughout the night but we don't use hot water bottles here we prefer the wheat bags. We wrap the each bag in a doubled over blanket and tuck them in at the ends so the pugs can't get to them. I guess you may get some dogs that would tear those wheat bags to pieces trying to eat the wheat but I've never had a dog try to do that yet. If they did we would have to move on to something else, but old dogs are quite sensible I've found, they are quite content to just feel the warmth and snuggle down to sleep. Some of the blankets I use are ones my grandmother made for me many moons ago and I think she'd be pleased that we are still using them today. I know I get a special feeling when carrying a wheat bag over to a bed that's wrapped in one of Nana Harpers creations, sure I'm happy when carrying them over in a store bought blanket as well because it makes no difference to the amount of warmth given the only difference really is in my own heart. But those Nana Harper creations are wearing pretty thin now a days so I'll stand there umming and ah-hing some nights with a blanket in each hand trying to decide if I am going to go with the emotion filled one or put it back on the pile so that it'll last a little bit longer. If I do decide on one of Nana's then as I am presenting it to the pug I'll tell them how special the blanket is to me and how very special the lady who made these blankets was. In my heart I do feel my grandmother is blessing the little pugs that are snuggling up to her blankets, I believe they may even be able to feel her love, sure those blankets have had a lot of washes over the years but love that strong can never be washed away and that is something I truly believe with all my heart. Amber by the way, as is the case with any pug that isn't well, was always given a Nana Harper creation because I feel sick pugs need all the help they can get.

But wheat bags just like hot water bottles only have a limited time of staying warm, they eventually cool down and for us that usually happens around two or three in the morning and over the years we've had many a pug that has woken us up barking at that time because they want their wheat bag reheating. So it's a quick ride in the microwave, a quick wrapping back up and the pug is fast sleeping in no time. Well most are right back to contented slumber in no time anyway, Baby always was, Zaney always is, but Amber just like Horton decided that a reheated wheat bag wasn't going to come even close to cutting it, they wanted much more than that, they wanted on the bed with us. I can clearly remember Amber waking up barking. It was around two o'clock every morning that we would hear her growly little woof and she'd be taken outside for a toilet break while her wheat bag was riding around the microwave. Then she'd come inside, be put back into bed, give the wrapped up wheat bag a sniff but instead of snuggling up next to it she'd just sit there woofing. For a few nights we let her go because we figured she would settle down eventually, which she did after half an hour. But over the course of a week that settling down period went from half an hour to a full hour then to an hour and a half and in the end I said to Dave we may as well just let her sleep on the bed with us all the time. He had been bringing her up on the occasional night anyway because he was exhausted and desperately wanted to get a few hours of sleep in before the alarm went off. I think we were both happier having Amber sleeping on the bed though, it was hard hearing her bark knowing she'd be sitting there looking up with her little tongue poking out just waiting for somebody to pick her up. I mean sure it was dark but we both knew what that gorgeous little face looked like and the thought of her sitting there on her own, well neither one of us could go back to sleep knowing that. Plus she was not for being quiet, I am sure that hour and a half would have very quickly become two hours and then three. It wasn't that she disliked the pen, in fact once Amber had gotten used to the routine of our life she would often wander over to the pen at bedtime, if we hadn't lifted her in first she would go over and stand in front of her pen waiting for one of us to help her in. I think what happened was over time Amber decided that she just really wanted to be as close to us as she possibly could. During the day she could get to us no trouble at all but night time was a different story and I guess she decided she wanted to fix that so began woofing to let us know. It was like "Where you sleep I sleep" so up she came. Once she began sleeping on the bed you'd not hear a peep out of her simply because there was no reason to speak. She was happy and contented so she closed her eyes and drifted off to sleep and I was thrilled to have her up there with us, happy to be able to see her all the time. On full moon nights I would sleep with the blinds open just so I could watch her sleeping, you have no idea how adorable the little mouse looked cast in the light of the silvery moon . Her little face shimmered. I do feel very sorry for dogs that are crying out to be with the ones they love but are locked in the laundry, which by the way is one of the coldest rooms in the house, or even worse left outside. Their lifespan compared to ours is so very short and they love us with all their hearts, we are their all and yet time and time again I hear about people locking them away, of course not everybody agrees about having a dog on the bed with them but surely putting a lovely warm soft bed right beside your own bed is not too much to ask. I honestly think it's one of the reasons I get such good ages out of my pugs and I 100% believe it's one of the reasons why Amber lived as long as she did.

Tommy and Amber

Amber slept in-between our two pillows with Tommy in front of her. She had already proven to me that she would be ok on the bed because she'd had plenty of chair time with Tommy. And when she wanted down she wouldn't ever try and get down by herself she would always ask, just sit behind Tommy giving out little woofs while waiting for me to go get her. I knew it'd be the same with her being on the bed and it was. Plus she was very good at knowing where the edge of the bed was, a lot of blind pugs will walk right off the edge and hurt themselves but Amber wasn't one of them, then again neither was Ruben or Billy. I stood close by watching both of them the first few times they asked to come up on the bed, stood right in front of them to prevent them from falling, I saw each one feeling for the edge and when they found it they would slowly draw their bodies backwards and go to sleep and I would encourage them to sleep close to the middle. Ruben especially knew what to do quite quickly, Billy needed a bit of training but then again Billy was a pug that had been made to live outside all his life before coming to live with us, he didn't know what it was like to sleep in a house let alone on a bed, but he soon picked up on what I was trying to tell him, he mapped the bed out and would sit waiting for me to lift him down each morning. And both of them learnt to woof for me when they wanted down. But even if I am living with a pug who is blind and not good at judging or feeling with their paws, as was the case with Arthur, I will not punish them by never allowing them to come up on the bed or couch I just make sure to be extra vigilant, never leave them unattended, they are only allowed up if I am right there next to them. I'll never leave them alone ever, even if I'm just getting up for a short amount of time they will still be placed on the floor for their own safety and I'll simply lift them back up again once I return. To be honest I am actually quite reluctant telling people about blind dogs on couches and beds for fear of them just hiking them up then leaving them there to fend for themselves because you can't do that, you need to use common sense, you always have to be there caring for them, being their eyes, making sure they are ok, blind dogs need special looking after and it's up to you to give it to them, no thoughtlessness ever, you simply can't afford it because it's the little blind soul in your care who will pay the price not you. Please remember this, please take your role as guardian of these little blessings seriously, they are too precious for you to be lax. Over the years I have taught many a blind pug to be safe when on a couch or bed. It does take time and you have to put the effort in but you can get to a place where they learn to stay away from the edge and also to call out to you for assistance when they want to get down or you can teach them to use bedside steps, specially made steps with sides on so they don't fall off. And when they've learnt don't go moving things as that'll only cause confusion, leave cushions and pillows where they are, once they have the bed and couch mapped out in their heads you can't go shifting things around. Put yourself in their shoes try and see things from their point of view or should I say not see things because if you can't see them with your eyes closed neither can they and that's how you have to always be thinking about things when sharing your life with a blind pug.

Once Amber began sleeping on the bed the wheat bag was no longer needed because if she felt cold she would just move closer to Dave, Tommy or me. But of course it wasn't so much the cold Amber was reacting to, sure the cooled down wheat bag may have been the reason she woke up in the first place but once she was awake she wanted to be where we were. Gone was the independent little darling who'd first arrived on the farm, her independence had disappeared as fast as the months had. Now she wanted to be stuck to me like glue, day or night it didn't matter, Amber and me we were glue. It was like she was saying "Where you are I am" and "Where you go I go", this little girl was led by her heart and I understood this because I am to. Once she had given me and David her heart she wanted to be near us all the time. I would say she never let us out of her sight but she didn't have a whole lot of sight so I'll just say that once The Divine One put her full trust in us, her faith in us, she wanted to be with us always. It had taken some time but she had handed her life over to us in a very beautiful way. She was in love with us and knew we were going to take the most excellent care of her and we thanked her over and over again for doing that. She'd given us a gift. I think it's such a special thing when a dog does this. They put their life into your hands and trust that you are going to give them a very good one. And we were going to give The Divine One the very best life possible like we do with all our dogs.

I remember one day during The Divine One's first spring here. Well it wasn't much of a spring really, more of an extended winter, but I was going to the shed to fetch some wood, the fire was roaring and the house was so beautifully warm. All the other pugs were either asleep in front of the fire or in beds that were as close to the fire as we allow them to be. I put my coat on and was about to walk out the door when I heard that all too familiar clunking sound behind me. So I turned and explained to Amber what I was about to go do and how long I would be gone for. I also told her I'd much prefer it if she stayed inside and she stood there looking up at me, beautiful grey face, mauve knitted coat on, tongue glistening because she'd just flicked it in and out a bit. I thought she understood and I also thought she'd probably want to be inside where the warmth was but as I turned and took another step I heard another clunk. The Divine One really did want to be with me and after the way she'd been when she first arrived there was no way I wasn't going to let her. So out she came and pottered around in the shed sniffing at this and that while I made my wood selection. I was looking for two pieces that would fit in no trouble once the two that were already in had collapsed down a bit and as I searched I was watching Amber wandering this way and that. She'd be by the wood pile with me then go off in search of something more interesting to sniff. She found a bit of loose hay on the floor so squatted down and had a wee on it, then she was off again sniffing near the BBQ, no doubt smelling remnants from the last time we used it and when I was ready I stood in the entrance of the shed and gave her a little shout. It took a few more call outs before she was willing to follow me inside though, I think she wanted to stay there as long as she could but it wasn't exactly warm in there, sure we were out of the wind but it was nicer in the house then the hayshed and when she realised I was really leaving this time she came over and followed me back inside. From that day on that's how it was all our years together. I knew I couldn't ever sneak out of the house without her so figured she may as well accompany me, if she was happiest by my side then that's where she was always going to be from here on in so I started preparing for taking her with me no matter where I was going or how long for. And the weather determined the amount of prep involved. Mild days were fine no trouble at all just out the door we'd go, summer days and out we'd go but be very quick and at all times sticking to the shade. Winter, well winter was when I'd need to have things well organized so that Amber was always warm, dry and comfortable. I did draw the line at taking her out in the pouring rain though and although she wasn't too happy about it I stuck to my guns for her sake. Couldn't let her get ill just because we needed to be separated for a little while and I always tried to be super-fast if I'd left her behind and not because I was getting soaked to the skin either because I like being out in the rain, it doesn't bother me at all, thrills me no end actually, rain always has. But what really spurred me on was seeing that tiny gorgeous face by the window. I wanted to get back to her as soon as possible, where once I may have lingered with the horses these days I found myself bolting back inside to be with my little love.

Gerald and Amber

If the rain was only light I would put Amber underneath my coat and protected her that way. She'd only have her head peeping out and be sniffing at the air, listening to the sounds. I'd have her in one arm and a biscuit of hay in the other. She could smell the hay and hear the horses and sheep talking to us as we approached their paddock. Then I'd fling the biscuit and go back to the hay shed for another one and another few after that, all the while chatting away to Amber as we went. It was the same if I was giving them a bucket of food, it was Amber in one arm and a bucket in the other, it took a few trips to feed everybody and yes much faster if I was able to carry two buckets at a time but Amber was thrilled being involved and time is not more important than a little pugs happiness is. The Divine One didn't mind being carried on those days, if she could feel a few droplets of rain on her head she knew she wouldn't be going down on the ground on that trip so enjoyed everything from up high. And that worked out pretty well for everybody. Amber really enjoyed coming out whenever I was refilling the horse water. She liked hanging around the water tank because there were lots of interesting things to sniff in that area, she could go off to the veggie patch, the side of the shed or the cluster of trees and always be in my view. The tank was a slow filler, we don't use town water for the paddock kids it's all rainwater and as with anybody who has a water tank knows they fill at their own pace and there's nothing you can do to alter it, the pressure comes from how full the tank is at the time, sometimes it took a while for the water bucket to fill. The slowness of the tank gave Amber time to have a good wander around and a good long sniff at everything and being blind she liked that, she liked the new smells that were out there each day. If the grass had been recently mowed she would go clunking off with fawn paws and come clunking back to me with green. And her paws would be green for a day or so until the grass stains faded. I guess I could have washed the stains off but she did look kind of cute walking around the place with little green feet and it was doing her no harm so I just left them as they were.

To be honest I don't think she would have felt the cold all that much when we were outdoors because I protected her from doing so. I protected her from being in the wind, put a thick coat on, kept her to the areas that offered the most shelter, always thought given to Amber, just did everything I could think of to help shield her from the elements and she was constantly on the move so that would have been keeping her warm as well. I wanted each trip out to be joy, joy, joy for her and I believe it always was. But sometimes the rain would start before I'd finished the job at hand. After the first time we got caught in the rain I began warming a coat up for Amber before we set of on one of our adventures, well it was chores for me but always the hugest of adventures for her. And I liked that she was having a blast but I also wanted to warm her up as soon as possible when we got back inside again and I've found that nothing in the world warms a little blessing up faster than being put into a pre-warmed coat. It wasn't the top of the Coonara that I put it on as the wool would may have ruined on there, it was highly unlikely that it would have caught fire as the surface isn't hot enough for that but I guess you just never know do you so you always play it safe. Can you imagine me burning the house to the ground and having to explain to the fire brigade and insurance company that I'd lost the house because I wanted to have a colourful little coat toasty warm for when my old pug came in from her walk, they would have thought I was completely nuts. And also would the insurance company have paid up if that was the case or would they have put it down to a crazy pug mother's own stupidity. Either way I took no chances. We had a coil heater at the time, electric, cost a fortune to run, but I'd drag it out of the cupboard, turn it on and place one of The Divine Ones coats over the top of it, never turned it up high, just high enough to warm it through. And I'd walk out blissfully happy knowing that when we came back inside again Amber would have a beautifully warmed up coat ready to be put on. It wasn't always due to being caught in the rain that I was doing this because even when there was no rain in sight Amber would still need the coat she was wearing taking off and a new one putting on. Because she was so close to the ground she would always get the underneath of her coat damp when walking over the grass, the grass wasn't overly long it's just that she was overly small. She would flick dampness off the grass up towards her tummy as she moved along so each trip outside meant a two coat change for Amber and I never minded that because she really did want to be out there having fun. Yes it was a bit of extra work but it allowed her to live life how she wanted to live it. She had a keen interest in things and I would much rather that than have her lying in bed with no interest whatsoever. For old dogs having an interest is a very good sign. Its dogs with attitudes like this who last a long time I've found. Them being interested in the goings on around the place helps keep their minds alert and their bodies active, it also gives them something to live for, a reason to get up in the mornings, something to make those little old legs want to stand up and get moving. I always think the dogs I take in are like little retirees, if somebody is used to getting up in the mornings, having somewhere to be, something to do and then suddenly stops and does nothing it's like they have nothing to live for and that can have an effect, it does something to the mind and I don't want that happening with my old pugs. I know diet helps a real lot too and also a huge amount of good looking after, but I do think I'm getting the longer years out of my little blessings because they actually have something to look forward to doing each day.

I guess sometimes I may have preferred Amber stay inside but there was no way I was going to squash or dampen that determined spirit because I felt it would have a negative impact on her if I did. All my pugs have different personalities so I work with them. Once they show me who they are I let them do what makes them happiest and always protect them while they are doing it. I'll make sure the experience isn't going to do them any harm and with The Divine One the coat warming thing really helped with that. Oh and you wouldn't believe how much that little blessing of mine sighed when I put the pre-warmed coat on her, she all but melted into that coat and the sigh of satisfaction told me she really appreciated what I'd done. The times I did leave Amber in the house were when she wasn't well and that was an easy thing to do because she didn't want to come out with me at those times. But as soon as she was feeling even the slightest bit better out of her nest she would clunk and yes there were times when even after she had recovered I still left it an extra day or two before allowing her outside and sure she didn't like that one little bit but I am the parent here and you have to do what's best for their health. Health comes first in this house because it has to regardless of how much they complain. I'd look down at that little face and say to her "One of us has to be the sensible one here and it is me" and she'd still try and sneak out the door, but she was always far too slow. I'd stroke her little ears, tell her I wouldn't be gone long then close the door fast. But I'd be able to hear her complaints as I was walking down the ramp and yes it was hard to listen to and yes it did make me feel sad hearing her calling out for me so I quickened my step until I was out of earshot because I knew I couldn't go back for her. And she was always there waiting for me when I returned, waiting in the exact same spot I had left her in. She hadn't moved an inch. She must have just stood there like that the entire time I was gone I guess in the hope that if I did change my mind and come back she was making sure she was easy to find. Then the next day or the one after that all was forgiven and forgotten because she was coming outside with me again and she knew she was because she could hear the coil heater being dragged out. It had a certain smell about it as it was warming up so that was a dead giveaway too. It also did this kind of clicking thing as soon as you turned it on. The Divine One would have heard that noise as well, in her mind there would be no mistaking what was going on. And I knew there was no mistaking because at this point Amber would be really excited because she'd begin woofing. Her head turned as I dragged the heater out and more often than not she crossed the room to investigate further. When I turned it on and the clicking sound started up sometimes she'd even do a clunky little stepping dance, it all depended on how long it had been since she'd last come outside with me. I think those first trips out after an absence were always the best ones for Amber. We'd be back to our normal routine, outside, inside, damp coat quickly taken off, new warmed up coat put on. The coat was quite wet some days on others it'd be only slightly damp. The flicked up water mainly stayed on the outside, didn't soak through, sure if I'd left the damp coat on her it would have soaked through in time and she would have gotten ill from neglect. So regardless of the level of dampness the coat was always changed and the first few times I was changing it she argued with me big time. Not sure if it was because I was picking her up or because she didn't want to be fussed with and a coat change could be seen as fussing to Amber at times, especially during the first few months she was here. So I'd be fast but gentle with getting the old coat over her head then walk to the column heater and grab the warm coat up. And again on the days she was being fussy I would be super-fast but super gentle when putting the new coat on. Some dogs just don't like wearing coats but it wasn't the case with Amber but I do think that somebody must have been rough with her head in the past, or even put a coat on that was too tight around the head and neck area like a lot of normal dog coats are on pugs, that's why they need special coats, ones that specifically fit the shape of the breed. Anyway after a few months of gentle handling Amber was no longer bothered about having her coat changed. It was a case of one off, another on and all was well in her little world. Down on the floor she would go, trot off to a bed and be contented to settle there, she'd had an adventure, she'd had her fill, I knew she was happy so I'd go hang the wet coat up to dry, nine times out of ten it was only wet not dirty so didn't need a wash. She'd not been anywhere near the mud just pottering around on the damp grass. After I'd hung the coat up I'd go and check on the pugs that had stayed inside the house. I'd seen them from time to time coming wandering over to the window to see what me and Amber were getting up to, they were curious but not enough to want to follow us around. They were contented to look on from the warmth of the house, no need to be fully involved, not in the depth of winter when the temperature changed so dramatically as soon as you stepped out the door. Once Emily did shoot out and came bounding over to us but then she bounded back inside the house twice as fast when she realised there was nothing more than a few jobs and a bit of sniffing going on. I often thought about what it would have been like if all the pugs had wanted to come out with me, some wouldn't have always needed coat changes because they were taller, much higher from the ground then their new little sister was, but I'd still have to go round feeling underneath their coats. I'd still have to have coats ready in case they actually all needed a change, imagine warming all those coats up, it'd then be multiple coat changing and multiple coats hanging up to dry. And yes I would have done it for them all but it would have been a heck of a job. It would have taken forever and by the time I'd gotten them all sorted out it would be almost time to go outside again.

CHAPTER TEN

No Sight No Worries

As far as vision went Amber arrived with very little and over the course of a few years what vision she had completely disappeared. Little by little it started slowly fading away and I use this term because that's exactly how it would have been for her, how it would have been on the inside looking out, as time went on she would have been able to see a little bit less until everything went completely black. And although writing the last sentence has made my heart lunge and feel sadness I do think blind dogs can live happy lives, well I don't just think it I know for certain that they can because I have been sharing my life with blind dogs for a good many years now. I have witnessed up close the kind of life they can lead. Yes they will definitely, definitely need some extra special looking after, they will need lots of care and attention, but they can be happy living life using their other senses and that is exactly what Amber ended up doing. And believe me it's a real joy taking care of blind dogs. When The Divine One first came here she could see shadows, make things out enough not to bang into them, well not to bang into them all the time anyway, and then when she got used to things there was no banging into things at all. But yes there would be an odd occasion where she got distracted and walked into the side of one of her siblings, but most of the time she was able to see enough to know where they were standing and simply walked around them, she did the same thing with trees and fence posts too. Came walking towards them then veered off when she got close, although the trees and fence posts got a good sniffing over before she continued on her way. Her siblings not so much, yes she'd sniff at them but only just so she was able to tell who was who and when she'd done that she'd merrily be on her way. She'd do the same thing when getting into a bed that was already occupied, sniff at who the body in there was and then if she wanted to she'd climb in beside them, if not she'd go find the bed that held the sibling she was searching for or she'd go find a bed of her own and settle down in that.

Sometimes when we've taken in a pug with limited vision we will use a lead to help them get used to things. Used a lead on the walks around the farm for the first few weeks, just so they can get to know the route we take, the layout of the land and how to navigate it. As they are walking beside us they will also be getting used to the different smells along the path and those different smells will help them find their way around the farm and find their way back up to the house again too. That's why I always walk the same path each time, it's done so that should one of the blind pugs be sleeping when we walk out the door they will be able to find us quite quickly when they wake up. And sometimes that'll happen not long after we have left the house because when we are going for a walk there is so much excitement in the air that a whole lot of tap dancing is being done as we file out the door and sometimes the vibration from that tap dancing is enough to wake a slumbering pug up, other times so deep is their sleep they'll still be snoring contently when we come back in the house again and that's ok I'll just take them outside for a toilet break as soon as I see their little old blind eyes open up. Such things are what we created this farm of ours for in the first place, it's things like this that I had been dreaming of my entire life. A loving home where little old souls could do whatever they wanted to do and not be rushed or pushed or bothered in any way, just giving each and every single pug the beautiful peaceful happy lifestyle they deserve. And it blesses our hearts so much to do that.

A lot of the time I've found that our new blind son or daughter will just naturally follow on behind their new siblings, be happy enough to sniff the air and shadow the pack. Yes they'll go at their own pace and they can take as long as they like, but I will always be there watching on in case they go astray. It's amazing how quickly a blind dog can get used to life on the farm, same path taken day and night regardless, no confusion then, they always know where to find us by using their nose and feeling the different types of ground underneath their feet. Our tree varieties have different smells and the rustling of their leaves make different sounds as well and a blind pug will be guided by these things. It's amazing what blind dogs use as their aides, things I would never have even thought about had I not shared my life with so many blind dogs. I've seen blind dogs walk off course and a few steps out they'll stop, sniff the air then turn and find their way back to where they are meant to be. Ruben did this a lot, he was a little guy that used his feet, his sense of touch as much as he did his nose, he would feel the ground underneath him changing and so to prevent himself from veering even more off course I'd see him pause, his head turning in different directions until he caught a familiar scent on the breeze then he would follow that. Sometimes I will allow a blind dog a little time before rushing over to help them, just quietly watch on observing their movements, seeing how they handle different situations tells me what senses they are using more. With all blind dogs their other senses are very much heightened, it's what helps them cope, but some will rely on another sense slightly more. That could be either their ears or their noses, yes most use everything, but I have noticed some slight differences in some of the blind pugs I've lived with, they are different in what they chose to use as their secondary sense. So I watch on, see what they need from me, see if they are able to bring themselves round on their own or if they are getting too upset or confused and need my assistance. I have a little one I'm living with now who will simply sit down if he loses his way. I'll be watching, seeing him sniff the ground, seeing him circling, wonder if he'll be able to find us and sometimes he can but if he sits down that's it I'm over there in a heartbeat because he's just informed me by his actions that he doesn't know where any of us are and would appreciate a helping hand. But he's new and in time that could change or he just may not be the type to race off on his own. He may always sit and wait for help and that's ok they are all different in their ways, but once I know what they need from me my role in looking after them becomes easier. With The Divine One there was no sitting down and waiting, she never held back, she'd take herself off on her discovery missions or "Divine Adventures" as we often used to call them. I would watch her familiarising herself with the place and I knew those Divine Adventures would benefit her greatly later on when all her sight had gone. Because The Divine One arrived with some vision it did make things that bit easier for her, sure it was only a small amount but it did at least help her with getting to know the layout of the house and land. And because we've had so many blind pugs living here we don't move the furniture around, so once she had mapped the place out it was firmly in her mind when her vision diminished. I have found that to be the case with a lot of dogs that go blind in the family home, go blind due to age, sometimes it can take their owners a bit of time to actually figure out that their dog's vision has gone because they will be there just wandering around the place like they have been doing for many years and that's because they are familiar with everything. Time and time again people have said to me that they have no idea exactly when their dog lost it's vision because they were behaving not much differently to how they normally behaved. Also if a dog's vision does go slowly they slowly become used to living that way. Slow loss of vision for a dog in their family home is a good thing I think, of course it's not good that they are losing sight I don't mean it like that at all, what I mean is that such a thing is easier on the dog. I take in a lot of pugs that are completely blind and I do find it takes them a little bit longer to figure things out. Figure out where everything is and it can be hard watching all of this but each and every one of them in time does get used to the farm and once they do life becomes a whole lot easier for them. I've found each dog differs in the time it takes for them to get used to everything and I do believe that has as much to do with personality as it does sight, they do tend to react differently to the situation they find themselves in, just like we all react differently to situations we find ourselves in, and it's ok, they are allowed to take their time, we just stand by observing and helping. It's important for them to know they are never alone, that we are always nearby should they need us.

I remember one day, Amber had been living with us for a year or so and she was sleeping when I walked out of the house, Casey was sleeping soundly too so I left the two of them inside and took the rest of the pugs for a walk. I had gone down the driveway then across the front paddock, but halfway across the paddock Arthur had lost his way, gone off course for a sniff or perhaps got confused, either way I veered off to go get him. Sort of did a letter "U" in my course to collect him then came back and carried on my normal path. But as I was about to turn and head up to the house I glanced behind me, if somebody is still in the house sleeping when I walk outside a lot of that walk will be done with me forever looking backwards watching for them, seeing if they are coming to find us and if they are then I'll stand and wait for them to catch up so that we can all walk together. Well this day when I glanced back there wasn't anybody in the front paddock so I started looking up the driveway seeing if somebody was making their way down. With the gaps between the tree trunks I could always see if somebody was coming. I always paused for a few moments, you have to because the little blessings who are coming could be having a bit of a sniff on their way down. Normally if they are coming out to find me it's done in a hurry as they always want to find Mummy fast and when they do they slow right down and catch their breath. But on the off chance they come across something that just has to be sniffed at I always pause long enough to see them when they take off again. The last thing I want is for them to have run all the way down the driveway then keep running across the front paddock. Casey could have handled it just fine. Amber with her little body, well I just didn't want her to be doing any fast running, sure she was fit now a days too but walking was best for her I thought and because she was so attached to me I knew she wouldn't be walking to find me she'd be trying to run flat out and at this point you may be asking why if I was so concerned about The Divine One did I not close the back door and lock her inside. And the answer to that would be because one, Amber was not the only pug I'd left inside and two, because Amber got really upset when she got locked in, if I was inside with her no worries, but if I wasn't in the house with her she used to get distressed. I knew when she woke up she would have already searched the house for me and when I wasn't there she would have then shot out the back door to come find me.

Through the trees I saw Casey come flying down the driveway, turn, then come flying across the paddock and I stood waiting for her with my arms wide open. I scooped her up and gave kisses when she reached me. She was panting a little but not much, more being out of breath due to excitement than anything else. So I kept her in my arms and gave more kisses as I studied the base of each driveway tree. At first there was no movement and I simply figured that Amber must have been tired that day, that we'd all get back to the house and find her still sleeping. I put Casey on the ground and was just about to walk away when I saw this little fawn slightly tippy down body racing down the driveway as fast as it could go. She looked like a rabbit, in size and colour she did anyway not in movement of course and she wasn't stopping to sniff at any of the trees. They held no interest for her that morning. The Divine One was on a mission to find me as quickly as possible. I instantly started striding towards her. I knew the path she was going to take so I figured I would meet her half way. Arthur was circling by the trees, not lost his way this time just having a bit of a sniff and happy to be doing so. I knew he'd be ok if I left him for a while. As I was striding towards Amber I saw her come out from behind the trees and set off across the paddock towards me but then she started going off course. I thought she had gotten confused, perhaps the wind had changed taking my scent and her with it. But it hadn't, what she was doing was tracing my steps and I mean my exact steps. Her little paws were now treading my exact footsteps. Her bloodhound nose was taking her exactly where it had taken me a few moments earlier. I watched on in amazement as she did the exact "U" I had just done when going to pick up Arthur. If Amber was merely following our route she would have come straight towards me. But her nose was telling her that I had gone off course so she was going that way too in the hope of finding me and I thought she was the most brilliant little darling for doing so, it meant that she could find me no matter where I was on the farm. It was the most beautiful sight to see too, this lovely little pug picking up her tiny paws like a champ and moving as fast as she was able to move all in order to find her Mummy. Well I just felt so blessed in that moment and proud as well, proud that she was so very clever and blessed because she loved me with all her heart, she didn't want to be separated from me as much as I didn't want to be separated from her. My heart was full to overflowing and because I knew exactly where The Divine One was heading I was there waiting at the bottom of the "U" for her when she came back down. When she reached me I lifted her into my arms, my voice was light and happy with praise, I gushed and she started kissing the side of my face in a frenzied manner and when she settled down a bit I began kissing her little ears and the top of her head in that same frenzied excitable manner. Even as I write this now I am feeling so much happiness in my heart, my heart started remembering the same time I did and as I typed the last paragraph it was like I was there reliving it all again, well more than that it actually felt like I was really there. My head knew I was recalling a memory but my heart felt like I was there for real and to be honest it was a beautiful thing to have experienced. I'm sitting here typing with an enormous smile on my face and I didn't even realise I was smiling at first but everything I've just told you about was the happiest of happy for me and I'm grateful to have felt all those feelings once again, so grateful that I started clapping. And I don't know who to thank but I feel that I can't move on without saying a very big "Thank you" to somebody. So I've said it out loud and I've written it now too and yes I am still smiling big time as I've done so.

Lilly Rain, Casey, Ava and Amber

As Amber's sight faded she began having trouble when out in the paddocks in bright sunlight. What little eyesight she had left to get around with well in sunlight that was lost to her, in the shade she could see better but in the middle of the paddocks in the middle of the day she started having trouble so I would go stand in front of her to cast a shadow across her face. That way she would know where I was and as soon as I did that she would come clunking over. She'd be in the paddocks sniffing around and come out of the shade of a tree and turn ever so slightly and be facing the sun full on. So she'd just stop still, trying to gage where I was, sniffing the air, trying to figure out where we all were. I'd call her name, no matter where I was I'd call out to her to let her know I was coming, and I guess from the sound she could tell how far away from her I was, most of the time I was close by but if I'd gone off to help one of the others then calling out to her let her know I was otherwise occupied and would be over to help as soon as I could. Not that she was overly bothered, she just wanted to know that I was still around and if I was taking a while she'd happily occupy herself sniffing the area she was in. Sometimes one of her siblings would saunter by giving a bit of blockage from the sun and she'd make good use of that, get her bearings that way too. Tommy was a great one for helping block the sun being that he was so big and all. But he rarely stood still, only paused for a few moments when he was doing his laps, whereas I would walk over and stand in front of Amber, cast a shadow across her face so she could see again and she'd look about then take off in the right direction. I didn't always need to be real close to her either, it all depended on the angle of the sun, the time of day, where the sun was sitting in the sky. I mean sometimes I needed to be close other times I'd just keep moving around until my long shadow was across Ambers eyes and she'd stand there waiting until she had enough vision to move on. It was handy that she was wise enough to wait, that way I didn't have to go chasing her across the paddocks, no fear of her running into things either, she'd just pause and wait for my shadow then her little legs would simply start moving again. If she misjudged things and stepped out of my shadow I would move over making sure shade was constantly across her face and she'd get back on course right away and eventually we'd be standing side by side again. It was a lovely thing to see, my little intelligent girl waiting for me to assist her and once she got her bearings off she'd go and if she had her back to the sun then naturally she was fine, there'd be no more assisting her on that walk but if she turned for some reason I'd have to go over and help her again, it all depended on what she found interesting to sniff at on that particular day. Whatever her little nose caught scent of that's where she would be drawn and if she was drawn I was drawn and if I was drawn everybody else was drawn in that direction too. So we'd all be following the littlest member of the pack wherever she went. And then the time came where standing between Amber and the sun no longer made any difference, she was fully blind now, but she adjusted to that too. Used her other senses, was guided more by her nose and what she could hear. Guided by the sound of my footsteps, guided by her siblings and the sounds they made too. She just did really well with the situation she found herself in, no holding back, her attitude was like "No sight, no worries" and if she could talk I think that's exactly what she would have been saying. Amber never let not being able to see prevent her from enjoying herself. She was an incredibly happy soul regardless and I've found that to be the way with most blind pugs. There's joy there, there's real joy there, of course they will need your help, but they just get on with living their lives. And that is why I have such a huge admiration for blind dogs. I am in awe of them. That's why when I'm asked to take a blind dog in I have no hesitation doing so. I look forward to looking after them because I feel it's a great honour and privilege to be doing that. To be able to share my life with these incredibly gutsy little souls, to witness every day their courage, determination and spirit, well believe me it's a really nice way to spend your days. And people may think it's me benefitting them. I don't think many people realise how much these little ones are benefiting me. But each one has added to my life and made my days incredibly special. I'm just so very grateful to be their Mummy.

CHAPTER ELEVEN

Blueberries, Strawberries and Carrot Juice Oh My

I have found with pugs that they are either going to be good drinkers or they are not, most of them are, only a small percentage are not, Amber was part of that small percentage. Well she was more than part of it she was the worst drinker we have ever had in the many, many years we've been doing this. And if there was a competition to be held here for the pug that drank the least then The Divine One would have been our reigning queen. She wasn't being awkward, she just simply did not like that taste of water and really if a dog doesn't want to drink you cannot force them to. Ok well yes you can, you could syringe it in and we have done that with dogs that are ill to keep them from becoming dehydrated while they are getting over their illness. But the thought of doing that with Amber every day was not very appealing, not to us and not to her either because it would have been unpleasant and there was no way I was going to deliberately go upsetting this little blessing of mine. So I knew I had to find an enjoyable way of keeping her well hydrated at all times. In the cooler months it was fine I would just add water to her meals to make sure she was getting fluids that way. I don't like giving them plain dry food, or kibble as I think some folks call it, we always add water to it here because in the back of my mind is the constant thought of kidney trouble, some keep it dry to help with their teeth and gums but we do that in other ways. Water is added to their dry food and soaks in while I am taking them for their walk and I would just give Amber a little more water than I did the other pugs. But we were coming up to summer, a vital time for fluids, our temperatures can get really high so for us summer is all about fluids, getting a good amount into them to ward of heatstroke. But of course with heatstroke it takes a number of things to prevent that.

Like you wouldn't give a dog plenty of fluids then leave them outside in the heat. For our pugs it's fluids and being kept indoors underneath the air-conditioning and very quick trips outside for toilet breaks during the day and only walking them early in the morning and late in the evening and sticking to the shade at all times when they are outside. It takes a routine of care to get pugs through hot Australian summers but we have never had a dog with heatstroke yet which is great because they can die from it. So here I was with this wonderful little soul who would not drink out of the water bowl and summer was just around the corner and they had predicted a hot one. I was trying to think of ways of getting more fluid into The Divine One and seeing as the weather was slowly becoming warmer I was adding more and more water to Amber's meals to the point where they now resembled soup and soup can be pretty hard for a little old pug to get down. One day I was making carrot juice for myself and was going out onto the deck to drink it, I knew the pugs liked carrots and I especially knew that Amber liked carrots so I poured some of my juice into a bowl for her and brought her up on my knee to drink it. At first she only sniffed at it, I guess going through her mind was "Liquefied carrots what the hell". But she eventually drank it all and barked for more. So I gave her a little bit more and was really happy because I now had a way of getting those much needed fluids into her during summer. To finally have her want to drink something was pretty great and of course as is always the case once one of the pugs has something they all want to get in on the act. So the next time I was making carrot juice I made extra so that everybody could have some and from then on carrot juice became a family event. Not all the pugs had it the same way though, some preferred a half and half mix, others like a quarter of juice with the rest being made up of water. It's a personal thing. Amber always liked hers full strength. I guess if there was even the smallest amount of water in it it'd be enough to put her off. But she was now getting fluids into her and instead of refusing it she was actually hurrying me up for some every day. The amount they would have would be equal to us having a glass of carrot juice each day. When I tell people I'm giving my pugs carrot juice I think they envision me giving each one a full glass but that's not the case. Over time I was able to get Amber to drink the juice with a bit of water mixed in but she always preferred it straight so I more often than not gave it to her that way and that was fine because she nor any of the other pugs were diabetic.

The Divine One got very smart at knowing when I was making carrot juice and no it wasn't just because she'd been smushing her face into the lower part of my leg for the past half hour trying to herd me into the kitchen so that I could make it for her. It was more like she had this little built in alarm clock inside her because each day somewhere between twelve and one she would begin her herding ritual and not stop until she heard the cupboard door opening and the juicer being set up on the bench. She was a good little herder too, did everything in her power to move me in the direction she wanted me to go and if she felt I was going astray she would run round the other side of me and smush her face into the other leg, just doing everything she could to make me walk in the right direction. When she heard the sound of carrot tops being cut off she would run around the kitchen floor doing excitable growly woofs. And she'd come over and beg up for a bit of carrot to eat while I was doing the juice, you know just to tide her over until her juice was ready. I guess to Amber it must have seemed like the longest wait. So I'd cut a small bit off for her and then a few bits off for the other pugs who had come over and were now lining up. Only a small bit though, well a few small bits because pugs like to have more than one of everything don't they, but I never gave them a bit big enough to choke on. The Divine One would run to the other side of the room with hers, eat it, then come running back and start asking for more. She'd climb my legs like a kitten if it wasn't coming fast enough, gripping onto my socks to gain leverage, used them to help hoist herself up. But she kept constantly getting her claws caught up in my shoelaces. And when trying to back away and untangle herself she would end up falling over and of course I couldn't have her doing that, not with how her back was, not with how her paws were, well not because she was an elderly dog either. I had to put a stop to it so I cut my laces very short to prevent her from hurting herself or pulling a nail out and I was only going to do it on the right foot as that's the side she liked best, that was her chosen side, the only one she ever went to when I was in the kitchen and I don't have an answer to the reason she did that, she just did and so I went with it, as you do. But then I figured it'd look pretty silly with the left shoe having long laces and the right one having short ones so they both got trimmed and I thought that was fine because at least they now matched. And the trimming of both laces did benefit Amber because if I was sitting down she would always go to the left side of me, always, so it was the right side if I was at the kitchen bench and the left side if I was sitting at the kitchen table. I thought it was funny how her mind worked. And wondered why she was doing it because she could easily get to both sides of me regardless of where I was. But she'd made her choice and it was not for me to question it but to just bend down and give her what she was asking for regardless of which side she was on and the loss of lace length made things so much easier for her. There were actually no laces hanging down at all now just a big knot at the top of each shoe which did look kind of funny but I got used to it over time. I had a child in the supermarket once who had the loudest voice, it was a long line at the checkout and I was about to go look for a shorter line somewhere but was hemmed in so stayed put. This little boy and his mother were in front of me and he became very bored very quickly as children of that age always do. Anyway he glanced down at my shoelaces, or should I say lack thereof and asked in a big loud voice for everybody to hear why I cut them off and before I could answer he followed up with "Is it because you haven't learnt how to tie your shoelaces yet? which made everybody in earshot roar with laughter. So I explained about my little old pug being blind and what she does to get my attention and he was very fascinated with it all so I swiped my phone and bent down and showed him photo after photo of The Divine One. He had a slight lisp and sounded adorable when he asked questions.

I remember one day being in the middle of making carrot juice and having to dash out into the paddock for some reason, maybe it was because the farrier had arrived early. Regardless I had to leave what I was doing and Amber wasn't impressed with that and neither were any of the other pugs. I could hear them all voicing their displeasure as I was walking away from the house. So I did what I needed to do and raced back as quickly as possible in order to finish the job at hand. But when I walked inside I found my sister had made the juice for me and was holding Amber while she lapped it up but I also noticed that Amber was drinking the juice from one of our good china cups. I asked my sister what she was doing, meaning using the good china, and she replied "She was thirsty" and I had to laugh because I guess it's best to use the good china for something rather than leave it sitting on the shelf doing nothing and no better use then giving a little blind pug carrot juice on a hot day. At least my sister was taking good care of her. And funnily enough that small china cup was the most perfect size for Amber's face, fit to her muzzle perfectly, little mouth in, long tongue flicking around all over the place and yet not one drop spilt even though the cup was being tilted on its side so that The Divine One could get every last bit. After that day I began using the china cups quite often for Amber as a way of helping her drink her juice, it was a lot easier and faster than using a bowl. During summer it wasn't unusual for Amber to have a permanent orange stain above her right eye where her tongue flicked up the juice she was having every lunch time. With the cup it wasn't happening as much. But that cup eventually broke and was replaced with another from the set and after we'd gone through each one of those six cups we went back to giving Amber her juice in a bowl which was fine because I have always loved watching little old blessings drinking carrot juice and when it's being lapped up from a bowl it's easier to see everything that's going on. I'll stand over them smiling until they are done then another one will have a turn and I'll be watching on again at them enjoying their little selves. Yes the standing and staring like that could be considered kind of creepy if I wasn't their mother. But it's all good, a lot of them are blind so they can't see the weirdo hovering overhead.

Amber not wanting her face wiped

We have killed our fair share of juice extractors over the years, I guess that's because they are in continuous use and they don't make them to last, well they don't seem make them to be up to the task of the workload here at Grace Farm anyway. We have tried cheap ones and expensive ones and find they both have around the exact same lifespan so now we go with the cheap ones only because we can't see the point of paying more than twice the price for something we are going to have to replace in the same amount of time. And when juice extractors die they seem to die the most agonising death, occasionally they'll go quietly, just a quick over exaggerated moan and it's all over. Some won't even do that, just a flick of a switch and they are gone, probably already floating up to electrical appliance heaven before I've even had time to walk outside and put them in the rubbish bin. We've had a real lot though that have wanted to be given an academy award for their efforts, they start doing the death rattle and all but fall off the countertop clutching their chests and it's those that stick in your mind. I woke up one morning to the smell of smoke and was about to jump out of bed and go racing around getting everybody out of the house to safety. I had been up most of the night with a few of the pugs so was really exhausted, I rolled over in bed and saw that David wasn't there and neither were the pugs that sleep on the bed. I was going to get up and investigate further but thought oh bugger it, whatever it is I'm sure David will deal with it and if the house is on fire well I'm sure he'll wake me, so I rolled over and went back to sleep. An hour or so later I woke up and there was still a strong smell of smoke in the house so I went to find out what it was. Apparently David had been making carrot juice for the pugs and the juicer started smoking then died, totally dead never to be revived. Well an awful lot of little flat faces were very disappointed that day and I mean really disappointed to the point of sulking. After that happened we decided the best thing to do was always have a backup juicer in the cupboard. That way as soon as one dies another one can quickly be unpacked and its business as usual. No sad little faces looking up at the kitchen bench expectantly. Just a bit of a delay that's all. I guess living on a farm with quite a drive to the nearest store it's the sensible thing to do. I remember once doing the lunchtime juice and it was a new juicer I was using, maybe a day or two old. So new that we hadn't had time to buy another one. Anyway this thing started coughing and spluttering a few carrots in and I thought oh no there's not even enough juice to keep half the pugs happy, even if I watered it down some of them would still miss out. And with no back up juicer in the house I knew I had to try and get this thing to work just long enough to fill the little plastic jug. Speaking of the plastic jugs it's funny but they outlast the juicers tenfold. They come with the juicers and are a perfect fit and we've got heaps of them in the cupboard, well we did at one time but in the end I had to start dropping them off at the op shop because we had so many. It's hard because they are of no use to anybody unless they have the exact same juicer we do, they don't fit anything else but I drop them off regardless in the hope that somebody will find a good use for them. Perhaps there's a little old lady who lives up the road from the op shop with a windowsill full of our jugs. I picture them lined up with fresh herbs growing out of them. It probably isn't happening but it's a nice image I have in my head whenever I'm dropping the latest round of jugs off. Anyway I kept giving this new juicer a rest in-between carrots to let it cool down because if the motor was cool it would work long enough to juice one more carrot. But only the one carrot and then it started coughing again. When it first started smoking I set myself up on the deck and juiced the last few carrots out there because I didn't want the house filling up with smoke. I grabbed the longest electrical lead we had out of the cupboard and the pugs followed me outside and we all watch on as smoke wafted across the paddock. It was the longest carrot juice I've ever made in my life but I kept persevering because of all those little upturned faces standing by my feet waiting for a drink. In the end that thing began smoking so badly I think our neighbours might have thought we were having a bonfire then again maybe not because electrical smoke it's not a nice smoky smell like a wood fire is. Electrical smoke has a smell entirely of its own and it's horrible. But I learnt from that, now as soon as they begin smoking that's it, out to the rubbish bin they go, no second thought given.

We did grow our own carrots one year but the sheep ended up eating them and that was the end of that, I guess we could have tried again but because carrots for juicing can be bought very cheaply we couldn't really see the point. Best to keep our local hard working farmers going, best to buy some of our produce off them, it's the less than perfect carrots that we buy, huge bags of them sold specifically for the purpose of juicing. For some reason people don't like buying mutant looking carrots. And carrots just like human beings grow in all shapes and sizes, come in all forms too and some of them not very appealing and we laugh our heads off at the sight of them, the carrots I mean not human beings as that would be rude. We've had some real deformities and a lot that look like pairs of legs and some look like they are in the act of dancing so we'll dance them across the countertop and right into the juicer. The short stubby ones can even look like people's heads and we'll stand there guessing who it is they look like, is it a movie star, a musician, a relative or even somebody who lives in town. But again if it is somebody we know we never tell them or show them for fear of hurting their feelings. It can be a lot of fun opening those bags because you just never know what you are going to pull out next. We grow strawberries here all the time and have had great success with them. All of our pugs love strawberries and I love growing them so it works out very well for us all. I like growing them in hanging baskets best, how pretty the look, big and bright with lush leaves hanging over the edge of the terracotta. Things like that give me joy, I get really excited as soon as I see those little white flowers form, the pugs don't get excited by these, they save their excitement for when the flowers are replaced with strawberries, especially when they turn from green to red. There can be confusion for the blind ones because strawberries start smelling like strawberries before they are ripe enough to eat and little blind pugs will be at my feet with upturned faces wondering why I'm not dishing them out. They don't understand the word "Tummy ache" they are led by their noses and probably think I'm being mean or even worse eating them all myself a thing I'd never dream of doing. We grow a real lot of strawberries here because the demand is so high, we 've had them in the veggie patch, in pots on the deck, in pots out by the carport, all over the place really. And the veggie patch and the hanging baskets the pugs can't get to but the ones in pots they can readily help themselves which some of them will and yes you do lose a few that in excitement get pulled off the stem too early by little anxious mouths. But after a taste or two they quickly get spat out and some will learn from that and remember and some won't so they'll be there again next season doing exactly the same thing.

Ruben John Comer was by far the best strawberry picker we've ever had on the farm. He was wonderful to watch doing his thing, no fear ever, just being led by his nose, he only had one eye and he was blind in that eye but it didn't stop him climbing into those pots and fossicking. And yes he did grab for the green ones a lot of the time but he never ate them, just quickly spat them out and because I felt he was enjoying himself so much and because I liked watching him helping himself I didn't really mind that he wasted a few. I actually thought he was pretty wonderful to be blind but so fearless up there in amongst the pots. I would always be there in case he needed help getting down which he did some of the time and let me know by having a little cry so I'd go over and lift him out, kiss the side of his face and put him back down on the deck. Ruben had no trouble getting in, just ever so slowly and gently picking up those long legs of his and climbing in. He'd feel his way around, feel the next pot over and move on to that, slowly step from pot to pot to pot never once falling. I think even if he'd picked every green strawberry and ruined the entire crop I would have still planted them for him because he was having as much fun searching as he did eating and I thought it was a good form of entertainment for him. He had been hit in his previous home and was very head shy when he first arrived so to see him out there enjoying himself like that, well there was no more heart-warming sight for me. I used to buy the odd punnet of strawberries just so Ruben could find some good ones every day. He always went to the pots outside our bedroom window, for some reason those were his favourites so when I saw him heading over, as he did most mornings during strawberry season, I would run ahead of him and put a few ripe strawberries where he could find them. He had a routine of finishing his breakfast then heading straight for the pots, pre-empting him wasn't rocket science so I'd stride ahead and be giddy with excitement because for me it was like hiding Easter eggs. I'd then stand and watch him searching, it never took him very long to find them, he'd be munching down in no time and then the green strawberry pulling and spitting out would start but he didn't mind because he'd already had a few good ones. Amber would be on the other side of the deck but she'd smell the scent of those delicious strawberries floating through the air. I'd watch as she made her way round. She'd pause, sniff the air then go and stand right in front of the pot Ruben was raiding. Of course she'd have been able to hear him too, hear him pulling the strawberries off their stems with a snap, hear him chomping down once he'd gotten them off and she wanted to be in on the act. Sometimes she'd woof too if they weren't coming her way fast enough and of course Ruben could hear her but such was his strawberry eating frenzy and his deliriously happy state he wasn't stopping for anybody. I think he was in his own little world up there in-between all the plants. But Amber kept on woofing because she was expecting him to pick a few for her. As far as The Divine One was concerned it didn't matter who was picking them as long as she got some. And Ruben was not a selfish pug, if he'd been able to detach himself from his mission long enough to sense she was there he would have been quite happy to chuck a few down. But being blind he couldn't see her and being mesmerized by strawberries after such a long period of time without them he wasn't pausing long enough to hear or smell that somebody was there. I'd go over and grab a few for her, not out of the pot Ruben was in because I didn't want to intrude on his happiness, I'd go a pot or two over and picked the nicest ones I could find then sit with Amber on my knee as she ate them. I'd break the bigger ones in half and flatten the half before feeding it to her. With the smaller strawberries I'd just squash them between my fingers and pop them straight into her little mouth. As long as they were flat and broken up a bit she could eat them pretty fast, I always flattened strawberries because of worry over choking. The pugs love them so much the last thing you want them doing is choking and the strawberries we grow here can be pretty big and I pride myself on that and thank the horses too as I walk by their paddock because their manure is a wonderful fertilizer. It takes a village.

Ruben hunting for strawberries in the pots.

Blueberries were something I introduced to the pugs well over a decade ago after reading an article about how good they were. I already knew blueberries were full of antioxidants, vitamin C and vitamin K and I knew they were full of fibre. But they also contain calcium, iron, zinc, manganese, magnesium and phosphorus all of which support the immune system and that's what I was very interested in doing, giving my elderly blessings immune systems a helping hand. But the article said something that really caught my eye, it said blueberries also helped prevent urinary tract infections. The reason being is that the fruit contains a compound that prevents bacteria from attaching to the bladder wall and tissues of the urinary tract. Well that was something I did not know and bladder infections are pretty nasty so if you can do something to prevent them I thought it was worth a shot. Unlike other fruits which are dangerous to dogs blueberries pose no toxicity risk to our furry friends. I must stress here that you really do need to do some research before giving anything new to your dog, it's just the responsible thing to do because foods that are perfectly fine for humans may not be ok to feed our canine family members. Because we are genetically different to dogs our food can have a very different effect on them. Some of the things we eat can cause anything from tummy upsets and vomiting to breathing issues, seizures and even death to our dogs so you have to be very careful. But blueberries are fine and I wondered why I hadn't thought about giving them to the pugs before. They are really just a little ball of goodness and being so tiny you don't worry as much about choking. I have always been extremely mindful that everything I give the pugs is the right size for them to eat so it doesn't end up getting caught in their throat. You have to take special care with pugs, well, with all little breeds of dogs really because it's a case of small breed, small mouth, small throat and with Amber being such a tiny girl it was even more important to cut her food into small pieces or break it up in my hands. Anyway I started feeding the pugs blueberries and at first they didn't go down so well. I gave Amber one first as she was closest to the fridge. She wasn't sure what I was giving her so didn't open up her mouth right away. She took her time, sniffed at the blueberry before eventually taking it from my hand. The look on her face told me she really wasn't all that fussed. Yes she ate it but it was a case of "Ok thanks Mum, but whatever" then she turned around and walked off. I gave the other pugs one too and their reaction was more or less the same and I thought to myself well that was a bit of a fizzer. I had expected a lot bigger reaction then that. I think I was expecting them to go nuts for blueberries the way they always did with strawberries but there was no excitement there, no jumping up, no woofing for more, as far as blueberries went they could take them or leave them. So I put the container of little blueberries back in the fridge and went off to do some jobs around the farm, as I worked I started thinking about things, realised the pugs had eaten their blueberry whole, they were only small so there was no need to break them up. I mean some blueberries can be whoppers it all depends on the years growing season but the first ones I bought for the pugs were tiny. I had made note of their size, realised they'd be fine whole and just started dishing them out. But with blueberries unless they are bitten into there's little to no flavour there, you are not getting the full benefit of a blueberry, no wonder the pugs weren't impressed. The next time I distributed blueberries I squished them between my fingers first, revealed the fruits delicious flavour before popping them into little mouths and it was an entirely different story. I got a very different reaction this time. Their little eyes lit up. It was a whole new flavour experience for them, lots of dancing around started being done, some shouldering, woofing and happy little squeals. I guess they smelt the blueberries and were expecting the same thing but this time the blueberry experience was different, it was as if they were now eating something completely new and in a way they were. They had two each and began licking my fingers to get every last bit. I looked down and said "Welcome to the world of blueberries babies" after that there was no looking back. Blueberries soon became Amber's favourite things in the world. She simply loved them, sucked them down at lightning speed. Because blueberries are low in calories I began swapping some of their normal treats for blueberries and being low in sugar blueberries are ok to give diabetic dogs. None of our pugs were diabetic but a friend's dog was and she was finding it hard to get treats that her dog actually liked. I had told her about green beans but Misty hated those, spat them out at lightning speed. She did the same thing with blueberries too at first so I suggested squashing them so Carol went home and started squashing blueberries for Misty and Misty decided she now loved them. Carol was pretty happy about that because she was able to give her diabetic dog a treat that she actually enjoyed, and she would be wouldn't she because that's the entire the point of giving your dog a treat in the first place. But one thing I forgot to mention to Carol was to do an internet search before feeding Misty anything different and I so wish I had of done because I got a phone call from her about a week after she'd started dishing out blueberries and in that phone call she proudly told me that Misty was now having raisins everyday too. And I said "NOOOOO STOOOP" you can't give raisins or sultanas to dogs, even small amounts are incredibly toxic. But I felt this was kind of my fault because Misty was Carol's first dog and because I know these things I just assumed everybody would know these things but she didn't and I should have thought to tell her. And with Misty being diabetic it was even more vital that I inform her of everything that could potentially cause harm to a dog. I had at least remembered to tell her about introducing blueberries slowly so Misty didn't end up with diarrhoea. Because I saw how excited Carol was on seeing how much my pugs were enjoying their blueberries. I didn't want Carol in her keenness to finally be able to give Misty something yummy buying a whole punnet of blueberries and feeding her the entire thing in one sitting so yes that was mentioned right away. I told her I had introduced blueberries two at a time with my pugs and built it up from there to a point where Amber was having ten or so blueberries every day. She'd have blackberries, raspberries and peaches sometimes too, but always always blueberries at lunch time. The other fruit was just because she liked them or if we hadn't been shopping and were running low on blueberries and her little face was tilted up sniffing the air for more food. That's when I'd be running back to the fridge to see what else we had in there that was safe for her to eat. As I searched the shelves I could hear her growly woof in the background eagerly awaiting my return. Once Amber was pacified and sleeping I'd ring David at work. Tell him that we had a blueberry emergency and he'd laugh because he knew exactly what that meant, it meant he'd be stopping at Safeway on the way home and raiding the blueberry section.

We did try growing blueberries here once but after a season or two our little bush never yielded much fruit and what little fruit it did give out, well the blackbirds always beat us to it. They were the first ones up in the mornings after all so I guess felt it was their god given right to feast while the household slept. Then just to add insult to injury they'd leave purple poo splotches all along the veranda's edge. It didn't worry Amber though because she more associated blueberries with the fridge not that pathetic little bush, she'd race from wherever she was in the house as soon as she heard the fridge door opening. Then stand there not moving in the hope of getting a few blueberries popped into her mouth. Amber knew the number of blueberries she wanted and if the amount you gave her didn't quite match up to the amount she had in her head she'd let you know by doing her growly bark. Keep her waiting and her woof would become louder and louder, like an alarm clock it was, an alarm clock that was kind enough to wake one from sleep slowly and gently, starting off soft and low then increasing if the snooze or off button doesn't get pressed. But there was no snooze or off button on The Divine One, she'd just keep increasing her volume until I gave her what she wanted. But it wasn't just Amber who received a few extra blueberries, yes she was the initiator but then everybody else would quickly get in on the act and I'd now be looking down on a pile of little old faces gathered round my feet, all with their heads tilted upwards and mouths wide open. I could dish out half a punnet of blueberries in one sitting if everybody was there. They got four or five each then the container lid was put back on fast so they couldn't smell them anymore. I'd show the sighted ones my hands to signal blueberry time was over, the blind pugs couldn't see my hands but they soon got the message when they heard the fridge door being closed and as the smell of squashed down blueberries became faint they one by one began moving away, went back to what they were previously doing, little old bodies toddled off in search of spots in the sun. Amber was always the last one to leave though, she was the first to arrive and last to leave. I think she was standing there that little bit longer in the hope of a score, ever hopeful of getting something extra and that is what ended up happening more often than not. Super quick the two of us were when sneaking her one more blueberry, we had to be otherwise the others would have known what we were up to and that wouldn't have been fair on any of them.

With blueberries Amber had them hand fed to her or put on top of her food. As she aged I would wake her up with blueberries in the morning, every morning I did it, she would be sleeping in as very old dogs tend to do and I never like to startle dogs awake, it's not good to do that to any dog of any age and even more so as they get older. If it was getting late and she still wasn't up I knew her bladder would be pretty full so I'd sneak into the bedroom and place two blueberries in front of her nose, put them on a face washer, then walk away to let her come round. I would squash the blueberries first so she'd be able to smell them better then leave her to it and a little while later I would hear her barking for me so I could go and lift her off the bed. I'd hear the bark and walk back into the bedroom with five or six plump blueberries in my hand. She'd be laying there sniffing the air waiting for me and especially waiting for more blueberries. One by one I would flatten them and pop them into her mouth while I was talking to her. She'd barely finish one before she was opening up her mouth for another. When she finished I'd let her sniff my hands then ask her if it was ok if I took her outside for a wee. I'd run my hands gently over her body so she knew I was about to pick her up and outside we would go. It was a nice routine for both of us, a lovely way for her to be woken up and a wonderful time for me hand feeding my little love. The other pugs would come outside with us, they'd already had their walk but were up for another one and Amber was in her mid teens at this time so she was only interested in a little bit of pottering, just long enough to find the most perfect spot to do what needed to be done then I'd pick her up and carry her back inside again or she would walk, it all depended on how she was feeling and how dark the clouds overhead looked. But she always had at least a little wander around because it was important to keep those dear legs moving and if they are up to doing it you let them and if they are not you help them, simple as that.

I mentioned earlier in the book about The Divine One being my little writing buddy and she was, well not just her but a lot of the pugs were and still are to this day. As I sit here now writing at the kitchen table I am surrounded by pugs, it's pouring down and thundering so I'm running on battery and hoping it doesn't go flat. I can hear the rain on the roof and see the gutters overflowing because it's coming down so fast, the pugs are snoring but the sound of rain is drowning most of that out, I can only hear them when the rain dies down for a little while and then it starts up again, but our water tanks will be full and I am grateful for that. The pugs I have now settle down pretty fast once they see the computer coming out. The pugs I lived with while writing my first three books, well it took a bit of organising before those little writing buddies were ready to settle down, especially when it came to Amber. A set routine had to be done before The Divine One would even consider having a rest. Things had to be done in the right order as well, Amber wasn't the type of pug you could mix things up on, no surprises for her, that little blessing knew the routine better than I did so I had to do everything the same way each and every day. It was a case of walk, juice, blueberries, bed, and the next day again, walk, juice, blueberries, bed, always in that order and each step had to be undertaken before even one key on my keyboard got tapped. When Amber and a few of the others were still with me one of my favourite places to write was sitting in the middle of the bed. I found our bed was the best place to be because I could have all the pugs up with me and they'd all have room to stretch and move around, it was the only place where we could all fit on one level and I liked us being together like that. I'd have pugs to the left of me and pugs to the right, pugs near my feet and pugs scrambling to get on top of the pillows that were behind my back. Each pug had their own special position on the bed, one that was chosen by them not me and I just went with the flow, went with the flow then and always go with the flow now. They know where they are happiest and wherever they are happiest is fine with me. Amber made sure she was the one closest to me at all times and god help anybody who tried to steal her prime position. She had no trouble at all herding the others away, in fact I believe she rather enjoyed it, some days I think she was just waiting for somebody to come over and try it on. Some would wander by on their way to their favourite spots but she seemed to know that's what they were doing, merely coming into her territory on the way to their own so she'd leave them alone. But if anybody lingered a bit too long that's when she'd intervene and as soon as she'd seen them on their way she'd quickly settle down and that little old head of hers was so warm on my knee in the middle of winter. David made me a table to set the computer up on. It's more like a tray with legs really, it's only tiny, just enough room for my computer and mouse pad. But it's all I need and I like that it's small because it means I can see all the pugs as I'm typing, nothing big and bulky blocking my view. Just before everybody is lifted up on the bed a midday walk is given, a good many wees are had and much sniffing is done. There'll be a chorus of woofing too should they be in a woofing mood and if there are birds about the pugs can't help but stand barking as they fly through the air. If the cockatoos are squawking well everybody starts going ballistic at that noise and I don't blame them one little bit. We'll come inside from our walk but if the birds are still being noisy the pugs shoot onto the deck to have another go. At times Amber will have already made her way into the kitchen, no doubt with the images of carrot juice, blueberries and strawberries dancing through her head, but on hearing the ruckus she'd turn fast and go clunking out the door, she wasn't going to miss out on having fun and the look on her face told me exactly that. She'd join her siblings in their chorus of woofing, running from one end of the deck to the other in a mad dash. It was nice for me to watch them out there enjoying themselves, once that was out of their systems they'd all file back into the house and it was time for me to juice some carrots.

The entire time I'm juicing the pugs will be circling around my feet. Once every last drop of carrot juice has been sucked down all the little dripping orange chins get a good wipe over and a lot of arguing and pulling away is done because they don't like their faces being wiped. The carrot juice is greatly enjoyed, the chin wiping not so much and everybody but Arthur makes that fact perfectly clear. Arthur will sit calmly in your arms as you clean him up, he loves having the underneath of his chin rubbed and it'd be nice if a few of the others felt the same way, but they don't so it can be quite the battle. I always have a towel flung over my shoulder during carrot juice time and just before they run off I'll be upon them and its dab, dab, dab before they know what's going on. I find that works the best, but you have to time it just right, you have to be ready to pounce just as they are slurping up the very last droplet. You go in early and that bothers them because they like to be fully finished before being disturbed, you leave it too late and they know what you are about to do so start scurrying away and then you'll be left chasing them all around the room leaving a path of carrot juice droplets as they go. I stand hovering above them with the edge of the towel in my hand, eyes fixated like a mad woman just waiting for that all important perfect moment to strike. Amber especially didn't like having her chin wiped, as little as she was she would fight me on it. Each day was the same, loved, loved, loved the juice but you'd try to wipe her face and she fought you like a tiger trying to get away. She was blind too so you'd think cleaning her face would have been a quick and easy thing to do but it was like she could sense the direction you were coming from and turn her head away just before you got there. But you do what you have to do, carrot juice really stains pug fur so you want to get to them with that slightly damp towel as quickly as you can. And of course it's never one towel with so many pugs in the house, you generally have three or four pre-moistened towels sitting on the benchtop ready to go. Once carrot juice time is over and faces are clean they'd all take off to the bedroom and stand swaying by the bed waiting for me to lift them up, there's a certain order in which they come up and if that's altered even in the slightest well those flat little faces are ill amused. And it was Amber's little flat nose that would be out of joint the most.

So now everybody is up on the bed. A few will settle down quickly, Ruben, Baby and Brian are no trouble at all and never have been, they get air lifted up then sink into the soft bedding and fall fast asleep, but others will need certain things before they can even think about settling. Nemo has always enjoyed being wrapped in my jumper during the winter months, well not so much wrapped in it but a nest is made out of my jumper then he goes and jumps right into the middle and once a good chin rest has been found that's it, he's settled and I can hear him snoring as I'm trying to organise Bromley. Bromley is one of those pugs that likes to play with a toy before he goes to sleep. He seems to need some winding down time before his eyes fall shut and it's up to me to figure out which toy is going to be his special toy that day. And a few can be offered to him before he finally takes his pick. So Bromley is now set, and Baby was too, she'd been happily sleeping in one of the dog beds but then Ava Lindy Lou climbed in with her and now she's no longer comfortable so I'll go and move her over, make sure her legs are not being squashed. Now those two are sleeping peacefully side by side. But Ruben has started crying because he too has decided that he would like to sleep on a nest made out of my clothes, it's normally what I was wearing yesterday. Nemo gets the top and Ruben the bottom, so a rearranging of my skirt or jeans is done and Ruben is once again back to being happy. And I am almost at a point where I can now settle Amber, who by the way has been sitting near my little computer table guarding her spot, but first I have to make sure that Steffy is somewhere I can reach her, she was the pug that always went next to Amber. Steffy's back legs were weak due to age, not bad enough for a cart but not as strong as they once were so I hold her steady and keep an eye on her until her head goes down. I always placed her in the middle of the bed, she stays close at hand in case she needs anything, but generally once she's asleep you won't hear a peep out of her and she's deaf so even if there is a commotion from the others Steffy couldn't care less because she can't hear it. And Amber didn't mind having somebody else next to her, as long as they didn't get in-between us she was happy. I think she actually liked the warmth from Steffy. A few other pugs were in beds on the floor, if they asked to come up I'd get them but if they'd already gone to sleep in the time it took me to settle the others then I'll leave them be, can't go disturbing them when they look so content. Once everybody was happy I'd start the computer up and being old it's a very slow process, slow to start up and slow to shut down. I guess if I'm being honest my computer should have been replaced some time ago, but it's the computer I wrote The Joy of Horton on, well not only that but all three books have been written on it and so too is the book you are reading now, it's very special to me for all those reasons so until it gives up the ghost of its own accord it'll continue to be used for the pure sentiment of it. As the computer lethargically hummed itself to life I'd be watching the pugs, Amber was usually the last one to fall asleep, I'd watch everybody's eyes and once the last pair of sleepy peepers has closed I'm at it, typing like crazy, typing until the eyes are all open again. It's like each pug even when sleeping is still well aware of the routine of our daily life, they all know the exact time of their afternoon walk. At 4.25 there is a little bit of movement, a slight stirring and then at exactly 4.30 just like magic every set of eyes springs open, it's a little bit like plugging in a string of fairy lights, and that's it I'm done writing for the day and we'll all be out strolling in the middle of the paddock enjoying ourselves by the time the computer finally shuts itself down.

"Sitting underneath my little writing desk"

CHAPTER TWELVE

Coats

Seeing The Divine One meandering around wearing one of her little coats was a beautiful sight. I always put her in the most girly colours too, pink, mauve and occasionally orange or yellow. But pinks of all shades were my favourite colours to see her in, I guess because she was so tiny it just seemed right that she should always be dressed very girly. Although sometimes I would run out of girly coloured coats that were the right size for Amber, being that she was adventurous I went through a lot of coats with The Divine One. And if it got to a point where all her coats were either in the wash or drying I would put one of her brother's coats on her and sure she looked cute in blue but I still thought she looked more adorable in pink. It used to confuse me sometimes when she was wearing a blue coat because I'd become accustomed to always seeing her in pink. I would often glance over her when she was in blue. A lot of the time I associate coat colours with the pugs, due to their different sizes I have set coats for each one, and it helps when you have a few pugs needing quick coat changes, that way you are not going to be wasting time putting on a coat that is too big or too small, you just see the coat you know is theirs, grab it fast and pop it on. Easy for me and easy for the pugs too because they don't like it when I'm putting one coat over their heads then taking it off just as fast because it's not the right fit. In our house it pays to have things worked out in advance. Come winter I'll have all their coats washed and ready for action. Those little colourful coats would be laid out in a straight line twelve coats long four coats high. Four coats for each pug is usually how I like to have it, as my way of thinking is this, one coat on, one coat in the wash, one coat drying and one coat ready to replace the coat that's on them but has just gotten dirty. Of course you will have a few pugs in the house that are exactly the same size so I will swap and change their coats as the need arises, say if one pug is more the type to run across a wet paddock while his similar sized brother sticks to the path as was the case with Brian and Bromley. Brian was a runner whereas Bromley was more than happy to stand and woof. So Brian was always borrowing Bromley's coats. It was mainly for the tiny and larger pugs that I first started sorting them in sizes and it worked, so I do it every year now. I do much prefer sticking to them wearing their own coats if I can as things can get confusing if I don't. We'd be out on a walk and I'd be looking all around for Amber, looking for that familiar pink coat and at times be in a panic wondering where she was and all the while she'd be standing right next to me in Rubens navy blue coat. I'd glanced at her a few times while looking and in not associating Amber with navy blue simply didn't recognise her at first. I even took off across the paddock one day thinking she'd gone the wrong way only to come back to the tree and find The Divine One standing there in pale blue with her little tongue hanging out and because she was wearing blue it made the pinkness of her tongue stand out all the more. And I did think about changing colours on her permanently and she did end up wearing blue for two or three days afterwards but I missed the pink too much so changed back again. Out of desperation I once put one of Brian's coats on The Divine One. She had gone through her own coats and was on to the second one of Rubens and I knew I needed to save the other two for him so I grabbed one of Brains from his pile and scooped Amber up. But when I put her back down again I realised it was far too big so I folded it over at the back end and held the front together with a clothes peg making it a more snug fit. I like a perfect fit because it can get pretty windy here and you don't want to have coats being lifted up on the breeze and little old backs getting a burst of cold air across them. Amber didn't seem to mind that it was held with a peg, she went clunking along regardless and the coat stayed put until we were about to come up the back ramp. Then one of the other pugs brushed against her, the peg fell off and the coat slid back and Amber just stood there waiting for me to come over and fix her up so she could carry on her way. But I didn't, being so close to the house I just picked up the peg, picked up Amber and strode inside pulling the coat over her head as we walked along and when we got inside the house was lovely and warm so I put her in one of the beds nearest the heater and that was that. When she woke up I had one of her own coats ready for her to wear. Winter on Grace Farm is about endless loads of laundry drying by the fire and the fire will be roaring 24/7 just to keep things ticking along. But we all benefit from a roaring fire, me because I like looking at it visually, David does too, and a fire always makes a place seem so homely I think. I personally always feel comforted when I've got a fire going. And of course we all benefit from its warmth. The pugs especially like coming inside after a walk and gathering round the Coonara together, and it dries things, dries them real fast, we'd never be able to keep up with the demand if we didn't have our beautiful big fire. Also old pugs tend to have a few more accidents in the house in winter so there are always more things to wash. But that's fine, you do what you have to do. And the final thing a fire is good for is keeping the paddocks clear, fallen branches are collected all year round, all the sticks are too so they don't go poking any of the pugs, sheep or horses in the eye. It's win win for everybody. I always say that the two hardest workers we have here on the farm are the washing machine and the fire. When I first start this sentence when talking to people they always assume

I'm going to end it with me and David and they laugh when I say no it's our fire and our washing machine, well the washing machine is by far the hardest worker of all because she goes all year round whereas the fire gets half the year off doesn't he.

Sometimes Amber would wear two coats when out on our winter walks and she looked like a little pufferfish when she did that. And if the top coat happened to be a red one David would call her "Little Miss Sheridan" as in a Sheridan football. He'd pick her up, snuggle her and say to me that we'd best not ever take her to a football match dressed like this because we don't want them mistaking her for the ball. And I'd smile over at the two of them thinking that yeah she did kind of look like a football but we had to keep her warm because she just wasn't the kind of pug who would stay indoors on cold days so I'd rug her up and off we'd go and if she started getting too warm halfway through the walk I'd take one of the coats off. Amber always wore a thicker coat to bed in the middle of winter and I didn't much care what colour that coat was, it was thick, that's all that mattered and really I couldn't see her while sleeping so what did it matter if the coat was putrid in colour, it kept her warm. In the mornings I'd take that coat off and place it beside my pillow ready for the next night then put a new one on before lifting her off the bed. Amber always slept in the middle of our bed so when I heard her stirring I'd call her name and she'd come clunking over to me. I'd be talking to her as I swapped coats, kissing those little ears, whispering into them that I loved her and taking care of her was all I ever wanted to do with my life. And then there would be those glorious mornings where she'd be going nuts giving kisses, ballistically kissing the side of my face as I was bent over her gently putting her little legs through the holes in the coat. She didn't kiss with that much enthusiasm every morning so I'd pause while she was kissing, when she was in the mood to offer such an outpouring of love it took a little while for her to calm down. And I didn't mind one little bit I was there enjoying every moment of it and was sad when she finished. Well I was sad but the other pugs were glad because now we would finally be going for our walk, well unless it was raining that was, if it was raining I would carry Amber out to the hayshed so she could have a wee without getting wet, I'd carry both her and Arthur sometimes and the rest of the pugs would trot along beside us, walking fast to avoid getting completely drowned. No rain meant we could go on our regular walk and although it was cold everybody preferred that. They didn't mind the cold so much, they were well rugged up and after a bit of movement were warm in their bodies and the paddocks offered many more smells then the hayshed did. I'd stand and watch them all wandering around in their colourful little coats. I'd be smiling the entire time and feeling blessed. Sometimes we'd come back inside and all the pugs would be fine other times some would be needing a clean coat putting on, and ninety nine times out of a hundred Amber would be amongst the ones needing her coat changed. It all depended on what she had gotten up to on the walk, she was close to the ground but she was pretty good at avoiding puddles, I'd see her step into them with one or two paws then simply turn around and walk back out. I don' think she had any issues with getting her feet wet I guess she just wasn't sure how deep that puddle was going to be so wasn't taking any chances. Well I know she never minded getting her feet wet because she would take off across the paddocks not bothering if the grass was damp. Amber was still going to have a sniff around regardless and because she was in pink she stood out against the green. I never had any trouble seeing where she was. I never had any trouble seeing any of the blind pugs actually because I always put the brightest coloured coats on our vision impaired blessings, put them on the deaf pugs too, pugs with special needs need special looking after, if they were in colours that blended in that'd be no good because you always need to be able to see them clearly across the paddock, it's no use putting a green coat on them as they'd be hard to spot, especially if they are standing still, just pausing and having a little think about things before carrying on walking which a lot of them tend to do and you'll only notice them when they start moving again and that's no use because sometimes they can be standing there thinking for quite some time and that's fine if they want or need to do that, they can do as they please here. But such a thing is not so good for me because should somebody need my help I need to know as soon as possible so I can go ahead and help. If I only had one or two pugs and was walking them on a lead around the streets it wouldn't matter much what colour they were wearing but here there are multiple pugs and they are wandering around in a large open area. For my sake and theirs I need to be able to sum everything up in one quick glance. This all started after

Amber entered the house, we already had little blind Arthur in the family but Arthur generally stayed by my side or stayed on the path we always followed and he walked nicely with the pack as well so Arthur was always easy to find and he had a set way of doing things. If I couldn't see him I always knew where to find him, I knew he would have had enough of a walk and already made his way up to the house again, Arthur was good like that he was a gentleman of routine and once I got used to his ways it was easy. But then Amber entered the house and she was such an independent little miss so I had to do something in order to be able to locate her whereabouts faster. I rarely left The Divine One alone but there was the odd occasion when one of the other pugs needed help or wanted to go back inside so I'd pick them up and take them indoors and come out to find that Amber wasn't waiting around for me, she had taken herself off on a little adventure. One day I made the mistake of putting her in a green coat, it was a perfect fit for her tiny body and I thought she looked gorgeous in it, fawn pugs do look nice in green. Amber reminded me of a little gherkin in that coat and I suppose I was concentrating on the cute factor only, giving little thought to anything else. I took one pug inside and as I was coming back out I saw another little face peeping round the corner of the house so helped that little blessing inside as well then closed the door behind me to keep them all warm. But when I went back outside I found that my little gherkin wasn't anywhere in sight. My eyes began searching the paddock in a panicked state, bright coat and she would have stood out like a beacon, as tiny as she was due to the colour she still would have stood out like a beacon and I could have crossed the paddock and been by her side in no time. When I did eventually find Amber she was sniffing by the row of trees, slightly tucked under one of them, really camouflaged she was. And as we made our way up to the house I decided that from then on it was going to be bright coats for all our special needs pugs. Although Amber still got use out of her gherkin coat. I kept it for her to wear when she was in the pup pup pen. We have a little penned off area that we call the pup pup pen, it's about the size of a suburban block and is handy for keeping pugs contained when we are getting a horse food delivery, they like to be out seeing what is going on and so that's why we put up the pup pup pen in the first place. It's also handy for when the sheep and horses are on the front paddock as the pugs can interact with them without coming to any harm. There are quite a few trees in that area and Amber loved barking at birds, she would often go out to have a woof and at those times wearing green wasn't an issue because she was easy to find. I would stand watching her from the deck as she ran back and forth, I loved seeing her enjoying herself, being vision impaired sounds were important to her and she sure did love the sound of birds. She'd be able to hear the sheep and horses too but birds were certainly her favourite, the sound of a bird would have her running out of the house down the ramp and into the middle of the pup pup pen in a matter of seconds. She knew the route well, no bumping into anything, just straight out there woofing and she'd run from tree to tree standing at the base barking depending on which tree held the noisiest birds. If they all fell silent for a little while she'd be there all bug eyed just waiting for one of them to make a sound, her body positon was like she was thinking "I dares ya, I just dares ya" and then they'd start up again and off she would run. When it was time to come inside I'd call her name and she'd stop barking, listen for a moment, turn her head slightly towards me, maybe even lift an ear, then a bird would chirp and she'd be off running and barking her little old head off once again totally ignoring me. And again I'd lean against a veranda post watching her on bird patrol. When the light was fading she did tend to blend into the grass but again no trouble at all finding her, she was rarely quiet when she was out there and on the nights I'd leave her to have an extra bit of fun I'd just go out and use her growly woofs to locate her. She really liked listening to the birds as they were settling into the trees of an evening because they were extra chirpy then, perhaps having one last sing before dark. Even when she was sixteen years old The Divine One still loved barking at the birds although she didn't run around then though more just stood underneath the trees and kept spinning round woofing when she heard the chirping, but still having the time of her life and still great to see.

When Steffy who only had the one good eye started to lose vision in it I decided it was time for her to be put into one of the brightest coloured coats in the house. Red and yellow it was, but the yellow was more of a gold colour or at least it looked gold against the red. I loved seeing Steffy racing around the place in that coat because it reminded me of Christmas. Sure we were many months away from Christmas but when Steffy was wearing her Christmas coat it always made me feel happy. Steffy was the kind of pug who could be relied upon to always stay with you, well if she had been the only pug in the house that is, if it had just been me and her I could have put her in any colour I liked and I'd only have to look down in order to find her. But she wasn't an only pug she was part of our pack and being full of empathy like she was she'd be constantly running from one of her siblings to the other, always checking up on everybody, always making sure they were ok and that was a very important job to her and it was for me too as I relied on Steffy quite a bit. So I'd be out walking with everyone and some would start to get a bit ahead of the ones who were lingering and out the corner of my eye I'd see this red and gold flash zooming across the paddocks, didn't even have to properly look up, I knew it was Steffy. I knew it was my little empathy filled blessing doing her self-appointed job and she did it well. Anything she thought worth being brought to my attention and I'd hear that all too familiar Steffy scream. Most times everything was fine but on the off chance it wasn't I had to check it out. Steffy never cried wolf. It was more what she felt was important and what I did were two different things, so I'd go see what was going on and sort it if it needed sorting. I think some of the other pugs may have known when it was a false alarm because not everyone followed me they'd just stand together in their colourful little coats waiting for me to return.

Over the years some lovely ladies made some beautiful coats for The Divine One, it all started the first year she arrived and having nothing in the house that was the right fit. My friend Sheryl made Amber a gorgeous mauve creation, knitted in little squares it was and made to measure so it was perfect and she looked gorgeous in it, wore it day and night and I'd wash it once we were all going to be inside for a few hours and try and have it dry by the time we went for our afternoon walk. Sometimes I'd be drying the last few slightly damp bits with a hairdryer just so Amber would have something to wear and I'd put a bigger waterproof coat on top to keep it from getting wet because that coat was precious, her first winter on the farm was a desperate one as far as coats went. By the time the second winter rolled around we were much more organised. We had a few tiny coats ready and waiting. My friend Sally made the most gorgeous coat for Amber, she made two actually one was pastel pink with a knitted white bow on top and the other one was a bumble bee coat with wings. Amber looked equally cute in both. That pastel pink coat is by far my favourite pug coat of all time and when I look at it today I see Amber so tiny soldiering along at sixteen and a half years old with the little white bow moving as she went. A real lot of fun was had whenever Amber was wearing her bumble bee coat. I remember David flying her around the lounge room the first time she had it on, he was making a buzzing sound saying that a little bubble bee had gotten into the house. He said to me "Quick get the door so it can fly back out into the garden again" he'd be flying Amber all over the house then shoot outside and fly her round the deck and the look on her face said that she was having an absolute ball. She loved playing that game. I think she liked the sound he'd be making as much as she did flying through the air. She had complete trust in David, knew he was never going to drop her that she would never come to any harm with him, she couldn't see where she was going but she could feel the sensation of being moved around in a different way, she could feel the air across her face and was enjoying it. There was a real lot of excitement in the air while she was flying,

I'd be laughing and following along so I didn't miss any of it and behind me would be the rest of the pugs. No wonder Amber liked the game so much she could hear daddy buzzing, mummy laughing and the frenzied pitter-pattering of her siblings on the floorboards. David would start making the sound before he picked her up. Amber would hear him approaching, hear the buzzing and start getting really excited, she didn't have a clue which way he was coming from but stood there all bug eyed with excitement just waiting for him to scoop her up. When he put her down she would sometimes start woofing because she wanted another go and really who could say no to her. She was blind and her tiny head was moving around trying to locate him, trying to hear and sense where he was and she was standing there in a winged bumble bee coat with her little tongue hanging out, she couldn't have looked more adorable if she tried. So David would walk round the lounge room saying "Did somebody let a bee in, did somebody let a bee in? and The Divine One would be giddy with excitement and he'd be calling out "Where is that little bumble bee, can anybody see where she is? The other pugs got in on the act too because he'd be looking down at them as he was asking the question, they knew something special was going on and started dancing around Dad's legs and jumping up for pats, so he'd lean down and pat them and ask them if they knew where the little bumble bee was hiding. And of course Amber was beside herself because she could hear all of this going on. Hear him getting closer and closer to her as he was calling out. I think half the time that's why he was doing it, so she knew exactly where he was and also to build up the level of excitement in the house. When he finally picked Amber up she'd start giving kisses, like she was saying thank you, but as soon as he got her into the flying position the kissing quickly ceased, her face changed, it was like she was readying herself for adventure. Sally said we could take the wings off if we wanted to and that could have been easily done because the wings were not knitted as part of the coat but made separately and sewn on. I guess she thought it could just be a normal yellow and black striped coat without the wings but I left them on all the time because they were adorable. Those two wings were made out of a different type of wool to the coat, very fine and delicate they were, like soft woollen lace, such pretty little wings, looked a bit like fairy wings to me. Amber wore the bumble bee coat for Halloween and was the best dressed pug in the house. Emily was totally fascinated with those delicate little wings though. Perhaps she heard me telling David that Sally said they could come off if we wanted them to because that's exactly what Emily tried doing every time she saw them. She just wouldn't leave them alone. Little Amber would be clunking along and out of nowhere Emily would come racing over, shoot out from underneath a tree and start pulling on those beautiful little wings. I'd try shooing her away so she didn't stretch and ruin them because they wouldn't have looked half as cute if one was hanging down all long and limp while the other was still small and perfectly formed. Emily was sneaky though, after she'd been told off a few times she'd wait until she saw I was busy with another pug then come running across and start tugging and tugging on them. She'd tug so hard that eventually she did manage to get one off and ran all the way round the paddock with it until the novelty wore of, Emily was so proud of herself that day and I had to go searching for the little delicate wing once all the pugs were back inside the house. Took me ages to find it, I'd almost given up hope of ever seeing it again when I spotted it sitting in the dirt by a tree trunk, partially buried it was and really filthy, but not out of shape like I'd expected it to be. I had shouted Emily over to me numerous times while watching her run but knew she had no intention of bringing it back to me, not after the weeks it had taken her to get the wing off. That wing was hers as far as she was concerned because she'd worked very hard acquiring it. She totally ignored me standing there calling out her name and my hands were on my hips too, a sure sign that mummy meant business. But she still went on galloping round and round. So I left Emily to it and concentrated on the incredibly pissed off one winged bumble bee standing by my side. The tugging thing would drive Amber absolutely insane that's why I'd stop it as soon as I saw it going on. But there was the odd time when I was too far away, off assisting somebody and couldn't get there fast enough to help Amber out. I was telling Emily to stop as I was running towards them but she was too engrossed in the game, she wasn't for stopping for anybody. Thing was Emily was a lot bigger than Amber, plus she could see so she had an advantage over her sister in that area too. But that didn't stop Amber from spinning round and telling Emily off. Sure she was little and at a disadvantage as far as sight went but she had no trouble sticking up for herself. Amber would feel the tug and turn her head fast and if her strike was good she'd gnaw on Emily's side, gnaw on it enough to make her abort the mission. The Divine One wasn't overly threatening but I guess she was just threatening enough to make Emily think twice about continuing on with things. Nobody likes being told off do they and Amber wasn't for backing down so Emily would immediately let go and run off to find herself some other mischief to get up to. I'd go over and pick Amber up, talk to her, give her a snuggle and kiss her little ears. I didn't like that she had been upset while trying to have a peaceful walk. If Emily had been the one wearing the bumble bee coat and Amber had tugged on her wings it wouldn't have bothered Emily in the slightest, she couldn't have cared less. But Amber did so I'd make sure she was ok and when I knew she was I'd kiss her one more time before putting her back on the ground. And she'd clunk off happily but the funny thing was she'd often be clunking off with pink dazzle lipstick on her head. A perfect print of my lips sitting smack bang in the middle of her little fawn head and of course not caring at all because she couldn't see it but she did look incredibly cute walking around like that and I'd vow to remember to just give air kisses on the days I was wearing lipstick and kiss them as much as I wanted to if I was only wearing balm. Then I'd start thinking to myself that perhaps pink dazzle lipstick was best left for teenagers and not a woman of my age but that thought would quickly be replaced with how short life was and if pink dazzle lipstick made me happy then I would continue wearing it. And also keep kissing the pugs with it on too because again life was short what did it matter of they ended up with pink foreheads at times. At least they were loved. And they sure did lean in for those kisses and it was lovely to see them doing that.

I did think of actually sewing the wings on with extra wool to put an end to the shenanigans, if Emily knew they would never again come off it may make her not half as interested. In my mind the most perfect solution to all of this would be for Emily to lose interest because she was a worry whenever Amber was wearing that coat. She could be very rough at times and I thought in trying to grab the wings she may have pulled Amber over, set her off balance sending her to the ground and I couldn't have that. But no Emily never lost interest she always had to be watched. If I saw Emily coming I would pick Amber up and after circling us for a few moments and realising she wasn't getting anywhere near Amber or the wings she simply walked off defeated.

Emily eyeing off those wings!

One day we were all heading out the door for a walk. I took a few steps outside and on realising how cold it was ducked back inside to grab another coat for Amber and just popped it on over the top of her bee coat as we were walking down the ramp. Emily had shot off in front of everybody, she was long gone by the time I came back out the door. I saw her in the paddock in the distance as soon as we cleared the house. Amber was a few steps behind me. When Emily saw that Amber was outside she came racing over no doubt ready to have a bit of fun at her elderly sister's expense. But when she got to us Emily just stood there with a look of bewilderment on her pretty face. She walked all around Amber looking for those wings, even peeped underneath her tiny sister to see if they were there, she seemed not to be able to take in that the wings weren't waiting to be tugged on. Clearly she had made note of Amber having her bee coat on when we all left the house and I guess she could smell the wool they were made out of so knew they weren't too far away. It was interesting watching her trying to figure things out, watch how her mind worked, her actions told me everything she was thinking and in the end they told me she was tired of looking because she wandered off.

I do think all pugs look cute in coats but certainly nobody could wear a coat quite like Amber could, I think it was that face she had, she looked beautiful in summer when there were no coats needed but you put her in a coat and the level of her cuteness instantly multiplied. Then again she looked pretty cute in a hat too, she only ever wore the one but boy did she wear it well. It was a Christmas tree hat, green and shaped like a tree with red decorations and a lovely gold star on the top. It was a beautiful hat and she looked magnificent in it. Although when I first saw that hat I didn't know Amber would be the one wearing it. I spotted it in a Christmas auction for an overseas Pug Rescue group and just knew I had to have it. My sister said she would buy it for me as my Christmas present which was great because it allowed me to bid higher then I would have been able to otherwise. I asked her how much I could go up to and she knew how badly I wanted it so she said do whatever it takes to get it. So I put a bid on and went to bed, due to being in Australia the auction was going to finish in the middle of the night. I know years ago David used to stay up when bidding on something on Ebay but I just didn't have it in me to do an all nighter. So I put my bid in, prayed and then turned out the light. The next morning I woke up and couldn't turn my phone on fast enough to see if I'd won. When I did I was ecstatic and starting picturing all the pugs wearing it. I had no idea how big it was going to be, but the pug in the photo looked like a decent sized pug so I was expecting the hat to be able to fit on everyone's head and the listing just said it would fit a pug so I assumed they meant all pugs but when it got here I couldn't believe how little it was. I said to David either this is a size small or the pugs in the USA are a lot smaller then Aussie pugs are. As soon as I opened the package I said "This is only going to fit the pug in the house with the smallest head" and we both instantly knew who that was. But it was even a bit too tight on Amber. Dave started stretching it but I said stop because I felt it would be all out of shape then and that the star on top would be drooping and that'd be no good, I didn't want her looking like Noddy. But he did stretch it enough to at least fit Amber comfortably. It was a Christmas auction and although it ended a few weeks before Christmas day the hat actually didn't arrive here until late January so we had to wait eleven months to be able to use it on our Christmas cards. And because our Christmases are in summer I took the photos in September because I felt it unfair to make Amber wear a woollen hat in the heat. So out we went with a handful of treats and took a few quick happy snaps and inside we came again. It was only the three of us that went out, we left the other pugs inside because we didn't want them pushing in front of Amber while we were trying to get a photo. Or worse lining up the perfect shot and having Emily race over grab hold of the gold star and try and run off with it dragging Amber with her as she went. Amber had the two of us and a handful of treats all to herself while those photos were being taken and she absolutely loved that. Loved the treats and loved the attention. It was hard getting her looking at the camera, being blind she was just following the smell of the treats but a few shots were taken and then we came onto the deck and I sat down ready to take the hat off. Amber jumped up to see if I had any treats left, put her front paws on the seat next to me and I started clicking away and those are some of the best shots we took that day and they were all pure flukes.

The pugs will wear their coats well into Spring and I'll keep them on hand a few weeks after they are not really needed just in case we have an out of the blue cold night, but once summer is well on the way all the coats are washed and packed away and I get so much joy when seeing them on the line. Just a row of little colourful coats blowing gently in the breeze and of course I've always got to take a photo of them. I washed the coats in lavender washing powder and they smelt so beautiful when I was pegging them on the line and they would smell so lovely when I got then out of the cupboard months later and was putting them on each pug. Then for some reason they changed the washing power, didn't mention on the box that is was now a new formula but I could tell it had changed. All the coats smelt disgusting, like they'd gone stale no nice lavender smell, I smelt it and Amber did too, she turned her head when I brought it near her, like she knew it was different. Maybe they were now using cheaper ingredients you know like companies sometimes do in order to cut costs. They don't think about the consumer so much as the dollar and I always think it's a shame when they do things like that. I mean if they do it they should tell you and drop the price too but of course they are never going do that. They do whatever they want to and think we'll not notice but I did and so did The Divine One, they couldn't get anything past us. So I rewashed all the coats and changed to another brand of washing powder. The pugs can look really funny when the weather first starts heating up. When they've been wearing coats all winter and you finally take them off they don't look quite right. They all look kind of naked. Like a pile of little gumnut babies running around the place until you get used to seeing them that way. And Amber looked so tiny after so many months being rugged up, it was like your mind forgot how very small she was. When I was changing her coat I really didn't take the time to concentrate on her size, more just getting the dirty or wet coat off and putting a new one on quickly so she didn't get cold. But now she was out and about clunking around the farm I'd smile down at her, at the size of her, my eyes watching her wandering about, walking like a boss. And then the temperature would fall again and out of the closet a pile of coats would come.

CHAPTER THIRTEEN

Sounds Of A Happy Home

Amber with Lilly Rain, Star and Ruben

Because I am always in the thick of things it's not very often that I get the chance to step back and listen to the sounds of my house. Of course I listen all the time to the sounds of the farm. The birds, the sheep, the horses, the wind and the wind chimes, the leaves on the trees rustling, the cows across the road mooing and the tractors and trucks going by and naturally I am always well aware of all the sounds my pugs make and that's everything from their growly woofs, the pitter-pattering of little paws on floorboards, the sound of toys being squeaked, the sound of the pugs playing with each other and the sound of them snoring. All these sounds make up my day to day life and I love them but when you are listening to them from another room it is all quite different. The only time I get to do this is when I'm not feeling 100% well, me being under the covers when it's not night time is very rare and so I do take the time to enjoy observing things differently to how I am used to observing them. Ok to be honest I am also listening to what's going on because I want to make sure things are being done right for the pugs. We have a set routine and routines are quite important to little old beings so even though I am not able to be physically there doing it myself I do like the keep things moving in the same order for the pugs sake. David does things a little differently to me and he's fine with that and some of the pugs are too, they learn to just muck in. But there are others, the most delicate of my little blessings that do tend to become quite upset if things are out of order and Amber was one of those blessings. She quickly let everyone in the house know that daddy going rogue wasn't going to cut it and when a few of the other real oldies and real delicates saw The Divine One playing up or heard her voicing her opinion they too started joining in. From my bed I could heard David in the kitchen, heard the different woofs and knew exactly who was encircling him. I knew Amber and Casey would be the main ones trying to hurry Dave up I knew Amber would be begging at the side of David's leg and Casey would be pushing her forehead into him. I knew Arthur would want things to move along too but not be so much in Daddy's face like his sisters would be. Arthur just like Ruben would want their dinner but would be content to wait quietly, well Arthur would be quiet but Ruben would soon start giving the occasional woof. It all depended how far behind David actually was. Dave didn't have to shout out and tell me who it was that was trying to rush him, I knew their personalities well, I knew their individual barks and I knew the sound each ones paws made on the kitchen floor. It wasn't hard at all for me to figure out what was going on in the other room and I'd be calling out to David, telling him who wanted what and what he could do to defuse the ever mounting situation. And he would call back telling me to either "Be quiet" because he "Had this" or be asking how I knew which ones were urging him on and I'd smile to myself then shout out "Because a mother knows, a mother always knows". And I also knew that he didn't really "Have it" half as much as he thought he did because if he did I wouldn't be hearing so much commotion filtering through the open door. But I didn't think it wise to point that out right now, he was doing his absolute best and the pugs were giving him a real hard time, me having an opinion on the matter may have been the straw that broke the camel's back and that camel was having a hard enough time as it was I could hear it in his voice. He was still softly spoken but there was mounting frustration creeping in and he didn't want or need me adding to it. The pugs were on his case, I could hear them all in there trying to sort him out. This made me smile too because I had stood in David's shoes many a time so knew the exact view he would be looking down on. My mind was picturing them becoming more and more exasperated as time ticked away, flat faces scrunching up, little old mouths forming into a woof. But Dave is pretty laid back, he is the type of bloke who one second would be feeling the heat and the next second be totally detached from the situation, not letting it get to him. I'd often hear the sound of my husband's laughter and I knew exactly what he would be laughing at. You get to a point where you are so far behind with the chores that all you can do is laugh and pick up the pugs and give them a snuggle then carry on doing the jobs you are trying to get done.

"Umm, can I help you guys?"

One Easter sticks out in my mind quite clearly. I had injured my foot and was frustrated about being laid up. Easter is a busy time for us here on the farm, for some it's all about a long weekend away, but for us its one last chance to get things done before winter sets in. That's why the Easter break is so important it gives you a bit of time to get all the jobs done that you've not had time to do previously. For me it was the worst time to go hurting myself and it was such a stupid way to do it too. But regardless of how it happened that was it for me as far as walking went for the next few days and it put an end to what I personally wanted to get done around the place so I was pretty annoyed that the goals I'd set for myself were not going to be met. If I'd had an accident with one of the horses or sheep well I would have been more ok with that, accidents happen right, but to do it the way I did made it all the worse I thought. All week we had been talking about what we wanted to get done, we had everything planned and were both looking forward to what we thought we could achieve but now I couldn't help out. David had to do whatever he could do on his own and I felt bad about that. I lay in bed feeling pretty pathetic for the first half of Good Friday. I was restless and bored. I watched David out the window and wanted to be out there too. By mid-afternoon I had come to my senses, decided to get over myself, I couldn't be productive in that area but I could be in another. I was writing The Joy of Horton at the time so got the computer out and carried on writing. I think I would have felt much worse if I had achieved nothing that weekend so I did what I could do and was happy enough with that. Plus I had my little writing buddies all around me so how could I not feel anything but bliss. They'd keep coming and going from one of us to the other, a lot of time was spent lifting them on and off the bed. They wanted to be with me but then they'd see David go by the window and be scrambling to get down and be out there with him, see what he was up to, so I'd set the computer aside and lift them all down and they'd be gone for a little while but one by one they would return to the bedroom so I'd set the computer aside again and lift them all back up and they'd be settled for a while, some would fall asleep then Dave would walk by again and somebody would woof and a little curly tail would wag followed by another and another and they'd be scrambling over to me so I could get them down and outside they would scurry only to be back a bit later jumping up at the side of the bed. So up they'd come again and all would be quiet for half an hour then I'd see David's head go by and so did they so I'd set the computer aside and lift them down once more only this time I'd be telling them that when they'd had their fill of being with daddy and wanted to be inside with me again that I would not be bringing them back onto the bed this time, that they would have to be content enough with settling down to sleep in one of the dog beds on the floor. Then I would see the shuffling bodies come filing back through the door once again and I would stick to my word too for all of about five seconds, then I'd look down and see those little grey faces swaying beside the bed, wanting to come back up, wanting to be nearer to me, so the computer got moved over again and up they all came. I probably only got a page written that day but still it was something wasn't it and besides those little old blessings were having a ball going from one parent to the other they wore themselves out with all their comings and goings and slept like babies that night.

Saturday morning brought rain so David decided he would do some cooking, we knew the rain wasn't going to last all day so he figured he may as well get our food sorted so he would be freed up to go back outside once the sky cleared. He decided he would make something that would last a few days. "At least until Monday night" he called out as he flew by. "Good idea" I said then watched on as a trail of pugs scurried after him, they weren't ever going to stay with me when they knew food was being prepared because no matter who is doing the cooking they know they will always be offered a little taste. But they did keep coming back into the bedroom with excited faces letting me know that important stuff was going on in the kitchen. It can be really great when Dave is doing the cooking because he is a pretty good cook and makes all kinds of special things that we normally don't have. He rarely has time to spend in the kitchen but when it all falls on him the pugs and I know that we are in for something very special. David likes to cook, it's a joy for him because he doesn't get to do it all the time. At first I'll hear the sound of many pots and pans rattling because David seems to like to use almost every pot and pan we have in the house and of course he would do wouldn't he because he isn't the one doing the washing up, he likes to cook but loathes doing dishes. I'm well aware of this so a good many images will be going through my head of a sink piled high and know that I'll soon be coming face to face with the exact image I have in my head. Dave always leaves the dishes for me because once he's cooked he's pretty much over it and doesn't want anything to do the washing up. "Your job" he'll tell me and I say "Ok" because to me it's the trade-off of for having something that I haven't had to cook myself for once and also for not being made to live off take away for days on end. After the pots and pans are out I'll be able to hear him humming a happy tune, the tune signifies that he's about to get down to business and from the sounds the pugs are making I know they are just as excited as I am to see what he is about to create. They keep running backwards and forwards, with their eyes they are telling me what's going on, so much joy in their mannerisms too, if they could talk they'd be giving a running commentary. I smile down at them then watch as they turn around and go rushing back to the kitchen fast so they wouldn't miss out on anything. For all they know a sample could have been dished out while they've been away from their post and they can't allow that to happen too often. They don't ask to come up on the bed at these times, far too much happening in the kitchen, the bed holds no interest for them right now. Because Dave wanted me to keep off my foot as much as possible I was having all my meals in the bedroom too. I had them on the little wooden computer table David had made for me to write my books on, it came in really handy when I was laid up. Gave me something to rest my food on and I could fit a drink on there as well. The Divine One was my breakfast, lunch and dinner date, she was up on the bed eating all my meals with me. You can't have all the pugs up on the bed when you are eating because it would be absolute chaos, so it was Amber at every meal because it was a special treat for her and for me too. I loved having her with me and sometimes Ruben would join us as well. Ruben was much quieter then Amber, he would be beside me half asleep half waiting to be given something, but Amber she wasn't quiet nor was she to the side, no she was front and center. Sat opposite me at the little wooden table, her head was just high enough so she could see what was going on, well she had limited vision so she was going by smell and her little mouth would open when she smelt food coming near. It was absolutely gorgeous seeing her face peeping over the top of that tiny table, eyes searching, nose in the air sniffing and the little tongue always hanging out. Just a lovely sight for me to see and if I wasn't feeding her as much as she thought she should be getting she would bring one little paw up, find the edge of the table then the other paw would join it and she'd stand there on her hind legs waiting for me to utter those all-important words "Are you ready for some more" and she always was and her mouth would open then she'd get down off the table eat her mouthful and be content to go back to sitting opposite me, quietly waiting for me to ask her that question once again. She was in her element eating on the bed, she knew it wasn't how things were normally done, she knew what was happening was something special and from the way she was acting you could tell she thought it was the best thing ever. It was such a beautiful thing for me to experience, it was at the time and it's even more precious to me now that she is gone and I am thinking back, remembering all of it. She was only little but she sure could pound on that table if I didn't keep the food coming her way, but it was fine she could pound on it all she liked, David had made the table solid and strong, it was never going tip over sending food across the bed.

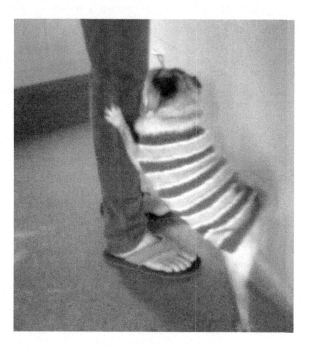

I always had a tea towel underneath my plate and because the table was so small those tea towels looked like table cloths, my little set up looked like fine dining to me and one day I got to thinking that I would really love to recreate the scene from lady and the tramp with Amber. We had a red and white checkered tea towel in the house I know we did so I suggested to Dave that he should make spaghetti and I could see his mind ticking over, seeing if he fancied it or not but when I told him why I wanted it he just laughed and shook his head. Looking back I so wish I had of gone ahead and done it and taken a heap of photos, imagine how great those photos would be to look back on now. It would have been a whole lot of fun and a whole lot of laughter would have taken place trying to get the perfect shot. Amber would have been having a ball, as long as she was eating she didn't care what she had, but she would have known something else was going on in the room too and been picking up on all of that. I would have had to be very careful with choking through. Amber wouldn't have known to take small bites or to simply hold the end of the spaghetti in her mouth for a few seconds while some photos were taken, she would have been trying to get that spaghetti down fast, get as much of it into her mouth as possible. Blind dogs tend to do that so their sighted siblings don't steal their food and really you can't blame them can you. My breakfast, lunch and dinner date would sit in the middle of the bed facing the doorway, at that point Amber was still able to make out forms so was no doubt waiting for that shadow coming through the door and when David wasn't appearing fast enough she'd sometimes ask to be lifted off the bed so she could go and sort him out. She'd indicate to me that she wanted down and I'd help her then watch her little shuffling back legs and uncurled tail go clunking out the door to go see what was taking so long. I would hear her approaching the kitchen, heard David say hello to her. Hear her clunking around his feet and hear her following him back into the room again but her step was far quicker this time because she knew he was now carrying a plate. One day David made the most amazing sausage rolls, so delicious they were and because he hadn't put onions in them I was able to share a little bit with Amber. And he knew I would that's why he had made sure to make them dog friendly. I never gave her any of the pastry though, that was rubbish food really and I would never give her anything like that, the middle bit, well that was a different story, there was meat in there but there was an equal amount of veggies too, so much goodness for my little girl to have, Amber loved them and I loved them, she kept woofing for more. She'd come over and rest her little chin on the table as soon as she smelt the food, eyes resting solely on me, even though she couldn't fully see me she knew where I was and those big glossy eyes of hers never drifted, always gazing in my direction, it was like I was on a date with the most beautiful girl in the world. I ate all my meals off that table for four days over the Easter break. And always there opposite me was The Divine One sharing my food. I think we both missed it when I was back to walking normally again. David wouldn't have missed it though I think he was glad to go back to work, get back to his normal everyday routine and let me and the pugs get back to ours. I think we would have driven him completely mad if he'd been made to put up with things the way they were one more day. I honestly don't think he had another day in him. The clock in the bedroom broke on Easter Saturday and I'd driven him bonkers for days after that. I'd be forever asking him the time. And I'd wait a little while and when nothing was forthcoming I'd be shouting out again and this time he shout back "Half an hour since the last time you asked" he also indicated by his tone that I shouldn't ask again for quite a while because he was busy trying to get things done. And I'd call out "You know you are running late don't you? And he'd shout back in a very irritated manner that the focus should be "Only" on the fact that things were getting done not on the time or the sequence of how they are getting done. After that I lay there trying to concentrate on counting my blessings, and no this time I do not mean the pugs, I mean the fact that I've actually got a husband who wants to help me, so I lay there desperately trying to keep my mouth shut and smiled sweetly when he re-entered the room an eternity later looking all hot and bothered. Thing was the cooking wasn't the only thing he was dealing with on his own, he was also doing absolutely everything single handily for the pugs and still trying to not let the Easter break be a complete waste as far as getting outside jobs done and yes that can be quite a lot for one person. But a lot of the time I wasn't shouting out to be annoying I was more making sure that the pugs were ok, it is hard being shut away when you are used to being there for them all day everyday looking after them and taking care of their needs. I just wanted to be sure they were alright, that he hadn't accidently locked one of the pugs outside because his mind was on too many things at once. Things like that can happen so I was constantly trying to make sure they didn't. I'd hear him going out the door and wait for them to all come back inside again, a few of the pugs would come running into the bedroom before following David outside for a walk, they were seeing if I was coming with them, and I would hold up my hands like I do when I've finished giving them a round of treats, letting them know that all the treats are gone or in this case that I wasn't walking with them today. I didn't have a signal for that so I used the "Treats all gone" signal instead and after a while they seemed to get what I meant. Saw my hands go up, heard me saying no walk for mummy and they'd pause for a second then turn and go running off. I would hear them all filing back inside the door and wait a little while before calling out. Just to give everybody time to come get back inside the house and some of them are lingerers and I knew this so would wait a bit longer but then I would hear the back door closing and just couldn't help myself, I had to ask, had to make sure all was well. So I kept my tone nice and light whenever I was calling out. "Are all the pugs in? I'd ask and due to the pitter-pattering of many paws sometimes David wouldn't be able to hear me the first time so I'd wait a little bit then call out again and he'd answer "Yes" but I knew that wasn't right because I had been listening intently and knew Ruben was missing. I knew it was him because he had a way of tapping the floor with one of his back legs, been doing it for years, sometimes because it was nearing dinner time and he was hungry, other times just because he was happy and then there were times when he did it for a reason I couldn't quite make out, but clearly he was happy about something or he wouldn't have been doing it. Anyway I knew the door to the outside world had now been closed and I knew that Ruben wasn't inside. I was about to draw David's attention to the fact when I heard the back door slowly opening again, no sound from David, he didn't call Ruben's name. I think he was trying to make as little noise as possible sneaking Ruben in so that I didn't know he had been left out there. But I strained my ears and heard Ruben shoot inside. Heard that all too familiar happy tapping and that's all I needed to hear. I knew he had been waiting by the back door by the speed at which he shot inside, not coming up the ramp, more that he was simply waiting for the glass door to slide along so he could gain entry. Maybe he'd even tapped on the glass alerting David to the fact that he was still out there, Ruben was old and he only had one eye and he was blind in that eye but he knew his way around the place and he knew to tap on the glass if the door was shut. I did hear the treat jar lid being lifted off though so I guess Dave must have been feeling a little bit guilty about locking him out.

By Easter Sunday I was well into the chapter I was writing and really enjoying listening to the goings on in the house. I was ahead of the new goals I'd set for myself but David was still behind with his and that's only because he hadn't readjusted, he was still going by the list we'd made during the week but with all the extra things he was now having to do that list was not ever going to be able to be completed. Never the less he was still trying hard to do it all and I knew how he felt because if it was him who was laid up and me out there doing things I too would be trying to get as much done as I possibly could. We are both similar in that way, once we have a mind to do something we will do everything in our power to try and achieve it. And of course he was still coming backwards and forwards doing things for the pugs. If I could do something by hopping I would do it but I didn't want to hop down the ramp with Amber in my arms, didn't want to accidentally topple over while carrying such precious cargo. I had been hopping to freshen the water bowl many times during the day because I know how often that needs refilling. The water bowl was easy, getting Amber to her special weeing tree safely wasn't so I'd call Dave in to take her. She really did love that one tree. To us it looked no different to all the nearby trees but Amber must have found something special about it to make it worth weeing on. And it wasn't like it was used by any of the other pugs. She wasn't going there because it had the scent of other dogs wee. No she liked to have a tree all of her own to wee on and it had me thinking that maybe it was more the lay of the land that she found easier. Perhaps that was why she was drawn. I am always aware of little old bladders, aware of all of my pugs urination patterns. I like to know how often bladders are being emptied, things like this can tell you a lot about what's happening on the inside so I'm constantly making note, that's how I knew when Amber had bladder stones. If you know things are out of whack you can start investigating, pay even more attention then you are already paying until you know what's going on. You can pick up on all sorts of things when you are constantly monitoring and that's everything from them getting a little dehydrated to urine infections and urine infections when left untreated can make a pug quite sick so you always want to get on top of things as quickly as possible. We have a very good vet for that, my job is to notice when something is wrong, his job is to treat the infection and get the little soul back to feeling better as quickly as possible. And in knowing how fussy I am about keeping an eye on such things David would always call out to me when he was taking Amber out, well taking all of them out, and when he came back inside he'd let me know who had done what. But Amber being a little fusspot with where she'd like to wee often needed taking out again to have another go, she'd been like that from day one and one of us would stand there waiting with her until she'd done what she needed to do and sometimes she could take a very long time to choose. Lots of umming and ahhing, lots of sniffing being done, lots of almost squatting because she'd found the most perfect spot then standing up because she thought she could find better. That's why the weeing tree became the place we'd always take her, saved a lot of time, if she hadn't gone when out with the pack then we would always head off for the weeing tree. Only now it was just David taking her and sometimes she'd need her coat changing when she came back inside. From the bedroom I could hear all of this going on, heard David trying to put a clean dry coat on and heard Amber telling him off for it in no uncertain terms. I could tell she was giving him hell. I'd hear him battling and asking The Divine One to be reasonable and could tell from her response that she was being anything but reasonable because she didn't realise he was doing it for her own good. In her eyes he was stopping her from getting back to me. But what she hadn't quite figured out was that by making the job twice as hard she was in fact the one who was preventing us from being reunited. So I shouted out "Be water" and Dave knew I was meaning go with the flow, water is soft and smooth, it just flows naturally and if it can't get there one way it'll find another. I kept on listening. Another round of "Be reasonable Buglet" was getting him nowhere but I knew what would be the case so shouted out "Get the fluffy pink one, she'll let you put that one on her no worries" and he shouted back "How do you know I'm not trying to put that one on now" I replied "Because she wouldn't be playing up so much if you were" and then added what had now become my Easter break catch phrase "A mother knows, a mother always knows" I heard him muttering under his breath something about me being a know it all. I couldn't quite catch it all but I knew what he was saying wouldn't have been all that nice so I didn't ask him to repeat it, he already had enough of a battle on his hands with Amber, he didn't need me chiming in again. The thing is I know my husband incredibly well, I knew he'd be in a rush with having so much to do. I knew he'd walk in the door, know to change Ambers coat and the one hanging on the back of my chair wouldn't have been the one he'd grab first because it wasn't the closest one to him. He'd not be giving any thought to the pug he was putting the coat on and how she was a finicky little thing with ideas of her own. And those ideas sometimes changed weekly with Amber, one week she'd like something the next she wouldn't and poor David wasn't up to date with things because I had forgotten to tell him. He didn't know that a few steps to the left and he could have gotten the right coat first up and avoided this little confrontation. I knew Amber couldn't tell the colour of the coat he was trying to put on her but she sure would have felt it, the coat he was trying to put on was a tighter knit coat, the other coat was no less warm but it did slide on easier and faster which was what Amber would have wanted. I knew she'd been out for a wee, I knew in her mind she would have considered it being away from me too long, yes she would have enjoyed being outside she always did but I knew as soon as she was in the door that she would want to be getting back to me as quickly as she could and the coat change was slowing her down. That's why she was battling him on it, she wanted to be back on the bed with Mummy and it wasn't happening anywhere near fast enough for her. A few moments later I heard my husband's voice again and this time he was telling Amber that her beauty was overwhelming so I figured he must have gotten the right coat on no worries and was now telling her how cute she looked in it. A moment or two after that The Divine One came clunking through the bedroom door wearing the fluffy pink coat.

I think the sounds I enjoyed listening to the most were when the pugs were being fed. Meal times are happy times here on the farm. Normally I am heavily involved in that, standing in the middle of it all filling up the bowls that are on countertop. And you don't notice it the same when you are in amongst it all, yes you are aware of what's going on but you are concentrating on what you are doing and when you get to hear it all from a distance it can be the most beautiful thing. You'll hear your husband happily talking to the pugs using the same tone you use when you are talking to them at mealtimes. You'll hear their joyful howls when their bowls are being filled and you'll hear their demanding little barks when they think he's going far too slow. Some of the pugs even resorted to running into the bedroom as if they were dobbing him in. And I'd ask if he'd done such and such a thing yet and he'd say no then ask me how I knew he'd not gotten to that bit yet and I'd shout back because they've all been coming to the side of the bed for the past twenty minutes telling me. Yes it's only twenty minutes but that can seem like an awfully long time to a little pug that's hungry. I could hear Dave laughing and the fridge door opening and closing multiple times because he'd forgotten something. Normally it was someone's medication I was reminding him of. Not all pugs are good at taking medication and I pictured the ones that were the worse rejoicing because they knew he had forgotten. I bet they were praying like mad that the voice from the other room would remain silent but it didn't so I listened on. I knew the rejoicing would soon be coming to an end when they saw he'd been reminded. I pictured Steffy pushing her head and neck against his chest, trying to peel herself off him and run away, doing all she could do not to have to take her medicine. He'd shout back "One down one to go" so I'd be listening hard making sure the next pug went well. And while all this was going on there was the constant sound of excited paws tapping on the kitchen floor because they knew dinner was only seconds away. In my head I could see Baby rolling around on her back by the fridge, a thing she does when she is incredibly excited, yes she'll be getting under his feet but she is happy so he'll be sidestepping her just like I always side step her and no doubt he'll be bending down every now and then to give her tummy a bit of a rub just like I normally do. I mean how can you not, she's adorable laying there looking up at you with that one eye of hers. I used to worry that somebody would accidently scratch her remaining eye while she was rolling but they didn't mainly because they were all on the other side of the kitchen where most of the food was and as soon as those bowls are on the move so is Baby, she'll flip herself over and be up on her feet in no time.

Baby

Arthur will be either crowd surfing or jumping up and pulling a drawer out then pushing it back in again, a thing he does over and over again to amuse himself while waiting for his dinner, he begs up because he now can since his back surgery and he begs up because he is blind and knows that once spotted neither Mum or Dad can stop themselves from putting a sneaky bit of food into his mouth, just as an extra treat you know because the little guys been through a heck of a lot.

Arthur

Amber no doubt will be gripping onto one of Dave's shoes and he'll have to move her off slowly so she doesn't slip down and hurt herself. The others will all be bobbing about, woofing, snotting, circling and dancing. Awesome or "El Screecho" as Dave used to call him at the time will be on top of the couch doing his girly bark which by the way is quite deafening. And I'll be able to hear David calling out to him, telling him to quieten down, that he's not winning any friends doing what he is doing. Lumen and Ruben will be barking too and they are because I can hear them. Lumen from her little pink cot and Ruben as he walks around the lounge room weaving his way in between the clothes horses, back leg tapping whenever he pauses and he does pause often while trying to get his whereabouts, but always with his back foot happily tapping, yes he's gotten himself stuck but soon figures out that if he walks backwards he will be ok. Some of the pugs will still be outside not wanting to come in just yet, one last sniff, one last wee and all the while David will be doing all he can to get their dinner bowls filled. So I call out to ask if this is what's happening and the answer comes back quickly "Yeah" and there's lightness in his voice because he is really enjoying his time with them, me well I live it every day I'm blessed that way and know it, but for David it's a holiday treat. You also hear when they are coming in to check on you again and you find yourself being very very excited when their little faces appear because you miss them, they've only been gone a while but you miss them all the same. You watch them turn and go scurrying out of the room, running off to have their dinner, you hear the doors opening and happy little paws dancing out onto the deck. And again there is a squealing of excitement as they are lifted into their eating pens and the bowls are lowered down. You'll hear them woofing when they've finished, the blind ones will be woofing asking to be lifted out of their pens. They've eaten their meal in peace and at their own pace too and they'll have also been given the time to sniff around the base of the bowl in case they've accidently pushed some of the food out while they were eating. But they've been in there long enough to have done all that so now they are telling dad they want out and I get really excited then because I know I'll soon be seeing their little faces once again. And yes The Divine One will be up on the bed sharing my dinner with me even though she'll have not that long ago had her own but that's ok because knowing it would be the case the food in her dinner bowl had been reduced a little.

CHAPTER FOURTEEN

Delicate Little Flower

Some pugs are delicate all throughout their lives and some pugs, just like people, become delicate due to age. The Divine One I believe had been delicate all throughout her life either that or her previous owners did a fairly good job of neglecting her. Perhaps it was a bit of both. I only met her when she was nine years old but she was delicate all the years she was with me. And it wasn't just her spinal issue either, after living with Amber for a few weeks it became obvious what a delicate little flower she really was and highly sensitive too. I knew this little blessing would be in need of a whole lot of special looking after and she had come to the right place for that because it's what I love doing. When I saw Amber's pound photo I had no idea this was going to be the case, yes I saw the dry eyes and knew she would need daily drops but I didn't know about her spine then or her other issues and that's ok, I'm always here ready to spring into action, I'm always up to the challenge. I thought it was good that Amber had come to me and Dave because she could have so easily gone to a home where they may not have wanted to put the effort in to caring for this needy little soul and that would have been really sad for her. She would have either been left to keep on living a life of neglect or been passed on to another home and maybe even another one after that. Either way her life wouldn't have been how it was here so I'm grateful she became our daughter. We both felt incredibly lucky to get her or maybe it was more than just luck maybe she had been sent to us and if she was well, I am very grateful to whomever it was that sent her our way. I remember Amber's first summer with us, she was out helping me in the garden, she was sitting better as far as her spine went and I was watching her pottering around. Her paws were green again because the grass had just been cut and the sun was shining but not overly hot, perfect weather for gardening and perfect weather for having a pile of little old pugs out there with you while you are doing it. At that point in her life Amber loved rolling around on the grass, she'd had her sessions with the physio so was feeling pretty good in her body. Of course it wasn't a normal dog roll, she was favouring one side more than the other but she was rolling all the same and in a state of rapture while she was doing it. At first I thought she was merely trying to scratch an itch but after a while it became very obvious it was more than just that. Maybe the first time she did it she was actually trying to scratch an itch but after realising she could now roll she started doing it all the time. The only thing was that sometimes due to her spine she needed help getting back up again but that didn't bother her nor did it stop her doing it. She'd just woof for me if she needed me but she really didn't have to woof because more often than not I was already on my way over to her, hands ready to pick her up and stand her upright. And when I had I'd keep my hands at either side of her for a few seconds until she started walking just to make sure she'd got her balance. I always had one eye on her and what she was doing but she didn't know that so would sometimes attempt to get up by herself and some days would simply flip herself over no worries, others days I'd see her try and not be able to do it, it all depended on the side she was trying to get up on. She looked a bit like a little turtle on it's back, legs kicking at the air, I'd be watching all of this as I was making my way to her and then all of a sudden she'd had enough, she must have realized she couldn't do it so stopped trying and lay there legs still then the woofing for me would begin. I thought it was fantastic that she was rolling to me it proved she was feeling good in her body and it told me that she was really happy too and if I was in any doubt I only had to look at her face to know how she was feeling. I could tell how much she liked being in the garden. She would always choose the grass patches that were the lushest and mid roll she'd pause and sniff the air, smell the grass, that little nose of hers was rarely still. Back then she was digging a bit too, not huge holes that had to be filled back in with a shovel just a little scratch at the earth here and there and she was so lovely to watch doing it. She reminded me of a little ancient chicken. Something on the ground would make her want to scratch so she'd be at it for a little while before moving on and I'd be walking behind brushing the dirt back in the holes again once she'd walked off. Didn't want any of the blind pugs stumbling on the uneven ground, Arthur was out there with us so he could have fallen and more often than Amber would come doubling back around, she would have stumbled in her own freshly dug holes if I hadn't filled them in. On her biggest digging days it looked like we had ourselves a gopher, not an adult gopher, more a baby gopher out on its first dig, like it would start a hole, get bored with it or think to itself that it could do better so moved on leaving a trail of half dug holes all over the place. It was wonderful to see Amber using her front paws that way because it wasn't so long ago that her paws were buckling or she was walking on the side of them, back then they were far too weak to dig holes. I'd marvel at how well she was doing. These days she flicked her paws outwards when she was walking then pause and start scratching at the earth. The Divine One was out there getting exercise and loving every moment of it. She'd come inside and sleep for hours afterwards with her little dirty paws hanging over the edge of the bed as she slept.

With Amber she was very delicate but she was also very bold, she wasn't a sook so you'd have to watch her, you'd have to always have it in the back of your mind the area's she was the most fragile in. Protect her from herself at times. And on the rare occasion she hurt herself she wouldn't come and tell you what had gone on she'd just carry on bobbing about until you saw it for yourself. Some pugs will definitely come and tell you right away, they'll act differently, come and sit very quietly beside you drawing your attention to them until you realise there's something wrong and check them out, it can be real handy when they do that but Amber wasn't one of those pugs. To me it was like she'd just shrug what happened off, think to herself "Whatever" and carry on her way, nothing seemed to bother her. One day I was repotting some flowers and Amber had wandered off on her own I'd been looking up from time to time seeing where she was, seeing where they all were and they were never too far away. All just scattered about the place doing their own thing. They'd already had their morning walk so were now just wandering around at a leisurely pace sniffing or sitting enjoying the sun then back to taking a few steps and sniffing then sitting once again, the way old dogs do. Then one by one they would make their way back to me and I greeted each one as they came. When Amber came back I noticed she had blood on her head which quickly burst the blissful little bubble I was in. I checked her out and it looked like she'd walked into a low tree branch. They are normally cut back, due to having so many blind pugs it'd be unfair not to ensure the farm is safe for them to wander around freely without getting injured. The silver birches are left low hanging because their leaves and branches are pretty soft, they'll just be brushed aside by the pugs as they walk by. We were in the silver birch part of the farm so I can only assume that Amber had gone a little bit further on her sniffing expedition then any of the other pugs had done. I went to the shed grabbed the pruning saw and walked back down to find the offending tree. Amber came clunking down behind me, she wasn't about to miss out on another walk and I was saying to her "Come and show Mummy which nasty tree attacked you". I walked by all the silver birches and was looking at the other trees yet I couldn't see any with branches low enough to have caused Amber harm. But over by the fence a gum tree branch had come down over night and that must have been what Amber had walked into. So the branch was taken into the shed to be cut up for the fire in winter and Amber was brought inside, had her head wiped with a damp cloth, antiseptic cream smeared on, two treats popped into her mouth and she was as good as new again. She was thrilled to bits too because they weren't the normal everyday treats that she was given, no these were from the special treat jar. We have two jars here at Grace Farm, a smallish one with super special treats in them, the ones given for special occasions and a bigger regular everyday treat jar. All the treats are very yummy though, we never give them cheap tasteless treats because what's the point of that, plus you don't know what nasty horrors are put into cheap treats. I've seen owners in shops grabbing for the cheapest dog treats on the shelf and think to myself "What are you doing, don't you care about your dog at all" All our treats are tasty but the ones in the special treat jar are out of this world delicious. I love seeing the look on a little blind pugs face when a special treat gets popped into their mouth. They'll already be there fully excited anxiously waiting because they know what's coming is from the special treat stash and they know this because we give the treats from that jar special names and use a slightly different voice too. The smaller jar gets filled with all kinds of different things but we'll always give them a special sounding name, whatever pops into our heads on the day really, funny names, silly names, meaningful names, or on the rare occasions the real name of the treat, but all are said in the most excitable of voices. Captain Crunches Super Duper Sparkle Clusters is the name we were using quite a bit back then. David made the name up one day and we both burst out laughing when he said it because it was like he was putting everything special sounding into the one sentence. He was oohing and aahing as he said it and it was a pretty long word for a little treat but the pugs were hanging onto every single word he said while I looked on from the sideline laughing at the scene in front of me "Who wants one of Captain Crunche's Super Duper Sparkle Clusters, who wants one of Captain Crunche's Super Duper Sparkle Clusters" and his voice was extremely enthusiastic so of course the pugs were going nuts scrambling all over him trying to be the first in line for one of those marvellous sounding treats and they were not at all disappointed when they got one either.

Amber was a little champ at taking medication but having her ears and nails done, well, you had to be extremely careful when doing those two things, especially as she got older. Being so delicate Amber could easily faint when she was getting her ears cleaned. We would only ever do one ear at a time then do the other on a different day and also remember to not hem her in, give her lots of room, plenty of airflow around her at all times. That seemed to help and we would always stop right away if we saw she was getting upset, you could prevent her from fainting if you did that and we always wanted to avoid a fainting spell if we could. When doing her nails we were quick about it, job done then back away as fast as possible and let her be. Pugs are very well known for not liking having their nails trimmed. I have personally found that 99.9% of pugs loathe it and Amber was no different to most pugs in that area, but because she was such a delicate little flower special care needed to be taken so that was always at the back of your mind whenever you were doing anything with her. We did everything quite differently with Amber because we had to. I have only had a couple of pugs who've never bothered about nail trims. One was because she was a puppy farm survivor and believe me she had been subjected to many worse horrors so a nail trim was nothing to her and the other one is Ava Lindy Lou. Yes Ava Lindy Lou doesn't really like it but there is no pulling away. She'll just quietly let you get on with what you need to do and I really wish all my other pugs were like her because it's so much easier when they aren't trying to fight you on it. The pugs will all be looking on watching Ava Lindy Lou having her nails done and I'll be saying to David that I hope they see how good she is behaving and learn that there's nothing to worry about but then their turn comes and all hell breaks loose and you realise that watching Ava's calm demeanour hasn't had the slightest influence on them. Pugs are far worse with nail trims then they are ear cleaning but with Amber you had to be extremely mindful doing both. She was finicky when she first came and steadily got worse over the years and due to health and age the last few years of her life we had to be so very careful when doing anything at all with her. She was given a light sedative when we were going to trim her nails, she was so old and so fragile that you just had to do something to take the edge off otherwise you could well lose her, she'd panic and die all for the sake of doing a few nails. And you had to time it right too, wait for the precise time when the medication had kicked in. You'd go in too early and she'd panic, start thrashing about and gasping for air, you leave it too long and the drugs because they weren't overly potent, would begin to wear off. You go in at the twenty minute mark and everything went smoothly. Yes she was still not 100% happy with what was going on but she was calm enough now to let you do it without freaking out as much. Such a tiny pug but it was always a two man job. Always done with both of us monitoring her and if she was getting too bothered that was it you'd stop instantly. I'd hold her and talk to her while David did the trimming then she'd be put down on the ground fast and go scurrying off trying to get away. She'd clunk to the middle of the lounge room then spin round trying to sense if you were coming after her, we weren't because we were wise enough to know she'd had enough and simply let her be. You'd watch her and she'd be listening for your footsteps and when they weren't coming she'd feel happy then about re-joining the pack, come ever so cautiously clunking over and once she realised all was well then she'd be up at the side of your leg wanting a treat. She was a funny little thing really, our vet thought so, he too would be trying to do things with her and she'd pass out, so he'd back off and she'd come good. When dogs get to this tender age you just have to do what you can do and if they are fighting you then you must simply draw back and leave them to calm down because being forceful is the absolute worst thing you can be. We found the best thing to do for Amber was trim one nail a night. No need to give sedatives at those times which was great because she did become a little bit wonky, well wonkyer than usual and you didn't want her falling off the bed. It'd just be a case of me picking her up and Dave being ready to give one single nail a quick trim then she'd be in her little nest before she even knew what was going on. We could do one nail quite easily this way, but only the one, you tried for two and she would have wised up to you by that time but one, well that can be over and done with in a blink. She didn't really have time to react to it, didn't have time to get upset, that's how fast everything was done, we became quite the experts at it because we had to be in order to keep The Divine One happy and stress free. Of course if Amber was going to see our vet for something then we'd get him to do her nails while she was there. Far easier that way, we've found they play up less when it's not Mum and dad doing the trimming. Sometimes it's like they know they can get away with more with you. And you'll stand there staring in amazement watching the vet work his magic like you can't believe your eyes and you wish it was the same for you but it's not so you just have to do the best you can when you are doing it, always being careful, never ever being forceful because much damage can be done when you are. A vet was telling us one day about somebody breaking their pet rabbits back while trying to do its nails, I didn't even know rabbits needed their nails trimmed I figured they'd just get naturally worn down with digging about outside, clearly I've never had much to do with rabbits, but can you imagine how horrible you would feel doing that, he said they were more concentrating on trying to keep the rabbit still in order to get the job done and didn't realise how much pressure they were putting on the poor little thing. When doing anything with animals force should never be used, it's the same with horses, if your horse is having trouble, being flighty, playing up, pulling hard on the lead rope isn't going to make it better, the very best thing you can do is loosen the rope, give a bit of slack, allow them to calm down and come to you. Force is wrong when dealing with animals. No matter what type of animal you are dealing with force is never the answer we need to always remember that.

Amber could get very congested at times, really snotted up, both nostrils blocked. We'd take her to the vet and she'd sometimes pass out when he was trying to clear them. Occasionally he was lucky and was able to do both but if she started getting upset when he cleaned the first one the other one was left alone because we knew the next step would be her fainting. With oldies you do what you can by working with them, you would only knock them out to do a job if the job was serious because sedation has its own set of problems when it comes to delicate elderly flat faced dogs. I found that if I got Amber to walk a bit, got her body moving she was very good at clearing her nostrils herself. Well with the help of antibiotics that is because you needed something to break up the congestion in the first place. Movement was good for her, she'd get some motion up and start sneezing and blowing out goo and I'd be rushing off after her with a handful of tissues. The second she blew it out I'd be there wiping it away fast so it didn't end up hanging off her tongue and being sucked back into her system. I didn't want her swallowing it. That little tongue was always peeping out of her mouth and she was constantly flicking it around. There was a heck of a lot of snot coming out once she started walking so from time to time it did end up sticking to her tongue. At those times both her nose and tongue got quickly wiped down and she'd be on her way again and I'd be right beside her waiting for the little volcano to erupt once more. It was great seeing all that goo come flying out, great that she was getting rid of it, she could breathe a lot better afterwards. Of course it came in handy that The Divine One was such a good little walker, she didn't need encouraging to move around, just did it all by herself even though she wasn't feeling 100% at the time. It would have been hard I think if she hadn't of wanted to walk, made it harder to get her decongested. And it wasn't like I could put a lead on her and pull her along, that wouldn't have been nice for her at all. Instead I would have had to try and think of another way to get Amber moving and again it would be done by working with the personality of the dog. And in knowing how much The Divine One loved barking at the birds I probably would have waited until I could hear them chirping in the trees then pick Amber up and put her on the deck. Chirping birds was a thing that always set her off running and barking so she could have decongested herself that way too and really enjoyed herself while doing it. But there was never any need to resort to other tactics because like I said Amber loved her walks and some days all she could manage to do was take a few small steps at a time but that was all it took to get things moving, she'd start blowing out goo and feel better in herself so would then feel like taking a few more steps. Some days she'd have a normal length walk, other days just to the shed and back but it was all benefiting her. She'd walk out of the house congested and back in again feeling better and I'd come back to the house with a handful of scrunched up tissues in my mum pockets and if the log fire was going at the time I'd waltz on over and chuck them in, then watch as they went up in flames. I'd walk out of the house with a pocket full of clean tissues on one side and eye drops in the other side pocket, of course they were for the other pugs as well but Amber was the one that needed the tissues most, the eye drops, well a few of the pugs were having them put in on windy days. Arthur with those big beautiful eyes of his was especially needing a drop or two of lubricating eye drops and he was blind so I'd go rushing over and stand above him and put a drop or two in each eye, he was always on the move but my aim was good because I'd had plenty of practice doing it, very few of those drops hit the ground.

Arthur never bothered he'd just keep on walking, perhaps he thought it was raining, sometimes he'd need more than one going at, he was never concerned either way. I'd watch him walking off knowing that his eyes were now feeling a whole lot better and then I'd quickly race back to Amber to see if she needed more tissues. You feel like a proper Mum at those times, pockets full of things your kids will need when out and about. I'd seen mothers at the park looking like pack horses with all the stuff they were carrying for their kids and on our walks I look the same. In fact these days when looking for a new coat or cardigan I will generally make my choice on the amount of pockets they have, a big difference on how I used to make my choices many years ago, back then it was all about colour and style now I clothes shop like a Mum. I've never yet found anything with pockets big enough to put pug coats in though which is a shame because sometimes I can be carrying quite a few of those especially during spring time when the temperatures are all over the place. You walk out of the house with a pile of pugs trailing after you in colourful coats then one by one they'll begin panting so I'll go over, remove their coat and be walking back inside with a pile of naked little pugs and a pile of coats hanging off my arm. Sometimes when one or two of the pugs want to be carried I've had to drop the coats on the ground and go and collect them later on, and that is a pretty cute sight to see actually, a big green paddock and in the middle of it a pile of colourful little coats just waiting to be retrieved and washed.

Giving Amber cough medicine was always a happy time for her, of course I wasn't happy that she needed to have it, but it was a joy watching her taking it because she just loved the stuff. David said it was like catnip for pugs but not all the pugs liked it as much as Amber did so I guess it was really just catnip for The Divine One. She loved it so much that she would bark her little old head off for it, especially if we were being too slow and she was already on the bed waiting. I don't think she thought about the other pugs we were taking care of, she just knew that she had cough medicine before bed and she was in bed waiting and as soon as she had it that was it she'd settle down to sleep, even if we were fussing with other pugs around her she didn't mind she'd gotten what she wanted so lay in bed contently, her little eyes were closed but she wasn't always asleep, more just settling down to sleep and her eyes were closed because she had no interest in anything else that was going on after that, she'd gotten her medicine and she was satisfied for now.

There were times when we even gave it to Amber as a treat when she'd had a nail trimmed, if she was to have her cough medicine at a certain time anyway we figured we may as well give one of her nails a quick trim just before the cough medicine came out. She had it in a little disposable plastic syringe as that was the best way of giving it to her, no spilt droplets then, not that there was ever any chance of even the tiniest of drops being spilled, she'd clamp down on the end of that syringe until the medicine was all gone. Even kept a tight hold on it for a little while afterwards, probably hoping there was a surprise bit hiding in there somewhere. I think she was afraid of moving her mouth away in case she missed that last droplet. It'd be a struggle trying to get her to let go sometimes and of course you couldn't go pulling on it, couldn't pull what few teeth she had left out by accident or anything like that, you just had to stand there waiting patiently until she let go all by herself and sometimes it could take quite some time for that to happen. So one of us would stand beside Amber gently holding onto the syringe and the other one would be racing around getting all the other pugs ready for bed. And whoever was doing the racing around would laugh each time they entered the bedroom on seeing the other one standing there holding the syringe while on the other end a tiny old pug was clamping down on it for dear life.

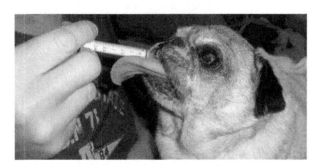

When The Divine One was on antibiotics they would sometimes come in a paste other times they came in tablet form but they got sucked down pretty fast regardless. The paste looked like melted milk chocolate but it didn't smell chocolaty at all, it didn't smell awful either, just not something I would ever like to eat but Amber had no trouble taking it. You are meant to smear the correct amount on the inside of their mouth or gums and Amber had such a little mouth, it would have been so hard giving it to her if she refused to open up, would have been difficult prying that little jaw open while trying not to hurt her teeny tiny mouth in the process. Such gentle handling would have had to be done, no brute force, but we didn't have to worry about that because she'd smell the paste coming her way and her mouth would spring open and she'd be licking it off your finger before you had time to make contact with her gums. Things went just as smoothly when she needed to take tablets. They were administrated in a different way but she'd take them just as easily. It was a two treat deal for Amber at tablet time. She'd take the first treat off you, the one with the tablet hidden in it, pretty fast but you always had to stand beside her with another treat in your hand to ensure the pill went all the way down. Be ready to give her the second treat very quickly after the first one was the best way of doing it. With the way her tongue was I didn't want the pill being flicked back out again so I'd stand beside her and if it looked like the pill was about to come shooting out of her mouth I'd hold the second treat near her face so she could smell it and when she knew there was more food coming she'd eat the first mouthful faster. She wasn't deliberately spiting it out or anything like that, it's just that due to how her tongue was it could sometimes get in the way and of course that wasn't her fault at all. It was just how this little girl was made and so I'd work with her and she was great at helping me out. Amber would even walk over to me when she heard me getting her two treats ready, she knew she had to have her medication before dinner so she'd wander over and sit in front of me with her little head tilted up. And I'd thank her for being so helpful and pop the first treat into her mouth and when the second treat had been sucked down I'd stroke her tiny head and thank her again for being such a great help to me and with that she'd wander off happily. There were days when she'd pause for a few moments with her head in the air, face still tilted up towards me, not waiting for another treat or anything like that because she knew that part was now over, more pausing while listening to what I had to say and so I would bend down again, gently cup her little chin and say "You is good, you is kind, you is Divine" then I'd stoke her little old head once again and she must have felt satisfied with the amount of praise given because she'd turn and go clunking off. I'd watch on as the little mauve coat disappeared round the corner of the island bench and a few moments later I would hear her growly bark, she'd gone out onto the deck and was now woofing at the birds but she'd shoot back inside again when she heard the bowls being filled. She always shot inside at precisely the right time, never missed out on anything, it was like she had one ear on the birds and the other one listening to what was going on inside the house. She'd hear a bit of commotion, hear one of her siblings sounding the dinner alarm and race back in lifting her paws up over the metal strip like a champ and be standing in amongst us all in no time.

One thing about Amber that I admired greatly was that no matter how she was feeling she didn't let it get her down, she made sure to enjoy her days no matter what and I have a positive attitude sure enough but Amber's attitude was off the chart. You couldn't be around her and not be affected by it. She didn't make a big deal out of showing you what she was doing or anything like that it was more that you knew how she was feeling so would be keeping an eye on her and see her pottering about doing her own little thing not letting anything spoil the day for her and I'd stand there and marvel. Amber didn't let the condition within herself or the conditions around her dampen her spirit. I'd watch on and be thinking to myself "You go you little optimistic warrior you" One day it was raining, rained all day long and the pugs had been holding their little bladders for the longest time just waiting for the rain to ease off enough for us to make it out to the shed. When I heard the heavy drops slow to a pitter-patter I grabbed a handful of treats and lured them all outside. The hay shed is a perfect spot for everyone to empty their bladders on rainy days, I'll throw some old hay down on the ground and they all start weeing on that and then we all shoot back inside again pretty fast. Well that's what normally happens most times anyway but this day Amber decided she hadn't had her normal amount of sniffing time and wasn't going back inside the house until she had. The other pugs knowing the routine ran from the shed and up the ramp fast and were all standing at the back door looking out at what Amber and I were doing. Not interested enough to join us, more just curious to know what was going on, but wanted to keep dry while doing it. But not The Divine One she wasn't going to let a few drops of rain stop her from getting a good sniff in. And I was ok with that I was expecting her to take a bit more time than the others because choosing just the right spot to wee on was her thing. Normally when it's raining she's a little quicker finding her spot but not on this day she wasn't. Clearly the rain was not bothering her as much as it was bothering me. Normally I love rain and am even known to go for a walk in it, a thing that still makes my husband shake his head. But this day I must have been in a mood or something because I just desperately wanted to go back inside the house. It wasn't cold out there and the rain was only light so I followed Amber around putting her under the umbrella instead of me making sure my little old blessing didn't get wet while she was sniffing about. Anyway I stood there with my face pulling in all directions and then I looked down at Amber, she was happy sniffing the ground and flicking her little tongue in and out and I thought what the heck am I being so miserable for, why am I not allowing myself to enjoy this experience as much as she is, so I lent my head back and let the rain fall lightly on my face and instantly became happier for having done so, in a matter of seconds my mood had changed. I took my lead from Amber and began enjoying this day I had been given. I had my eyes closed but was always listening out for Amber scuffling off so I could keep her under the umbrella, but the whole experience became so much happier for me. When Amber finally indicated she'd had her fill I picked her up and kissed her grey face and thanked her for what she had just allowed me to experience. I walked inside the house feeling lucky and blessed. Sometimes it takes a little old pug with a much better attitude then you yourself have to remind you of how very lucky you are.

I remember our 24th wedding anniversary clearly because we spent the evening at the vet with Amber, she was really ill that day, lots of trouble breathing and I thought we were going to lose her. She had been sick for a few days and on medication but it wasn't helping her much. I'd not slept well for a few nights as I was constantly worrying about her and checking if she was ok. Then she took a turn for the worse on our anniversary, so I called David home from work in the afternoon and we set off for the vet. Amber had been booked in for seven that evening but we called ahead and said we were coming in early and they said fine we'll just fit you in when you get here. X-rays showed there were no growths on her lungs but her left lung was infected, that's what I had been hearing, an infection not a tumour and we were relieved about that. So Amber had a few injections and we got sent home with a fistful of new medication.

On the way home we stopped off for a quick chicken burger and Amber sat happily on David's knee sniffing the air and eating little bits of chicken. She'd not eaten much of late but as soon as the injections started to kick in she became ravenous and was letting us know by her soft little barks. It was like she was saying "Hey I've had my injections now I want a reward for being a good girl" We couldn't cool the chicken down fast enough for her. Both of us were ripping bits off and blowing on them like crazy. She'd gulp a piece down and a second later her little head would shoot up and she'd be sniffing the air again and woofing for more. It was wonderful to see her appetite had returned, that made both of us happy, because she'd not eaten much all day she was quite hungry, and quite hungry to a pug is practically starving. They miss one meal and feel like a great injustice has been done. Amber ate most of the fillet out of my burger and was still looking around for more, well not looking because she's blind but sniffing and woofing and licking her lips. I was more than a bit hungry myself yet there I was madly breaking the hot fillet up and burning my fingers doing it. But my hungry sick child spurred me on so I was blowing on the food with all my might so it wouldn't burn her sweet little mouth and she was impatiently barking her little old head off for more and more as she sat opposite me. I'd brought a towel with me in the hope that Amber would want to eat. Towels can be so handy when you are feeding pugs in cars, especially when you are feeding blind pugs in cars because they drop bits of food all the time and a towel catches them nicely before they disappear between the seats because once they disappear it can take almost half an hour to fish them out when you get home. Like a little bird Amber sat perched on her Daddy's knee squawking and opening her mouth for food as soon as she sensed my hand near her face. David and I were so pleased she was doing that because it gave us hope. Sure she was being demanding but neither one of us cared. Dave rolled down the car window and hung his hand outside to cool the chicken down faster. The Divine One wanted food and at that point we would have given her anything, peeled prawns and hand fed them to her if that's what she had wanted to eat. When she was carried into the surgery our vet said he thought she was on her last legs but as Amber was carried out the door again she seemed to spark up a little bit and I think it was because she knew food was on its way, because food is always on its way after a visit to the vet and Amber knew the routine well. I did feel real sorry for her though because being blind she didn't know what was happening so the x-ray was an ordeal, a few different people were handling her, passing her from one to the other in order to get the job done and she was very jumpy afterwards. Not feeling well and the strange sounds and smell of the vet surgery wouldn't have helped either. Whenever anybody touched her she'd jump a mile because didn't know who's hand it was, eventually it was solely mine and David's but she still jumped regardless and it took a while for her to settle down, the chicken helped a lot because after she'd eaten a few mouthfuls she didn't jump at our touch anymore, her mind was now on the food she was receiving and she knew exactly who was feeding it to her.

Amber slept soundly all the way home. Her tummy was now full and by this time she was breathing a lot easier too and her breathing continued to improve throughout the night. When we pulled into the driveway our neighbours came walking down to the gate, they said they were having a big anniversary party on the weekend and that we might like to make sure our horses and sheep were put in a paddock not too close to their house, they didn't want the loud music frightening them. We thanked them for letting us know then smiled as we drove up the driveway, we thought the differences in our wedding anniversaries was amusing, similar amount of years were being celebrated but both were done in very different ways. We thought they would have laughed if they'd known our celebration was a vet visit and a chicken burger and theirs was a party for a hundred people with a live band. But they didn't even know it was our anniversary, they had only recently moved in, such things had not been discussed. We came up the driveway with yet another vet bill in our hands but we were happy and content. Well not happy that Amber was sick but happy with the way we live our life with our little pug family. We did not for one second begrudge the people next door their big party, we were just relieved we hadn't been invited. We'd dodged that bullet and were thankful. We are not party people, we never have been, quiet nights at home with our pugs suits us just fine and we were really thrilled that night because we made it home before dark, just in enough time to grab a quick cup of tea and go sit on the deck to watch the sun going down. That's the kind of things we live for, quiet nights with the pugs while mother nature entertains us with her finest glories. The following weekend wasn't so peaceful, that party went on for hours, we were glad the horses and sheep had another paddock to escape to. Whisper is a very nervous horse, Gerald couldn't care less, he was probably wishing he had been invited to the party, but as far as the sheep and

Whisper went they were very glad to be kept away. We gave them extra food so they wouldn't have to worry about grazing, they could go and feel safe near the trees at the far end of our property, as far away from the noise and lights as they could get without venturing onto somebody else's farm. What I remember most about that weekend is Amber standing in the middle of the lounge room barking her little old head off at the music that was ringing loudly in the air. I remember looking down at her and being grateful to have her feeling somewhat more like her normal self, she was a ball of energy that night, the injections had done their job and the antibiotics were doing their job too. She was running from one door to the other then racing out onto the deck in a frenzied manner, the noise of the partygoers was something different for her to bark at and she was really enjoying her little self. Seeing her like that made my heart smile especially after how she'd been in the last week. To be honest I think she was having just as much fun as everybody next door was having and who knows perhaps Amber was trying to sing, she could hear the partygoers singing and maybe my little mouse thought she'd give it a go.

CHAPTER FIFTEEN

Bunnings

Most of the work we do around here we do ourselves because it cuts down on labour costs, we feel our money is better spent on vet bills and animal expenses but even if there weren't so many vet bills and animal expenses I think we would still try and do the work ourselves, most people would do wouldn't they. And we like doing work here because unless the job at hand is dangerous we can have all the pugs around us sniffing and watching on, work, just like everything else on Grace Farm is a family affair. But there are always going to be times when you cannot do the work yourself so we will go ahead and call somebody in. We've had a few workmen here over the years but I think everybody's favourite was definitely Bunnings, everybody loved Bunnings especially Amber. And the thing was he loved her as much as she did him, she very soon became his favourite. But even though he knew she was a girl he always referred to her as "The little fella". Amber would be standing there in the pinkest coat we had in the entire house and he'd still bend down, stroke her greying ears and say "How you doing little fella" but Amber didn't care, she was getting attention and that attention when given by Bunnings usually came with a treat so really I don't think she cared what he called her to be honest. When Bunnings was first called out to the farm The Divine One had been living with us for quite a few years so of course felt she was very much in charge of the property and had to investigate everything that went on in it. She was quite a good little guard dog actually, never held back when approaching somebody, no fear there, even though she was approaching them with little to no sight she'd still clunk up to them with all the confidence in the world and would stand a few feet away using all her other senses to get a feel for them. She knew the farm like that back of her paw, had it all well mapped out in her mind and she had a great little nose on her too so instantly knew whenever there was somebody different here. She'd find them in no time and suss them out, some interested her more than others did. I guess it all depended on who they were and if they were animal people or not because dogs, especially blind dogs can tell these things about strangers pretty fast. And if they didn't like dogs Amber tended not to waste her time on them, I figured in her mind she was thinking "Your loss buddy" and off she would go, clunking her way back into the house without a backward glance. But Bunnings was a definite animal lover all of us could tell that about him pretty fast. Bunnings wasn't his real name but by the time he crossed my path he'd been called Bunnings for so long I don't even think he remembered what his real name was. Bunnings was recommended to me by a friend, "A bloke you can trust to do a job" he said then added "And not only that but do it properly and not rip you off" well that sounded pretty good to me so I called the number I'd been given. It had been scribbled across a ratty bit of paper pulled out of a pocket in the middle of a paddock. On first go I'd called the wrong number, not my fault, just had trouble reading the last digit written down, I thought it was a five but on closer inspection realised it was an eight so called again and listened to the gravelly voice saying hello. At first I felt kind of uncomfortable calling him Bunnings, I figured it was a nickname made up by his friends and because I didn't know him I felt I had no right to use such familiarities. But Bunnings was the only name I'd been given so I had to go with that. At first I figured it was his surname and almost called him Mr Bunnings and I believe if I had done so he would have roared with laughter and repeated the story many times over. In time I came to learn the real reason people had started calling him Bunnings though. It was on account of his ute and shed, well mainly his shed, it was a massive shed he had on his property and it was full to the brim with this and that. Mainly building materials, end of line items, things you couldn't get anymore, tiles, light fittings, bricks, pavers and taps stuff like that. Outside there were sheets of corrugated iron leant against the shed wall, walk a few feet and you'd find fence posts, wooden sleepers and the odd farm gate. And yes he even had a kitchen sink, had a few of them actually. It was like if Bunnings didn't have it nobody did and that was how he'd gotten his name. And in your mind you may be conjuring up a heaped mess but it wasn't like that at all, everything was neatly placed, tidily stacked, he'd built proper shelving and the shed was set out in isles, it really did look like the inside of a Bunnings store. The only thing he didn't have were shopping carts for people to use, well he did have one old shopping cart but that sat over by the trunk of a huge tree with bits of red gum in it. Everything in his shed had a place, nuts and bolts sat on shelves in jars, the shed didn't have a lock on the door, had done at one time but it was broken and he didn't feel the need to replace it because country folk don't steal from one another was the answer I'd been given and I hoped he was right because Bunnings was such a nice man I'd have hated for anybody to have done the wrong thing by him. But I do think if somebody had done wrong by Bunnings the entire town would have tracked them down and made things right. Everybody knew Bunnings, he was liked and he was relied on. People generally dropped by his place first before going to the store. And on the very rare occasion Bunnings didn't have what you were looking for he certainly knew where you could get it and if you were willing to listen to one of his stories he would eventually tell you. Bunnings didn't always sell things, he often traded them. Traded them for anything really, items from your garden, your shed, your paddock and even things you had made yourself. And more often than not it was Bunnings who came off worse for wear but he didn't seem to mind, he liked helping people and he liked talking to people. I think half his fun was gotten from talking to people while the bartering was being done. I'd often drive by his farm and see people working off their debt and working right there beside them, working harder than anyone else was Bunnings himself. When farmers were selling up, selling up for good not just moving on Bunnings was called in first to see if they had anything he wanted and he was rarely charged for what he took, they let him have it for nothing because then he owed you a favour and Bunnings was the best person in the world to have owe you a favour. And he could owe you that favour for years before you called it in but he always responded, he always remembered those he owed. Sometimes I'd go out to look for him and find he'd walked off half way through a job, a little note scribbled on an offcut of wood telling you where he'd gone and what time he thought he'd be back, clearly he had come up to the house to tell me but when he couldn't find me he left a note. Bunnings was somebody you could count on in a crisis, just call his number and he'd drop what he was doing and come and help you out. I've found blokes like this are never short of friends and he sure did have a heck of a lot of friends.

I don't know what his true profession had actually been but by the time I met Bunnings he was a jack of all trades. He'd often refer to himself as a master of none, but that wasn't right because he had a great knowledge of a good many things. And the work he did was brilliant, no matter what the job was he did it well and you'd complement him on it and he'd brush it off with a wave of his hand, he wasn't good at receiving complements. He liked getting them though you could see it in his eyes because they smiled when you praised him but as for a response, well I just don't think he knew what to say so he'd wave you off but I reckon when he got home that night he would have remembered every single word you'd said to him and gone over it in his head a good many times while he was eating dinner. More than likely told his wife about it too when she was still alive. "I'm a generalist not a specialist" he'd tell me, but I didn't believe that for a second. If I had to guess I would have said that Bunnings had started out as a carpenter but as with all blokes who work on building sites, they don't just stick to doing the one thing, if their job is finished and somebody else is still going they'll jump in and give them a hand, it's just what people do, well it's what people of Bunnings generation did anyway, I'm not sure if it's still the case now. But you can learn a lot by doing that which is exactly what Bunnings had done. So he'd not only be able to tell you all about woodwork he knew things about plumbing, tiling, plastering, bricklaying and electrical work too. He was in fact a very intelligent bloke, you could have a conversation with him about absolutely any subject and he'd enlighten you with all these facts, the way his mind worked was quite remarkable. You can have some fantastic conversations with people like this and that's exactly what Bunnings and I did over the course of our association. The first time I called him out I had no idea what sort of man was about to get out of the ute. I'd kept the pugs inside because some of them can go completely nuts when meeting new people and I didn't know if he was up to having a pile of pugs setting upon him in a circling licking jumping up manner. I don't mind things like that but some people do so I held my lot back until I knew the kind of person I was dealing with. Also some people can be really clumsy around small dogs, not look down when walking, not do the slow shuffle I often do, if you are not used to being around so many elderly dogs you will not be aware of where you are putting your feet and I didn't want any of my little blessings getting trodden on. It was best for me to meet this workman on my own and if he ended up being a dog person then I would explain to him about my old, blind, deaf pugs and then allow him to come over and meet them once he knew how to behave. And in writing this sentence I've realised that I've made myself sound like an old and very strict school teacher but what I mean is how to behave around dogs that have special needs. To be respectful of them at all times.

I always put an image to a new voice when I hear one, been doing it since I was a kid, with the radio mainly but I do it with new people on the end of a phone line too and that's exactly what I'd done as I was talking to Bunnings, but the man who got out of the ute didn't match my image in the slightest. My phone Bunnings was tall, sandy haired and slender, the real Bunnings was none of these things, he was a peculiar looking fellow, but he didn't seem to be aware of it and so I pretended not to be too. Short and round he was, especially in the middle, reminded me a bit of a spinning top. I'd see him trotting past the veranda, his head level with my hand and I so wanted to lean over, grab hold and spin him and I reckon if I had of done he would have spun round that front paddock for the longest time. I never told him any of this of course because such things are best kept to oneself, but I thought about it a lot, especially during the first few months I knew him, after that I guess I just got used to him being the way he was. He gave me a quote on the job and it wasn't as high as I had expected it to be so what I'd been told about Bunnings was true. He wasn't out to rip anybody off, a fair price for a fair days work were the rules Bunnings lived by. The day of the quote Bunnings didn't get to meet the pugs. No doubt he would have heard them woofing, but he did what he was here for and was on his way in no time. It was arranged for him to come out the following Wednesday to do the job and that's when he did end up meeting everybody. When he drove up I didn't realise it was him at first because he was in a different ute and his clothing was different too, I realised I had met him in his quote clothes and now he had overalls on. Seeing as he wasn't dressed as smartly I figured letting the hounds loose was an ok thing to do and it was. He instantly dropped to his knees and began receiving each pug as they came filing down the ramp and they wandered down at different intervals, on this particular day there was no rushing, so he was able to give each one a far bit of attention before the other one's decided to come down. Amber was the last one to venture outside to meet him, she had been on the front deck sunning herself and was in no rush to move. But I guess at some point she figured she may as well go see what all the fuss was about because none of us seemed to be coming back in any hurry and she must have gotten tired of sitting out there by herself. She came clunking down the ramp and stopped a few feet from where Bunnings was kneeling, suddenly her little face came up and she began sniffing the air. He had cows on his property and I think that's what she could smell on him, my dad has cows too so after pausing for a few moments The Divine one must have just figured it was grandad so walked over to sniff his boots the way she always did with my dad, but the hand that reached out to stroke her wasn't grandads so she gave the unfamiliar hand a long lingering sniff. As the pugs had come down the ramp I'd been giving Bunnings a running commentary on each one, it was a bit like a fashion show only I wasn't describing clothing I was relating each ones name and whether they were blind or deaf or not. Just so he knew how to behave with each pug as they approached him. Amber seemed alright with letting him touch her, she didn't wag her tail, due to her back she wasn't much of a tail wagger. But she was content enough in his presence, not as ecstatic as some of the other pugs were but she was not unhappy either, her mannerisms told me she was ok and the longer he was patting her the more ok she was with him doing it. Bunnings hadn't seen Amber coming down the ramp because he was busy patting and re-patting all the other pugs. He may not have even heard me saying her name or that she was blind. He only became aware of her when she got closer to him "And who is this little fella then" he asked. Amber was wearing a two toned pink coat, clearly looking very much like a little girl but I think the term "Fella" was what Bunnings used to call a lot of the animals he came across. Maybe because he wasn't good at remembering names and in our house you couldn't blame him for that. The coat Amber was wearing was knitted in two types of wool, a smooth kind and a shaggy kind, four or five rows of each. A friend said it looked like strips of bacon and as much as I didn't like the fact I had to admit that it really did, same colour same striped pattern, after that every time I looked at it I could hear my friend's words. Anyway Bunnings didn't seem to see the coat he only saw Amber and he liked what he saw. The little tongue hanging out of her mouth drew him in just as it had drawn me in a few years earlier. She looked simply adorable standing there looking up at him. In my mind I imagined her thinking to herself "Grandad but not Grandad" as she sniffed his boots.

After the initial meeting and seeing how gentle Bunnings was with all the pugs I knew it would be ok if I left the door open while he was here working. I told him the pugs were used to coming and going as they pleased and he nodded his head. I also told him that he must let me know whenever he was going to move his ute so I could make sure all the pugs were safely inside the house. He nodded his head again and said "They'll be ok with me, I won't flatten um" and I walked back inside thinking well thank god for that. Most of the pugs left him alone when he was working, once a fuss had been made and a pat had been given, the novelty of having somebody here wore off pretty fast and they'd come waddling up the ramp and hop into their beds. Amber was the one who was most fascinated with him though and that was because he used to share his yogurt with her, he did it once and that was it, she wanted to share it all the time from then on. He'd let her lick the empty container and she loved doing that. The first day he was here I saw him scrap that container clean but after Amber showed an interest he didn't scrap his spoon around as many times as he used to do, he always left a tiny bit for her. And sometimes she'd be standing there for the longest time licking at it, making sure she got every last bit but he didn't seem to mind holding the container up for her, he'd even tilt it on different angles if he thought she'd missed a spot, just doing all he could to make things easier for her. I would watch Bunnings studying Amber. Listening to the sounds she made and watching her little face trying to get as far into that empty yogurt container as it could go. He'd sit on the ground smiling down at her and she'd be there having the time of her life. And while Bunnings was looking at Amber I'd be studying his terry towelling hat, at first I thought he was wearing the same navy blue hat every single day but over time I came to notice that each one had different paint splotches on them. He had seven of those hats, one for each day and I came to know the paint patterns on each and every one of them. Some had a few speckles in certain areas whereas others were completely covered. Mostly white paint but some had a few different colours mixed in. Sometimes as he was talking I would be studying the paint splotches more closely, like make eye contact every now and then, just to let him know I was listening and then back to the paint patterns my eyes would go wondering what job he was doing when they happened and for whom. I also wondered if he spent as much time talking to them as he did to me. I think a lot of people liked listening to Bunnings talk. You paid him for the job not for the hours spent so people didn't mind at all that he was a bit of a talker. No job was too big or too small for Bunnings and he worked each one at his own pace, you couldn't hurry him along, not that I ever tried, I liked that he lived his life like that, not too many people do that these days, some because they can't afford to and others because they don't want to. We live in a fast world that seems to be getting faster and faster all the time which in a way is kind of sad I think. I do believe people would be a lot happier if they slowed down once in a while because it does the soul good. Anyway Bunnings was a bloke who lived his life well and I liked that about him. Another thing I really liked about Bunnings was he always cleaned up after himself because a lot of workmen these days don't tend to do that. I don't know if it's due to ignorance or always being on the clock but when you have pugs wandering round the place you need to have somebody who cares enough to not leave shavings on the ground to get stuck in little old paws. I liked that I could rely on him. I'd often go out and pay him while he was cleaning up, you'd hear the broom going and know he would soon be leaving for the day so I'd make sure the pugs were safely inside then tuck Amber under my arm and stride out there so we could say goodbye. Because Amber was his favourite he always wanted to say goodbye to her. Most days I'd stand talking to him while he was finishing up but if I was busy doing something and hadn't heard the broom he'd come up to the house and shout "Oo-roo" through the back door or an open window and that'd be it for the day, he'd be on his way.

Bunnings liked smoko to be on time, made that pretty clear from day one "Smoko's at ten thirty on the dot" he shouted out to me before getting on with the job and that's where the sharing yogurt with Amber thing all started. Each day at ten thirty he'd have a tub of yogurt and a cup of tea. He'd supply the yogurt I'd supply the tea. He was offered a seat in the house but declined, a lot of workmen do because they don't like to make a mess in the house, it's not just their boots that are dirty, if it was that would be an easy fix they'd just leave them on the doormat and come on in. It's their overalls they are thinking about, they don't want to sit down and mess up the furniture. So I'd take a cup of tea out for myself as well and sat on a bale of hay talking. Amber would follow me down the ramp because she knew what smoko meant. Bunnings always brought a small pale blue foam esky with him when he worked, white lid, rope handle, and whenever I saw that being taken out of the ute that was my signal to put the kettle on. He knew what I was doing so would set his lunchbox to one side and carry on working until mine and Amber's face appeared in the entrance of the shed. A few times I missed seeing him going to the ute, didn't even realise what time it was until I saw him at the kitchen window, when he finally caught my eye he'd hold the esky up and I'd nod in acknowledgment and off he'd go. Sometimes I wondered how long he had actually been standing there for. One day I was cleaning ash from the fire so I could get more logs in when the temperature dropped, clearing out the ash isn't exactly a quick job and I know I was enthralled in what I was doing. Well I guess enthralled isn't really the right word here, more I was concentrating on getting all the ash out without dropping any and my mind was on something or other because it always is, but time had gotten away from me that morning and because the pugs were used to Bunnings being around they didn't alert me to the fact that he was standing there. I guess he could have knocked but I think he was too polite to do that, didn't want to interrupt me while I was busy so waited patiently until I turned around and when I did I almost shot through the ceiling. Being off in my own little world of thoughts I had completely forgotten there was a workman on the property and he was in the shade of the veranda so it was more a figure of a man I was looking at from the shoulders up, other than wearing a hat there were no other visible signs it was Bunnings. And besides a lot of blokes in Australia wear hats. To me it looked like some strange man had wandered up to the house and I was just weighing things up when I recognised who it was. It reminded me of a decade or so back when David was on holidays. I go into my own little world an awful lot, always thinking about something or someone, I've been a deep thinker all my life, these days I'm usually thinking pugs and people I have loved and when I do that I get quite absorbed to the point of not being aware of anything else. Anyway David was in the study and both of us entered the hallway at exactly the same time, both at different ends and I looked up and saw this big bloke in the darkened hallway coming towards me and his frame was huge, his head was close to the ceiling. I was so used to David being at work that I'd forgotten he was home, he is a quiet sort of a bloke so that's an easy thing to do and when he wasn't working he did spend an awful lot of time in his study. I didn't recognise it as being my husband at first so my heart started racing. I thought we were being robbed and knew I had no hope in hell of fighting a bloke as big as this one off. I only had Sarah and Harper back then and we were in that little red brick house, our very first home but for a second or two I was really worried about our safety. I actually let out a god awful scream when I saw him which made David, Sarah and Harper all physically jump. He said "What the hell are you screaming for? He'd never heard me yell like that before, I don't think he knew I could scream so loud and if I am being honest up until that point neither did I. But everybody got a fright that day and after I'd settled down we had a good laugh about it. You have no idea how relieved I felt when it was David, to go from fear and uncertainty to realising it was somebody you know was such a relief. It was only a few seconds of unrecognition but in those few seconds so many thoughts went racing through my mind, what to grab to try and defend myself, whether I could turn and make it out the front door with Sarah and Harper before he caught us and also trying to remember if any of the neighbours were home at the time so they could come and help me. Well Bunnings didn't scare me as much as David had done but it was still unnerving seeing a man staring in your kitchen window. After that I always made sure to be on time and a couple of times Amber was even ahead of schedule, I guess she must have wanted her yogurt and wasn't in the mood for waiting. She'd rise up from her bed and clunk out the door at around ten or ten fifteen in search of Bunnings and it never took her very long to find him. One day I was watching on, saw The Divine One get to the bottom of the ramp and assume the position and by assuming the position I mean she paused and her little nose shot into the air and begin sniffing, she was listening for him too I could tell that by the way her head kept tilting ever so slightly in different directions. Bunnings was always tinkering with something, so she'd sniff for him and listen for him and then followed the sound pausing every now and then to sniff the air again. When she found him he was kneeling on the floor doing something with a pipe so she marched up to him and sniffed his legs. I saw him turn, stroke her head, say "Hello little Fella" I always thought Amber was far too pretty to ever be mistaken for a boy but clearly Bunnings didn't. He started talking to her as he put his tools down. "Would you like a treat little fella" Amber wasn't for moving so I guess he realised that she did so went and grabbed his esky from the passenger seat of his ute. Amber was still standing where he'd left her so he walked over and put the esky on the ground. Amber's little head came up to sniff the air but the lid wasn't off the esky yet so she couldn't smell anything and I imagined her being pretty unimpressed with that. I saw him take out a banana and offer it to Amber to sniff, well she really did love bananas and from her reaction he could tell this so began peeling it and sharing it with her and seeing that the two of them were having a nice time I went and put the kettle on.

After the banana eating incident we didn't see Bunnings for a while but we did have two other workmen come here one day and Amber was able to con food out of them too, well once she'd befriended them she did anyway. When she first approached she was doing her usual guard dog thing, the way she walked up to them it was like she was fully ready to take these newcomers on and I smiled because the only thing she would have been able to do was pull on their socks and I doubted that'd be enough to wrestle them to the ground but her stance said she was up for giving it a go should the need arise. Looking at her standing in front of them like that made me smile all the more, tiny, ever so tiny, beautiful but funny little body, no sight, tongue hanging out and yet she was the only one out there defending the farm. Amber had a way of standing like she thought she was ten feet tall, and I imagined her thinking to herself as she stood there that "You can't trust anybody these days can you" I think she felt it was her duty to protect her family and she wasn't about to let lack of size or lack of vision stop her from doing it. Everything about her posture was saying so. Her approach, her stance, even her little growly woofs had a bit more of an effort put into them. She was out there oozing confidence and the workmen looked down at her like she was the funniest thing they had ever seen, but their laughter didn't put her off she clunked a few steps closer and began sniffing their boots and the two of them couldn't stop laughing. One looked up and said "Is this your idea of a guard dog" I smiled and said "Are either one of you game enough to take her on" they laughed and said they wouldn't dream of it. One of them asked what her name was and when I said The Divine One they laughed even harder. Amber was in her element when it was smoko time for these two though because they had the most wonderful things to eat, where Bunnings had yogurt and bananas these workmen had chips and sandwiches with delicious fillings. Bunnings brought sandwiches too but because of his dodgy stomach his fillings were kind of bland. But these two blokes were young and their stomachs could handle anything, they were at least thirty or so years away from having to worry about dodgy stomachs so Amber would hang around them while they ate. They'd sit on bales of hay and she'd stand in front of them growly woofing, demanding they give her some of their food. I went to bring her inside because I could hear what was going on and I wasn't sure if they were going to be as kind and generous as Bunnings was and I didn't want my little blessing being disappointed. I thought I'd just bring Amber in and give her a treat, not the normal everyday treats but a treat from the special stash, I knew she would be happy enough with that. But as I was walking towards the shed I heard one of the electricians say to his mate "Give the old blind dog the other half you heartless bastard" He must have only given her half a chip at first, it was a pretty big chip so maybe he thought she couldn't handle the whole thing being so little. But what they didn't know was that Amber would probably have eaten all their leftover chips if they'd left them unattended. I found out that she'd had two chips and a bit of roast beef from one of their sandwiches and I figured that was enough for her for one day. I thanked them for sharing then picked Amber up and brought her inside and she told me off all the way back to the house because she didn't want to come inside she wanted to be out with the workmen where all the fun food was. But her mood didn't stay sour for long because they were cutting hay over the road and she loved woofing at the sound the tractors made, couldn't see what was going on but loved the smells and sounds. She'd run along the veranda when the machine started up, then spin round and come running all the way back. Then they'd stop for a bit and she'd come inside but as soon as she heard them again out she would go as fast as her little legs could carry her. By the end of the day she'd completely worn herself out. Then a few days later when they came back to bale the hay she was out there again woofing up a storm. And I thought it was good that she'd gotten a few days rest in-between because she really did need it.

A year or so passed before we saw Bunnings again. But then David went into hospital and came out worse for wear so Bunnings number was dialed. He was told over the phone what needed doing and knew our place well so didn't need instructions. I saw his ute in the driveway but he wasn't sitting in it so I popped my head inside the shed and saw that he was busy summing up the situation. I figured I'd leave him to it and took off in the direction of the horse water and started filling it up. I put Amber on the ground to have a wee and she was sniffing about near the trees when Bunnings finally joined us. When he went over to stroke her head she jumped back a little because she wasn't expecting it. I think in his absence he had forgotten she was blind. As soon as he realised he'd startled her he remembered though and you could tell he felt really bad about frightening her so from then on he would lean in and let her have a sniff of his hand before touching her, that way she knew what was coming and she loved those pats I could tell she did. But what she loved more was what Bunnings kept in his esky. I think that's what she remembered about him most and if she could talk I have no doubt she would have been asking him if he had his esky in the ute and if he did what he had in it that day. The job he was doing was a four dayer so Amber got to have smoko with him quite a few times. And she didn't have to be reminded either, the first day Amber must have heard the ute door open and close because she took off and was clunking down the ramp before I caught up with her, she had a mauve coat on that day, I could see this little prettily dressed figure disappearing down the ramp as I grabbed the two cups of tea off the bench. And she wasn't for stopping, no waiting for mummy that day. I think she would have made it all the way to the shed by herself if I hadn't caught up to her, she was doing a very determined walk, it was raining lightly but she didn't seem to mind, she wasn't about to let such a thing stop her from getting her treat. Bunnings had seen her coming and when we both walked into the shed he was sitting on a bale of hay and beside him was an empty yogurt container with a nice thin layer of yogurt left around the sides for Amber.

"Having a play"

CHAPTER SIXTEEN

Ho Ho Nooooo

It was early December and I was talking to a friend who was telling me he was dressing up as Santa Claus for a pug rescue event he was attending the following weekend. He had already tried on his suit and was laughing about how it made him look, with him being so short he said it looked like he was wearing his big brothers hand me downs, so a lady from the group was busily taking both the pants and the sleeves up for him. He was really looking forward to playing Santa and I knew exactly why that would be, imagine all those little pugs being placed on your knee for a photo. I thought it was a brilliant idea, brilliant that all the pugs who had been adopted out by that particular group got to meet up once a year for a big Christmas party. It would be a chance for both the pugs and their owners to catch up with one another and to me that was a really beautiful thing to do. Personally I would be looking forward to an event like that all year round. Imagine the level of happiness there, the joy and excitement in the air, the younger pugs all running round playing with each other while the older ones sat in prams sleeping or watching them depending on how they were feeling. It would be a wonderful time for everyone involved. And due to my friend they would all be going home with a photo of their pug sitting on Santa's knee, to me that made it all the more special. I really wished I had been able to attend the party but the event was overseas, I had no chance of going, not with all the little old pugs I had to take care of here. And in knowing of my commitments he promised to send me lots of photos so I didn't miss out and I was happy enough with that, but the next day when I was out walking the pugs I started thinking about our conversation and I decided that I would love some Santa photos of my own. I have always done Christmas photos here on the farm, pugs in hats or chewing on dog treats that look like candy cane, I've also got some beautiful photos of the pugs laying underneath a heavily decorated tree and pugs rolling around in tinsel when the tree is being taken down. I've got a great photo of Emily sitting on the couch chewing a Santa toy and Arthur with little white antlers perched on the top of his blind head. And the photo of Tommy sitting with some low hanging baubles around his ears is actually one of my all-time favourite Christmas photos. I think it is a draw with the one I have of Horton sitting on our ottoman in front of the tree, it was Horton's second Christmas with us and he was so little that I had to bring him up to the height of the tree branches so the ottoman was moved over and he sat there like a little champ while I took a couple of happy snaps. Then I picked him up and gave him a few treats. He didn't have his nappy on because December is summer here in Australia so he was having a bit of nappy free time as he generally did when the weather was warm. Anyway he ended up having a little bit of a wee on me while I was feeding him the treats and I smiled when he did that because I knew he was enjoying himself. So I changed my dress, gave Horton a quick bath and we all went out onto the deck so he could dry off in the sun.

I couldn't wait for Dave to get home from work so I could share my idea with him. I was so excited about getting a pile of photos of the pugs with Santa because it was something we'd never done here before, I don't know why I'd never thought about it but I hadn't. One year I did think about taking some of the pugs to have their photos with the pet store Santa but some of them were really old and I knew they wouldn't have been comfortable with all that noise and all those people. They are used to a quiet life on the farm, something like that would have been far from how they normally spent their days, some of them would have been petrified. Besides I couldn't take everybody down there at the one time and I didn't think it fair to only have two or three pugs done. In my mind it was everybody or nobody so up until now it had been nobody but all that was about to change and I was ecstatic about it. I was telling a friend what I was planning to do and she said "If you can't take the pugs to Santa then you bring Santa to the pugs" and I said "Exactly" and again couldn't believe I hadn't thought about doing something like this sooner. When I talked to David about it he wasn't so taken with the idea, well he was until he realised it was him who would be dressing up. His response was "No, noooo, hell noooo". And I said to him who else do you think would be playing Santa? Me? I mean I could do Mrs Claus and would have had a great deal of fun doing that but it just wouldn't be the same so I left David with getting used to the idea and set about finding a Santa Claus suit for him. The one I found was a bit cheap and crappy but I was in a rush the day I went to the shops so I shot into the first store I came across that looked like it would sell what I was looking for and it did so I bought it then got back in the car and headed home. It was the pugs I was rushing to get back to. A few were clingy that morning so I really didn't like leaving them but I had to go out as I had an appointment that couldn't be cancelled and I wasn't going to waste time looking for a slightly better Santa suit because I figured they would all be more or less the same. I mean unless you are going to play Santa every year then you really wouldn't put money into a suit that was made of better material and I was having enough trouble getting David to wear a suit this year the chances of him agreeing to do it every year were incredibly slim. Besides those heavy Santa suits are more for continents where it snows, white Christmases and thick Santa suits go perfectly well together but our Christmases are hot. On Aussie Christmas cards Santa wears a singlet, shorts and thongs. There is no snow to encourage one to want to put on a thick suit and beard. This was one of the many issues David had with playing Santa, he doesn't like the heat as it is and having to deal with it while dressed from head to toe was not thrilling him in the slightest. I told Dave my friend in America was really looking forward to it and he said of course he would be, he's not doing it in soaring heat is he. But even though David was grumbling I wasn't for backing down, I couldn't, the images in my head of all my little blessings having a photo with Santa Claus was spurring me on. I even thought about trying to hire a snow machine to make the photos look even better but that thought only lasted half a second, one because it would be really costly and two because I didn't really want the pugs getting their little feet cold. Dave would have been thrilled with it I know he would be, I imagined him face planting himself in the snow in order to cool down or making snow angels while a pile of pugs jumped all over him. Imagine how wonderful those photos would have been. Well that is if the snow lasted long enough for me to take them and the heat we were experiencing that year told me it would not. It'd melt as soon as it hit the ground, not even last long enough to give a good covering, it would give the grass on the front paddock a pretty decent watering but that would be about it. Or would it simply burn the grass leaving bald patches all over the place, that'd probably be more the case. So the snow machine idea left my mind as fast as it had entered it.

When I presented David with the Santa suit the look on his face told me everything he was thinking and he hadn't even taken it out of the bag yet. He poked a hole in the plastic, felt the material and his face became slightly worse than it had just been so I pretended one of the pugs needed me and slowly backed away so I didn't have to hear him complaining. And a few days later when it was show time I was really glad he was wearing a beard because it meant I didn't have to fully look at his face, see his crumpled expression, the most of him I could see that day was his nose and eyes and his eyes were glaring at me like fire. I saw his eyes squinting in a smile when he was looking at the blessings but then he'd glance over at me again and the fire would return. Thing is of course he would be smiling when looking down at the pugs, you just couldn't help but smile when seeing how much they were enjoying themselves, they are always happy when treats are being dished out and because I wanted to get them all looking at me when I was taking the photos I had an entire jar full of treats tucked under my arm when we all walked outside. We went to an area of the farm where the most amount of trees are because I wanted it to be cooler for everybody, but the trees weren't fully grown at the time so it was mainly the pugs who could stand underneath and that was ok because they were the ones we had to worry about most. If I had thought things through properly I would have bought a Santa suit sooner and taken the photos earlier in the year at a time when the weather was colder, taken them in winter perhaps. But then there would have been no leaves on the trees, not as much greenness, just stalks and sticks and having them in the background of the photos would have been kind of depressing. I think my eye would have been drawn to them for years to come. As it was everything looked lovely and I knew every time I looked at those photos I would be really happy with them. Also in winter the ground would be sopping wet so Santa's chair would have been sinking into the ground and my Santa was grumpy enough as it was, imagine how much worse he would have been if him and his chair toppled over into the mud. Also we never hang around in the cold with elderly pugs, it's always a quick dash outside for a toilet break then back inside by the fire for a nap, no time to take photos, no time for hanging around.

On the day we took the photos I left David on his own in the bedroom getting changed while the rest of the family waited in the lounge room for him. I figured he would be faster getting dressed if he didn't have one of the pugs swinging off his pant legs, a thing Awesome and Casey really liked to do. Casey went through a stage of doing it almost every night when Dave came home from work, turned it into a bit of a game she did, he'd be walking through the house with this little black sweetheart hanging off his leg and she wouldn't let go until the excitement of him being home had finally worn off and depending on her mood and how much she had missed him that could take a while. We never tried to make her loosen her grip for fear of her losing one of her teeth, she was pretty old after all and she didn't have a lot of teeth left so she never made a hole in the fabric, just hung on for dear life with that incredibly strong jaw of hers, her little curly tail going ballistic in the process. She wasn't trying to bite him, merely escorting him through the house, dancing like mad alongside him while holding onto the only part of him she could reach. And then that was it, she'd quickly let go and he'd bring her up for a kiss and a cuddle.

From the bedroom I could hear a whole lot of cursing, even with Christmas carols playing and me singing along I could still hear my husband airing his views. Then after what seemed like an eternity Grace Farms one and only ever Santa Claus stomped into the room. I didn't have to see the flash of red and white out of the corner of my eye to know he had joined us because the air in the room quickly changed. It didn't even look like the figure was David's normal height, it was like his mood had shrunken him down a little. Or was he just not standing up straight because he wanted his pose to reflect how he was feeling. I wanted to both look at him but not look at him because I could sense his disposition. Even from the other side of the room I could sense it. But I couldn't avoid it any longer, I wanted to know what he looked like so I glanced across and burst out laughing, which by the way did not help his mood at all. A few of the pugs had flown over to him, clearly they had not picked up on his mood the way I had, or if they did they weren't for caring. I watched him bending down patting pug after pug and with him not looking at me I studied him more closely. He looked like a kid who had outgrown a school uniform and whose parents were making him wear it again the following year because they didn't want to buy a new one. The pants were fine but the top was not. It looked to be a lot smaller than the pants were, if this suit was not a "One Size Fits All" like it said on the pack but had come in a small, medium and large sizing then I would have said somebody had made a mistake and put a size large pants in with a size medium top. The fact that the pants were a perfect fit really surprised me because if anything it was the pant length I was most worried about. Due to David's height I had expected them to not even make it to his calves and figured I'd have to have a few pugs sitting in front of him to hide that fact, but these pants were great. The top was far from perfect, it barely did up, he had to wear a t-shirt underneath to fill in the gap and the sleeves fell short, didn't even cover his wrists. The belt looked awful, it was only just fastening and it was a thin belt too, not thick and chunky like a proper Santa belt should be. When he sat down the belt completely disappeared from view. I almost expected it to snap and go flying through the air taking somebodies eye out in the process. Not one of the pugs, in my mind it was going to go higher than that, perhaps giving an unsuspecting bird concussion. I'd have thought they would have made things the other way round, the top bigger and the pants shorter. I mean David is above average height, clearly they were not thinking of the average person when they cut the cloth for this suit. And the top, well a lot of Santa's like to wear padding and there were no allowances made for that. David tugged on the sleeves in an irritated manner "Bullshit one size fits all" was what he kept repeating as he came across the room. When he reached my side he started coughing saying the beard was nothing more than cheap cotton-wool, it kept going up his nose and making him sneeze and every time he spoke the beard lifted on his breath and I tried not to laugh any harder than I was already laughing. I asked him if he was ready and he said "As ready as I'll ever be" then he told me that I should hurry up taking my photos because he was already way over it. But he didn't have to tell me that I already knew this was going to be a very quick photoshoot because they normally are if we are doing something different, I don't like messing the pugs around so everything is done at lightning speed, especially if it's one of the pugs that's wearing a costume. I told Dave he was behaving worse than our most uncooperative pug and he just grunted and stomped across the deck.

When we got outside I went and stood next to one of the trees and tried to get as many of the pugs underneath as I could and because I was close by most stayed exactly where I had put them. "You'll need a chair" I told David then watched as grumpy Santa stomped up onto the deck and came back with a chair. He positioned it in an area that he thought would do but I asked him to move it a few feet as the view was better there, more trees in the background, more exposed sky, more fluffy clouds that were now reminding me of Santa's beard. Normally David is a very obliging man but by his mannerism you've have thought I'd asked him to give me the world. So the seat was picked up and plonked down again with a huff and it wasn't exactly where I'd pointed to but I didn't have the guts to ask him to move it again. It'll have to do I thought to myself as I made my way over to where David was standing. A few of the pugs were wondering why they hadn't been given a treat yet and began woofing to remind me of what I had tucked under my arm. From the house you could hear the sound of carols playing, not too loud, you'd just hear the odd tune when the pugs quietened down, just enough for me to hear what carol was playing but that was all I needed to be off singing again. I know most of the words anyway, I've been singing them long enough and if I get stuck I make up my own. Sometimes they are fitting with the carol at other times I just make stupid things up and David will normally laugh but he was in no laughing mood today. The sun was blazing down and getting hotter by the minute so I looked around to see which pug looked like they wanted to be first. I figured we'd get the black pugs done first up that way they could then go and stand back underneath the tree or even be whisked inside the house where the air conditioner was. Billy was near my leg so I scooped him up and placed him on David's knee, he sat nicely and I clicked the camera fast, I was not going to stand there and size everything up, not going to make a black pug sit out in the sun any longer then they had to, being blind Billy could smell the treats, knew exactly where I was standing so he faced me full on and was back on the ground eating his treat in no time. A few of the old fawns were still lying where I'd put them so I guided Billy back over to the tree to be with them. Seeing he was ok I looked around for Casey, she too was an easy shoot, limited vision due to age, she sat comfortably on her dad's knee. Again I wasn't for taking any longer then I needed to, I aimed as best I could but I knew not all of these shots were going to be good ones and I was ok with that. I figured they would be special regardless. Next came Lumen, she had been quietly sitting in the shade watching all that was going on with those little cloudy eyes of hers. She loves the birdlife here on the farm so her little head kept looking around whenever she heard chirping. She was certainly having a ball but Lumen is not a pug she's a fluffy terrier cross and her fur is thicker and longer then a pugs coat is so I had to be mindful of that. As I handed her over to Dave I said that I was going to take her back inside and put her in her cot as soon as her photos were finished. I knew she wouldn't like it, she would have much preferred staying outside with us, so when I did take her in I brought her cot over to the window so she could watch what was going on. As the rest of the pugs got their photos taken I kept looking over at the window, seeing her there, her black and white coat really stood out against the pink of her cot. I smiled every time I glanced up at the house and sometimes I waved to her, she looked so beautiful sitting there and she was happy too because I'd occasionally hear her woofing whenever she saw something she thought worth woofing at. When I'd taken Lumen inside I'd brought David out a cup of water which he gulped down fast, lifted his beard and drank it then slung the plastic cup to one side, as soon as it hit the ground

Awesome pounced on it and carried it away to chew on. I didn't mind because it was one of the last cups from an old picnic set, we rarely use glasses here because I'm always worried about them getting broken and one of the blind pugs walking through the shards.

Now it was time for the fawn pugs to have a photo with Santa. Santa had cooled down a bit once he'd had a drink. I decided to do the oldest fawn first and work my way down to the youngest, it was a way of keeping track of who had been done. I figured it'd be easier and quicker too. I wouldn't end up taking somebodies photo twice while somebody else missed out. Imagine how horrid that would be. I'd be sitting at my computer looking at all the shots then realise somebody was missing and I knew there was no way David was going to allow me to put him through it all again. So this way of doing things was perfect, I'd give the pug a treat then go and get the next eldest, easy really. Amber and Ruben were both the same age, but he was still by the tree whereas Amber had followed me out and was standing by my side. I was aware of her and kept blocking her with my shadow so she didn't get too hot. I picked her up and placed her on David's knee and she looked up and sniffed the long white beard, felt its texture on her face, blinked a few times feeling the cheap imitation beard against her eyes and nose, she pulled a face, scrunched her mouth up like she didn't like the feel of it. As far as Santa beards went this one was a fizzer, nobody seemed to like it. Dave bent further down, closer to The Divine One's face and this time she leant in and sniffed his temple, felt the side of his glasses with her tongue and this amazing look came over her little old face. It was like she knew it was Daddy but wasn't sure why he was different. I was standing in front of them, camera in hand, watching and waiting to see what unfolded. To be honest I wish I had videoed it but I didn't think of it at the time, I was too busy enjoying myself, absolutely loving seeing her reaction. Amber was a thinker and I knew she'd be able to tell me everything that was going on in her mind by her facial expressions. Also, I was standing ready in case she needed me to lift her off his knee fast, if she showed that she was getting upset or too confused then I would have quickly gotten her out of that situation and to hell with the photographs. But she wasn't fazed, yes she knew something wasn't quite right here but she was happy enough to sit and sniff and figure out what it was. After a little while David lifted up the beard and Amber leant in for another sniff and on finding his proper face started going ballistic giving kisses. The Divine One had a look on her face like "It's back, its back, he had something weird on his face but now Dad's normal face is back again" before that she was probably just thinking to herself that this frizzy faced mutant wore the same aftershave as her Daddy did. Feeling David's normal face made Amber ecstatic, perhaps she was worried that she would have to put up with the beard forever and clearly didn't like the idea of that. With blind pugs the toss or tilt of a head indicates so much and Amber had a way of tilting her head when she wanted me to come over, like if she could see she would have been looking right at me. Amber always knew where I was standing, well not only me she always knew where everybody was standing at all times, she used her senses to know where her family was, it's a thing all blind dogs do. And she could tell I was close by on this day too, she could sense me there, hear my breathing, her little ears were well attuned to that and she would have been able to smell me too, smell my perfume. I've been wearing vanilla perfume for many years now. I look like a sugar cookie so figure I may as well smell like one too. The perfume is nice and the pugs can find me wherever I am on the farm because my smell is very distinct, I'm the only thing that smells like vanilla here at Grace Farm. Well Amber did the head tilting thing indicating she wanted me to come closer, her face looked like she wanted to tell me what she knew so I stepped forward and stroked her grey ears. Then cupped her little face and said "Well done sweetheart you found Daddy". As I stepped back two of the other pugs started jumping up at the side of David. Amber must have been able to feel them there and she looked down as if she knew something they didn't, like "Stop what you is doing everybody, I have an announcement to make" and she coughed like she always coughed but because of where she was and what was happening at the time it was like she was clearing her throat, the way one does when they are going to give a speech or make a very important announcement. That's the only reason it was so funny, if she'd coughed before I put her on his knee or after I'd lifted her down it probably wouldn't have even been remembered all these years later, it's because it happened at the most perfect moment that it's come to mind again now. But it made both David and me burst out laughing and I thought thank goodness something has been able to change Santa's mood. I quickly took a few photos and gave Amber her treat then lifted her down and she trotted off happily and kept to the shade. She coughed less when she was on the ground which made me realise that David was in fact not just moaning for the sake of moaning but was actually telling the truth about the cheap nasty white beard. David looked over at Amber standing by the tree. I think he was going to ask if she needed some help, he watched her for a few moments and then picked one of the other pugs up. I guess he realised she was ok he knew Amber was a cougher and todays cough was only a little one. I think it was the only time she had coughed at all that day and I knew the reason for it but wasn't for saying because I could see the beard being cast aside if I did and who is Santa without a beard, he's just some twit in matching pants and top with a funny hat on his head. So no, I was not for owning up to why Amber had coughed, not until all the pugs had had their photo taken I wasn't. I just set about getting those last few photos taken very fast and as soon as they were over I figured I would get the beard off my husband's face and chuck it in the bin. I suppose I could have left it in the shed for a mouse to make a nest out of because that's about all it was good for but we do not encourage mice to breed here because mice and rats bring snakes and we do not want snakes to call our property home.

In the span of about five minutes the rest of the fawns got their photos done and that was a good thing because by this time Santa

Claus was sweating like a pig. As I placed each pug on his knee I was becoming more and more aware of just how hot David was, at one point I thought perhaps we should have taken the photos inside the house. I could have easily set up a chair by the Christmas tree and I don't know why I didn't think of doing that as it would have made for some pretty good photos. I guess because we have so much space outside and so little space inside I was more thinking about that. And again because we are in Australia there is no need to be huddled inside the house at Christmas time. But it was alright for me wasn't it I wasn't the poor soul in the suit, I was wearing a cool cotton dress, I didn't tell David what I was thinking because I knew he would be less than impressed. I was just glad the photoshoot was over. The fawns like the blacks were really good about looking my way, a few of the sighted ones did get distracted once or twice but as soon as they heard the treat jar madly being shaken they quickly stopped looking at what had caught their eye and started looking back at me. It was a huge amount of fun getting those photos taken, a whole lot of excitable squealing was being done and I am not ashamed to say that most of it was done by me. I was in a state of complete and utter rapture, even if David wasn't. His mood could not dampen my spirit and because I was so elated so were the pugs. They were feeding off my enthusiasm and feeding on a heap of special treats, the atmosphere was charged with joy. They'd be begging up at my leg wanting a treat, wanting to be picked up, wanting to have a go on David's knee and so I'd lift them up and they'd jump all over Santa. Some were not content to be simply sitting on his knee they'd be climbing all over him. I thought a few would have torn the beard with their claws but they didn't. They'd sniff his face and lick his nose as that was the part of Daddy that was real and as soon as they settled back down I'd take their photo. I got some really beautiful photos that day and not all there taken on David's knee because while the pug he was holding was settling I was also clicking away at what the other pugs were doing. While writing this chapter I went and looked at the photos again, a thing I haven't done for a long time and I was amazed at the shots I had totally forgotten about. There's Ruben way in the background walking around, if I had only concentrated on Santa I would never have remembered that he had taken himself off on a little sniffing expedition once his photo was done. There are lots of photos of pugs sitting or sprawled out underneath trees and pugs playing with each other. I also forgot that there were large round bales of hay in the paddock over the road. They are in the background of a few of the photos and really nothing says Aussie country Christmas like a paddock full of hay bales.

As soon as the photos were over Dave said "Are we good? I nodded that we were and walked over to take the beard off his face but he beat me to it, he ripped the hat, beard, belt and top off at an alarmingly fast rate then Grace Farms one and only Santa Claus sat there in his t-shirt, boots and pants. There were a few more clouds in the sky by this time and some of them were blocking the sun so it was cooler for everyone. David was now in no rush to leave, he sat there relaxed and happy watching the pugs milling about. Seeing as the sun was now blocked I decided to go bring Lumen back outside to be with us, it would have been unfair to leave her in there on her own when there was now no reason for it. Baby who was sitting by David's side pawed at his leg to come up so he put the beard, belt and hat inside the Santa top and loosely folded it across his knee then lifted Baby up and sat her on top of it. I think he wrapped everything up so the pugs couldn't get at it, he like me knew that beard was not good for them to be chewing on, neither was the hat because the bob was made out of the same stuff as the beard. I think if that Santa suit could talk it'd be saying "Cheap, cheap, cheap" I know I was thinking it every time I looked at it. I stood in front of David chatting away, the conversations were happy ones because he was overjoyed to be finally free of most of the suit. I couldn't wait for the photos to be loaded up on my computer so I could see what they looked like. A few of the pugs were wandering around, others had come over from the base of the tree and were now siting underneath David's chair. Awesome was on his back kicking at the air with Nemo, Brian and Ava Lindy Lou on top of him. I kept the delicate oldies next to me, out of the way, so there was no fear of them being accidently kicked in the face. Baby kept moving around on David's knee and by doing so had undone the mound she was sitting on. The belt peeped out. Awesome noticed it before we did so jumped up and started tugging. David pulled it all the way out and gave it to him and he ran round the paddock with it in his mouth. The belt may have been no good for Santa but it was a big hit with the pugs. We watched the younger members of our family playing together. Awesome had the buckle in his mouth and running behind him hanging onto the end was Ava Lindy Lou and Brian. Not far behind them little bandy legged Nemo was doing his best to get in on the act and he was succeeding too, well, as well as a limited vision pug could succeed, but he was having a blast you could tell by the look on his face. Nemo liked it better when the younger pugs tired themselves out and came to a stop. He jumped all over them when they did, grabbed the belt a couple of times too but mostly he was happy to just jump all over Awesome and Awesome being the big docile boy that he is was more than happy to let him. Side on to them and a little distance away was

Bromley watching everything and woofing. A thing Bromley really likes to do, he's never been one for getting involved in the thick of the action but will egg everybody on from the sidelines. And then there'd be times when he'd sneak up to the edge of the pack and lunge at somebodies stuck out leg. He rarely makes contact with the limb because his aim isn't all that good but he's enjoying himself regardless and really that's what it's all about for him. After a while the belt was no longer any fun, they'd all had a chew on it and it now lay in scattered pieces. The rolling around with the siblings thing was wearing a bit thin too so they all came back to sit underneath David's chair, Billy was under there taking up most of the room but he welcomed a few of his siblings in and the others lay panting nearby. Once they'd rested they stood up and started sniffing, Brain went over to a tree for a wee and a few of the others followed him, no doubt thinking what he was doing was a good idea, the little girls squatted and a few legs got cocked then they all slowly made their way back to us. Again Awesome looked up at David's knee, this time it was the beard he spotted so flew through the air and grabbed it. It was tucked underneath Baby but he spotted it all the same, spied the tiny bit that was hanging out, the younger pugs have perfect eyesight, to me it looked more like part of Baby's tail but Awesome knew what it was and took off with it. Within seconds Awesome had torn that beard to pieces and quite a few of the pugs were now running around with it in their mouths. I said to Dave that it really wasn't a good thing for them to be playing with, didn't want anybody swallowing it and choking or having it stuck in their intestines. I could see a trip to an emergency vet happening if they did. Dave put Baby on the ground and took off fast. I looked up, tried to preempt the direction the bulk of them would be going in and started running. If I wasn't trying to cut them off I would have been taking a photo of it all. It did look kind of funny five pugs running flat out with bits of white beard in their mouths and behind them a half dressed Santa flying across the paddock at full speed. The ones who were too old for running slowly followed me out as I approached two of their siblings and tried to take the beard out of their mouths but they weren't for handing it over until a treat was dangled in front of them. So an exchange was made. I looked up to see how Dave was going with his lot and two had been caught and the beard retrieved but Awesome was still going strong. Acting like it was a game. I think it was the best fun he'd had in ages, a weird fabric beard to play with and Daddy running after him, the faster Dave ran the faster Awesome ran. I guess he thought the aim of the game was to run faster and faster so he was just playing along. The way they were running you'd never have guessed it was a warm day. Ava Lindy Lou saw what was happening on the other side of the paddock and started running and on her way spotted a bit of beard that somebody had cast aside. I stood watching and waiting for one of them to come my way. I knew Ava Lindy Lou would soon be getting tired. She doesn't quite have the same stamina as Awesome does so I concentrated on her and sure enough she soon came to a stop so I ran over and shook the treat jar in front of her face and she couldn't spit that beard out fast enough. Awesome was still running flat out and he had the biggest bit of beard in his mouth. I have always thought Awesome had the stamina of a racehorse and he was proving me right that day, he was showing no sign of ever slowing down. As I ran across the paddock Awesome zigzagged around me. Not close enough to allow me to catch him, more like he wanted me to get involved in the game too, I think he was ecstatic that Dad was playing with him but wanted both of us to chase him now. But there was no way I was going to do that so I got a handful of treats and the next time he headed my way I scattered them on the ground in front of him. I knew he was looking at me as he came flying over. I knew he would see those treats fall. I also knew it would be too tempting for Awesome not to stop and try and eat all those treats before any of the others pugs got to them and that's exactly what he did. So while he wandered around looking like a sheep grazing I went and grabbed the beard. When he finished eating he didn't even go looking for his new toy instead he headed straight inside the house for a much needed drink. I then did a few laps of the paddock looking for any bits of beard that I'd missed. I had a real good search around too because the smallest bits were the ones that were more dangerous for the pugs.

I had put a bit of red and gold tinsel on one of the fruit trees because I thought it'd be great to have an outside Christmas tree that year. But it didn't get in many of the photos and it was no big deal that it didn't because I had decorated that tree a week or so earlier and with the sun being so fierce it had already faded the tinsel. By the time we got out there it did look kind of tired and pathetic. An embarrassment of a Christmas tree if anything, it more or less looked like exactly what it was, a fruit tree with faded tinsel clinging to the branches, absolutely nothing magical about it at all. As I searched the paddock I passed it many times and each time it seemed to look more and more pitiful. At the time I didn't think about the harshness of the sun, in my mind I was getting a job done early and I did think a decorated tree would have looked pretty special in our photos but it was not to be. Instead it was avoided like the plague in the main shots but it's there off to the side in some of the more relaxed photographs. There is even a photo of Amber going to the toilet underneath that tree and I remember Dave pointing it out and laughing saying to me "Well you can tell exactly what she thinks of your outside Christmas tree". After Santa had gone into the house some of the pugs stayed sniffing underneath his chair. I had a feeling one or two treats had been accidently dropped there and they were not coming inside until they had been found. I took a few photos of that scene too and it made me smile when seeing it again. And to think all these photos were taken a few months after I lost my Mum and David lost his. I guess the reason for the Santa suit was because I wanted to do something really special that year. I suppose I was trying to make a very hard Christmas a little bit happier, find something to smile about, something to bring joy. It was the first one each of us would be celebrating without our Mums. Looking back I can't believe we actually did that so soon after suffering such loss, I suppose it shows we were a lot stronger than we thought we were at the time. I'm proud of us for doing that and I think both of our mothers would be proud of us too and hopefully they were both looking down at all the antics happening in the front paddock that day. Santa gave me the thumbs up before turning and walking back into the house. And as David strode across the paddock he was smiling, really smiling, he had enjoyed himself, truly enjoyed himself I know because I took a few shots of him walking across the paddock and his grin was wide. He may have been protesting on the way out but a very different man was walking back inside again. I guess the pugs would have done that to him. I mean you can't be around all those happy little beings without some of it rubbing off. I knew I would never be able to talk him into dressing up as Santa Claus again but I do think he was glad he had done it one year at least. The sight of him walking off smiling made me happy. The shots of him were taken without his knowledge but those photos are some of my favourite photos of my husband. I think it's because of what he did for me that day, clearly didn't want any part of it but was good enough to participate all the same. He had the rest of the Santa outfit scrunched up in his arms, no need to fold it neatly, we had no intention of keeping it for next year, we both knew it was going straight into the bin.

CHAPTER SEVENTEEN

Feisty Pink Princess

It became apparent pretty early on that Amber although a very tiny pug was definitely not ever going to allow herself be walked all over. Not when she first arrived and not as she got older either. During her settling in period she was quite the placid little princess, just an innocent little blessing walking round the place with her tongue peeping out. She was unsure of everyone and everything and she wasn't feeling too well either, but as soon as she was feeling more settled in the house and as soon as she began feeling better in herself physically, that's when her true personality came through and she revealed to everybody on the farm that yes she may have only been small in stature but there was an enormous personality being housed in the teeny tiny body of hers. The Divine One could be a little bit bossy at times, but she was not ever what you could call overly nasty, no that wasn't who she was at all. It was more that she was full to the brim of sass, had an incredible attitude and spirit, one that couldn't be dampened by anybody or anything. The perfect word to describe The Divine One was feisty, and her feistiness went up a few notches with each passing year. When she first arrived on the farm Amber was simply sticking up for herself, letting her siblings know where she sat in the pack and no it definitely was not at the bottom as some of the other pugs assumed it would be. When Amber first joined the family Sarah was still with us and she was certainly top dog, no doubting that at all, everybody knew she was the reigning monarch and they all respected it. But I do believe that if Amber had arrived here with full vision and full health things could have worked out quite differently for her. No she would never have been able to steal Sarah's crown. Sarah would never have allowed such a thing to happen but Amber may have taken over the throne after Sarah passed on, if, like I said, The Divine One had not been lacking in vision and health. We lost Sarah a few months after Amber joined the family and for a little while the pugs were all living in limbo as far as a leader of the pack went and I've found that can sometimes happen with certain pugs, it's as if everybody is used to their roles, each one is very contented with the way things are so are perfectly happy to carry on living that way, which is exactly what happened at the farm until Ruben John Comer arrived on the scene. With Amber it was more that she wasn't going to let anybody get away with something she did not like them doing and a few tried it on and I know it was due to her size and because she couldn't see very well. They could tell that Amber was disadvantaged in a few areas so tried to benefit from the situation but quickly got told off for it, got told off in no uncertain terms and after realising that she was not an easy target they never tried to take advantage of the littlest member of the pack again. Although a few needed to be told off more than once for the message to fully sink in. The first time I actually saw The Divine One sticking up for herself was during treat time. I watched on as one of her full sighted siblings shouldered her out of the way putting themselves in-between Amber and the treat. They did it in the hope of that treat ending up in their mouth instead of hers and at first she simply let things go, perhaps because she thought what had just taken place wasn't on purpose, that somebody had accidently gotten in her way. I saw her thinking about things for a moment or two, saw that little mind of hers ticking over and then she set off walking around the offending sibling, side stepping their body to come and stand in front, she sensed where I was and was trying to get closer to me, well more closer to the treats and could smell I had them so was doing her best to let me see that she was there. I guess she sensed she had been blocked and was doing what she could to rectify the situation. But what she didn't know was that I'd never once taken my eyes off her, I was well aware of what was going on and still had one treat left in my hand with her name on it. I bent down again ready to give her that which was rightfully hers and The Divine One was just standing there blinking waiting to receive it when all of a sudden she was shouldered out of the way again. Well this time Amber's little face changed, changed very quickly, I knew she'd just realised that what had taken place was no mere accident and I was just about to take control of the situation myself when I saw my teeny tiny new daughter turn and begin going nuts gnawing on her siblings shoulder. It was sudden and out of the blue but it did the trick, out of shock the offending sibling jumped away fast and Amber was happy enough with that, she got her treat and carried on with her walk. Some dogs won't let things go, they'll hold a grudge, tell somebody off and have a bee in their bonnet about it for quite a while afterwards, but not Amber, she didn't make more of it than it was. Never gave chase, no point doing that, no reason to, she had sorted the situation out, let them know her thoughts on the matter, informed them in her own way that such behaviour was not on and was able to let it go. But yes a few did need telling more than once and Amber was more than happy to keep on telling them. Emily needed telling off a whole lot of times before finally accepting that the little one would not allow herself to be messed with. And because it was done without any real malice I let it happen, let the situation sort itself out, but I was always watching on though in case the mood changed because you have to do that. You always have to be ready to intervene. Some of the pugs Amber was putting in their place were much bigger than she was and I didn't want one of them deciding to turn around and have a go.

But the pack Amber had joined were all pretty laid back and besides they fully understood why the little one was going all psycho granny on them, they had tried to stop her from getting a treat, they knew full well that such behaviour was wrong and so took it on the head when she told them off. Some of the pugs were huge against her tiny frame and they had full sight as well but they let themselves be reprimanded regardless. That little jaw of hers couldn't really go in for a big shake of somebody, most pugs will grab hold of the side of a neck and give that a quick tug in order to gain some control but Amber's jaw couldn't stretch that far so she'd gnaw on the side of their shoulder or the top of their leg and really was just about as harmless as a blowfly bouncing across a window pane. If she was able to she would occasionally reach up and grab hold of somebody's ear, but those ears were pretty hard to keep hold of, too soft and silky, too hard to keep in one's little mouth for very long. The Divine One was cunning when she needed to be. We had a pug enter the house who was very, very large and over time with good nutritious food and plenty of slow gentle walks around the farm they slimmed down quite nicely. But they were left with plenty of lose skin and The Divine One in her own little creative way must have sussed this out. She was standing next to the ex-chubber one treat time and Amber knew who everybody was due to their unique smell. Well this pug jumped right in front of Amber as I was dishing out the treats, took the treat right out of my hand even though it was only inches away from Ambers face. Clearly Grace Farm's slimmer of the year was feeling extra hungry that day and simply couldn't stop herself if she tried. I felt a bit sorry for The Divine One because there she was, little, old and mostly blind, just standing with her tiny mouth open ready for me to pop that tasty treat in but the pug beside her was way too fast for both of us. I was about to fish around in my pocked to see if I had anything in there to replace the stolen treat with when all of a sudden Amber turned sideways and lunged at this pug. She knew exactly where to strike too because she went straight for the loose roll of hip fat and chunked down on it with all her might and the pug was so stunned by what happened that she dropped the treat and I was able to pounce on it and give it back to Amber but I had to get her to let go of that roll of loose skin first and she wasn't letting go of it so easily because getting her treat stolen one too many times had really annoyed her. I was holding the treat in front of The Divine Ones nose and blowing on it to so she would be able to smell it better but she still wasn't for letting go, she was too intent on tugging on that roll, deeply committed on bringing the treat stealing pug into line. I began wafting the treat around and blowing on it even harder but Amber was so incensed that a whole lot of wafting and blowing had to be done before she turned my way. It amazed me that she knew exactly where to strike, but she got that roll of fat first go, no stumbling around in the dark, lunged straight at it as if she could see exactly where it was and then held on for dear life.

Amber and Ruben

So that's how it was from then on with Amber, she'd sort a situation out when it needed to be sorted and then sometimes the same thing would have to be done again when we took in a new pug that also made the mistake of thinking that the little one was an easy target. It's all about settling into the pack really, everybody working out their position in it, each pug finding out where they stand in the pecking order. No matter what the species there is always going to be a hierarchy of dominance, a sorting out of where one stands within in a group. Every living being on the plant does it, even us humans although we are a little less obvious about it. Chickens, or chooks as I call them, are extremely obvious when doing it and I guess this is where the term pecking order came from. A higher ranking chook will peck at hens they consider to be lower in the flock. It's a serious game amongst chooks and apparently starts when they are as young as six weeks old. Bigger, stronger, healthier chooks with more aggressive personalities will bully their way to the top by pecking others into submission. Although if you watch them for a while you will notice that a lot of the time they'll first try to gain control by squawking and strutting about with their feathers fluffed up but if that doesn't work they'll resort to pecking and sometimes will pull a few feathers out. I've never liked the feather pulling. I think it's a pretty nasty thing to do to one another and it can be horrible watching it happen but once each chook has worked out their positon the flock will start to live in harmony. After that it'll only take a quick glare or a slight peck from a higher ranking chook to keep everybody in line. Although the pecking order will change if the hen in charge gets sick or goes broody, if that happens sorting out who is boss will have to be done once again. I don't have chooks here on the farm at the moment, it is part of a future plan, but if I did I would make sure to give them as much space as possible, no small cages here because one I wouldn't do that to any animal and two because the less space chooks have the more violent they become when sorting out who's boss. That's what I've been told anyway and it does make sense to me, the more room one has to move around the less territorial you need to be and the more joy is gotten from living, it's the way I look at it anyway. I don't like seeing any type of bird in small cages. If I had an aviary it'd be an enormous one and if I had chooks they'd be spending their lives free ranging. Free range chickens are the happiest chooks on the planet I think. As long as you make sure to put them in a secure coop at night so the foxes don't get them then let them out again first thing in the morning because chooks like to get moving at first light so you'd have to be up pretty early in order to keep them happy. But I can see myself doing this in the not too distant future. I reckon I'd have them in a red hen house, a barn type set up, but not quite as big as a regular barn as there'd be no need for it to be. Just enough room for a few nesting boxes and they'd have to be up high as chooks like to sleep up off the ground, it makes them feel more secure. I can just see myself calling them in at the end of the day with a bucket of food in my hand, see them come running at me from all over the farm. I'd count them as they made their way inside, making sure I didn't accidently leave somebody out all night long as I know they wouldn't be there in the morning, not with the amount of foxes we have round here. Imagine the joy that could be gotten from seeing a pile of chooks wandering around the place scratching at the ground. I grew up with chooks and it was my job to feed and look after them but I didn't see it as a job, it was far too much fun for it to ever be thought of as a chore.

Amber and Awesome

In the animal kingdom establishing a hierarchy comes with the territory. It is very much a part of their life. I've seen it taking place in the paddocks with the horses and the sheep do it too. It's just a natural occurrence and with horses it's magnified because they are so big. But it's generally sorted out pretty quickly. It'll be dealt with in the first few weeks of a new member of the heard or pack being introduced. Dogs will do it with other pets and even their owners will be included in it too, that's why you have to make sure that you are the pack leader. It's very important that your dog sees you as leader of them all. When I take in a new pug I know the dynamics are about to change, the pack is going to be different to how it was before so I need to be constantly keeping an eye on everybody to ensure things go smoothly. There is always a period of settling and adjusting, not just for the new pug but for everyone else in the pack, although it is a little harder for the new family member because they are getting used to a lot of things at once while the others are just getting used to one more dog. Also my dogs are old and for some the time of adjusting can be a little bit overwhelming, you have to be patient and understanding and watch, watch, watch. I'll be constantly observing them until the hierarchy has been sorted out. Most times the pugs will sort it out themselves in an orderly manner but I have had the odd occasion where I had to intervene and you have to act fast, sort the situation out quickly before it has time to escalate. You can't let it intensify or let them think that such behaviour is ok because it isn't ok, it is far from ok and you as pack leader need to let them know what is and isn't going to be tolerated. Mostly it'll all just be a load of hot air being blown, a whole lot of huffing and puffing and strutting and stomping around and a whole lot of shouldering each other too because pugs are well known for doing that. But if you know your pugs you'll be able to read them like a book, you'll more often than not know what's about to take place before it even happens. I would always stand close to Amber because she was the neediest and because of the personality she had she sometimes needed to be protected from herself. When a strange dog is settling into a new pack it will make note of the smallest and the most fragile members because they are the easiest ones to dominate. They always start at the bottom and work their way up and how far up they go depends on the dogs living within that pack, their health and their personalities. It's all about working out where they sit and it's a very natural thing to do and it's a thing that does need to be done, it's how dogs live. It happens with all packs whether in the wild or in the home, wherever you have multiple dogs you will have the pack mentality and it's not always horrible and nasty like you see on nature documentaries. I've found it to be a watered down version with most domestic dogs and an even waterier version in my home because most of my pugs are elderly and really it can just be like a pile of old folks in a nursing home having a bit of a squabble over something. A bit of a huff and puff then due to age and common sense most times it'll be all over before it has begun. People who have younger dogs and dogs of different breeds, well it'll be a completely different matter for them and I do worry when there is a pug or any other flat faced dog living with dogs that have long snouts because they are at a disadvantage there. I worry about owners not being fully aware of the situation and leaving them all together when they leave home instead of being sensible and separating them, keeping the small needy breeds safe. Problems can happen for many different reasons. Sometimes you'll get a dog who doesn't understand how things work, some have never lived within a pack before, they have been only dogs all their lives so the working out where they fit is a little bit harder for them. They'll need a whole lot of special understanding until they learn how to live with us and it can get out of hand if you have a very domineering personality. That is why you need to have your wits about you, you need to watch how they are all acting and reacting towards each other, basically it's all about acting and reacting when a new pack is being formed and it's your job to oversee things until they are once again living in a harmonious state. But it doesn't end there, keeping that harmonious state going year after year, that is your job as well and things are forever changing. The dogs in your pack will be constantly altering, they will be aging and with age comes change, changes in their health, changes in their bodies, changes in their minds and their little personalities they too can change somewhat too due to all of this. And you as leader of the pack, as their guardians, as Mum and as Dad have to be fully aware of all of these changes as they take place. You can't sort a situation out if you are not aware of it and the only way to be aware is by watching what's happening and sometimes you have to leave things a little bit to see how they unfold. It all depends on what's going down and how it's affecting the rest of the dogs but yes I can say with absolute clarity that changes will always be taking place.

Casey and Amber

I think Amber was just amusing herself a lot of the time when she was being feisty, like it was all some kind of big game to her. She did seem incredibly happy when she was telling somebody off. Some days she got a real kick out of it, other days she couldn't care less. It all depended on how she was feeling on any given day. Sometimes she could spend an entire day being a little control freak and when she was in that kind of mood it didn't take much to set her off. I had to be constantly aware of where she was and what she was getting up to and take her in hand if she was becoming too much. David would watch on sometimes and shake his head and I'd stand there telling him my views on the matter or maybe I was just making excuses for my little Divine One. I'd be saying something like "Amber has a big personality you know" and he'd just stand there looking at me. So I'd tell him that I thought the personality she'd been blessed with was too big sometimes for such a little body to contain, that she had to let it out somehow and being bossy was her way of doing it" "Yes that's exactly what is going on here" I'd say before carrying on my way, usually with a huffing and puffing Amber tucked under one arm because more often than not she was still trying to tell people off as I carried her away. Telling them off in that groaning growly coughing spluttering way that is uniquely Amber and I don't know if David believed me or not but I wasn't for looking back. I'd just carry Amber off and distract her with a walk down the driveway or a little trot along the deck. I thought of Amber as one of these feisty old ladies who believed that due to how ancient they were they could get away with anything. Like they now had a rite of passage, it was as if in Amber's mind old age had given her an excuse. She was in amongst some younger dogs and probably thought she knew a thing or two about life, knew a lot more about everything, a lot more than they did that's for sure and her attitude reflected that. I believe she thought she could do whatever she wanted and everybody should just fall in line and the funny thing was that more often than not that's exactly what they all did. Ruben may have been boss, our top dog, but Amber was very good at getting everybody else to do what she wanted and Ruben didn't seem to mind. I guess he felt what she was doing wasn't hurting anybody and certainly wasn't interfering with his role in the least so he left her to it. I did however notice that Amber never tried anything on with Ruben. I guess she knew he shouldn't be messed with. So you'd have Ruben doing his thing being in control of the room and there in amongst it all was little Amber being forceful whenever it took her fancy. With Amber I felt her sassiness, her feistiness, her days of wanting to rule the kingdom was actually what was keeping her alive at times. I think if she'd hadn't had such a feisty spirit dwelling within then she may have given up the ghost a long time ago. Most of her siblings knew who she was and ignored her, most knew The Divine One could be a little bossy boots, but an inoffensive little bossy boots, they knew she was all huff and puff for show, not many teeth, no harm to be done. Time and time again I would watch them standing there staring into space until the little spitfire had worn herself out and the older she got the faster that would happen. It was like engage and retreat and a few hours later or even as late as the next day or the one after that it'd be engage and retreat again. All the pugs in the pack knew Amber really well, they knew her episodes of bossiness would be over in a matter of seconds. So they'd stand there and she'd be all feisty against the side of their shoulder and then she'd suddenly stop and go clunking off and everything was once again back to normal. Amber never minded being ignored either, unlike human beings who are being bossy and ignored Amber didn't let such a thing infuriate her. If she could have shrugged her shoulders she would have as that's kind of how she responded to it all. She paused, rethought things, then turned and clunked off. Or sometimes she'd carry on being bossy for just that little bit longer, carried on amusing herself until she'd had enough and only Amber knew when that was going to be, so I'd watch and take each session as it came. Take a quick assessment to see exactly what was going on.

I believe The Divine One's bossiness started when she had her treat stolen and, well, she wasn't having any of that so sorted them out and when she had done so I guess she must have thought to herself "Well that was a bit of fun I must try that again some time" so she started to do it a bit more after that and yes all the while she was aging and weakening and she was so very little. Due to her size and strength she could never be what one would call threatening. Like I said Amber was nothing more than an annoying little fly or mosquito buzzing around, a bit irritating when it was there and ok when it had gone away and like all annoying little insects they go off and annoy somebody else then come back round again. And you have to 100% know your dogs and if she had been a different dog or if she had been really upsetting the others then I would have taken the situation in hand because I am all about having harmony in my home. Yes allowing each dog to have their own personality, that is their right, everybody living in this house has a right to be themselves but they must live in a harmonious way, be respectful to one another, I expect my little family to work well together. I won't let the balance of our home be interrupted. That would be not only unfair to the dogs but to David and myself as well. Amber was a harmless fireball, nothing more than just a harmless ball of fire that was extinguished almost as fast as it was ignited and when she'd worn herself out she'd go and have a little sleep. And it wasn't like the entire household was terrified of her, to be honest nobody in the house was terrified of her, maybe there were times when she hoped that they were but nobody was. Didn't stop her being feisty though, I think with Amber it was more that she liked things done a certain way, her way, and if the others weren't doing what she thought was right she had no trouble at all letting them know it. Most just gave her an extra wide birth whenever she was in one of her super bossy moods and it wasn't an all-day every day event because she could go weeks and even months without being set off, then something or somebody would irritate her and off she would go again. The other pugs would see, hear or feel her clunking around and when she was in a super bossy mood there was an extra bit of clunk in her walk letting the others know the best thing to do was keep out of her way for a little while. Which was a pretty easy thing for most of them to do, with Amber being blind and a lot of the others fully sighted they could quite easily avoid her and she'd just be there sniffing the air searching for them and sometimes by the time she actually found somebody her mood had already changed so she'd sniff at their heads or shoulders and climb into bed next to them and that was the end of that.

I actually thought it was good that The Divine One wouldn't allow herself to be walked over, she was an only dog before she came here after all and sometimes they are the ones who actually do let others lord over them but not little Amber. But due to her being who she was we'd have to leave her locked in our bedroom whenever we left the house. Because she was so tiny I worried that one of the other pugs may have taken it upon themselves to sort her out while there were no humans around to protect her and I didn't want that. She'd have never survived it. So we put her in one of the beds in the bedroom and Arthur and Ruben went in there with her for company so she was never alone. Those two boys were always so lovely with Amber. Arthur was completely harmless and yes Ruben was top dog but he never saw Amber as a threat because the truth was that she wasn't. I assumed Ruben had reasoned it out in his head that "The Little One" could be a grumpy old broad at times and that was just how some women folk are. When we got home we'd often find Amber, Ruben and Arthur sleeping in bed together and they were in a real deep sleep too so we didn't ever disturb them, just let them wake up naturally and come wandering out to find us when they were ready. Being younger than the other two Arthur was usually the first one to wake up so we'd take him out for a wee and give him his treat, we never return home empty handed, we always bring something special back and we'd put a treat aside for those who were still sleeping. The slumbering blessings never missed out no matter how long it took them to wake up.

There were certain times though when I did need to rein Amber in and because I dressed her in pink it was very easy to keep track of her. I didn't have to look twice I knew that flash of pink was her so I'd fly over to see if the one she was telling off was ok or if they needed a bit of help and if they needed some assistance I would help them. We had taken in two more pugs and these two bonded souls were very sensitive beings. I noticed right away how delicate in nature both of them were. I also noticed they reacted differently to how the other pugs were reacting to Amber. By reading their signals I could clearly tell that they didn't see her how the rest of the pack did, where the other pugs more or less just ignored The Divine One our two new blessings didn't. Over the course of a few days I noticed they were becoming increasingly upset and I couldn't allow that to keep happening. It wasn't fair on them. Amber regardless of being tiny could be pretty intimidating to extra sensitive souls and these two poor darlings didn't know how to cope when she got in their faces. They weren't up to telling her off, if they had of done she would of taken heed and that would have been the end of it. But neither one of them had it in them to stand up to her, they were old and tired and not in very good health when we first took them in. Basically they both just wanted a bit of peace and quiet and it was my job to ensure they got it. I believe each pug needs to be able to feel happy and content in their own home, it is their right. As much as I loved Amber I couldn't let her go on upsetting my new son and daughter so I stepped in. These two pugs were much bigger in size than Amber but I've found that size has little to do with it, it's more about the personality of the dog. I have found in life that sensitive souls need protecting from influences that harm and I have also found that a lot of things can be considered both hurtful and harmful to extra sensitive souls. I know this because I am one of those souls. I knew exactly how these two pugs would be feeling so I intervened, I knew the times Amber needed reigning in and when she was fine being let go. With the ones who weren't affected by her, which by the way was everybody else we had living in the pack at the time, I knew it was ok to let Amber go, let her get it out of her system. But with Buddy and Baby I always stepped in. Well at the start I did anyway but after a few days of being told off Amber decided it was best to leave the two new souls alone and whenever she did go near them she was wise enough to take a much more gentle approach now.

She'd only ever clunk over to them when she was ready to have a rest and after a bit of apprehension they both allowed her to get in bed next to them.

Baby, Amber and Ava

There were times when I would lift Amber off the couch and noticed the side of her coat was wet, not wet as if somebody had accidently had a wee and she had been laying in it but certainly wet enough to order a coat change. I knew exactly why it was wet too because we had a pug at the time that got their thrills from licking everybody's coats. It was the texture of the wool they liked and they'd spend hours licking away at the side of somebody. Some pugs do this kind of thing because they are stressed or because there is something else going on with them, but I checked the pug out thoroughly and no, nothing else was going on there, they simply just liked the texture of the wool. I found the whole thing quite irritating to be honest, really put me off my writing. I had to put ear plugs in more than once just to be able to finish a chapter. I tried blocking it out and concentrate on the story I was telling but the more I tried to ignore it the louder it became. I did move the licking pug over a few times but they just snuggled up next to one of the other pugs who was wearing a coat and began lick, lick, licking again. I thought about taking my computer out onto the deck and writing out there but it was a cold day and besides within a few seconds of setting myself up outside I would have been joined by all the pugs because where I am they want to be also. So the ear plugs became my saving grace. Anyway The Divine One had been sleeping the afternoon away right next to the obsessive coat licker so I took her gobbed on pink coat off and because all the other girly coloured coats were in the wash I had to put a blue coat on Amber when we went for our afternoon walk. And it was a lovely walk too, yes it was cut short due to the threatening rain clouds that seemed to be following us around but because it was coming up to dinner time none of the pugs were the least put out by it. Nobody even blinked an eye when I turned and started heading back to the house, one by one each little body spun around, no complaining woofs, no nose out of joint snorts, nobody in a defiant manner attempting to shuffle off in the opposite direction, not one little blessing resisted my decision, today we were in unison. It was like they had all been thinking the exact same thing I'd been thinking. That we'd better head home fast before our luck ran out and the raindrops started falling. We all raced up the back ramp and shot into the house and a few moments later we heard the sound of rain on the roof. As soon as I got indoors I went round drawing all the blinds because I wanted to keep the house as warm as possible, the fire was now dwindling and I was well aware of that fact. I knew getting the fire going again needed to be my top priority, it would be the first job done before lining the bowls along the kitchen countertop. I was crouched on the floor busily shoving twigs into the fire when out of the corner of my eye I saw a blue blur fly by and because it was blue I didn't think too much of it. My mind identified it as being one of the placid boys moving position. I figured they were going to find a bed that was more appealing to them until a commotion on the other side of the room told me otherwise. I closed the door on the Coonara and set off to see what all the fuss was about and there was little Amber in a blue coat going nuts at the side of somebodies shoulder. It was Awesome she had bailed up this time. Clearly he had done something to set her off and she was letting him know it in that little granny way of hers. There was a good ten year age difference in Amber and Awesome and he is a very big solid pug, he was back then and he still is today, to run into the side of him would be like hitting a brick wall, you'd feel it more than he would. But regardless of his size and strength he just stood there like a solid mass letting his teeny tiny aging blind sister tell him off. I do think Amber was very conscious of what Awesome was, how could she not be, she was very much aware of the differences in their bodies, but Amber also knew who Awesome was. She knew he was a big softie and that she could get away with anything with him. When Awesome first entered the house he was only a baby and The Divine One just like everybody else had given him a good sniffing over, but just like all the other blind pugs in the family Amber had lingered and Awesome simply rolled around on the floor with a toy in his little mouth pawing at everybody as they gathered round. Amber had been right there beside Awesome as he grew, she would have sensed the changes taking place in his body, sensed him growing bigger, felt him getting stronger, heard him racing round the farm barking, building up strength while running along the fence line with the horses, she would have been able to hear the differences in his body as he moved around the house, his steps would have become heavier, louder, made more of a thud as he went running by. Amber may have been blind but she would have been very much aware of everything that was going on with her baby brother, you may think blind dogs are not aware of anything but from my observations I've found they are very much aware of everything that's going on, even more aware then fully sighted dogs are because they are paying that bit more attention, where a sighted dog will sometimes just look, a blind dog will be using all the senses they have left to work things out and by doing that they will have gained a whole lot of knowledge. The Divine One would have also felt Awesome's ears getting higher and higher from the ground, where once they would have been level with her face and could be tugged on at will, they were well out of her reach now. And that too would have been noted, she would have known the pup had grown. She also would have felt how his body was when she was leaning up against it or sleeping beside it, no more giddy puppy with jiggly body fat, now he was pure muscle, a big solid block of it. Still she had no trouble putting this annoying youngster in his place when he needed it and that had as much to do with Awesome as it did Amber. Sure Awesome was a very big, fit, young, healthy dog but he was also incredibly docile, just a big sook really, yes he wanted to play but he would allow himself to be told off when he got too rough and puppies can very easily become too rough without even realising they are doing it. To Awesome Amber would have been like a grandmother, a great grandmother even. There were a whole lot of differences in the two of them. I guess there were times with him being so young and full of robust health that he really got on her nerves. I don't think he would have gotten on her nerves half as much if he was just racing past being silly and yes he did that a lot of the time too but he also would go over and try and initiate The Divine One in play, paw at her sometimes if woofing at her side was getting him nowhere and well, old dogs don't like that kind of thing, it can be very annoying and even upsetting to them, they like to be left alone a lot of the time. They have lived their puppy years and have matured. And some will have a personality as strong as Amber's was and those dogs will be able to stick up for themselves no worries but you will have others that will need your help with keeping an annoying little puppy at bay. The more sensitive natured dogs will need you to help keep their life as peaceful as possible when bringing a puppy into the home and that's fair isn't it. They after all weren't the one who went out and bought the puppy in the first place you did. So it is your job to keep harmony between the two of them, know when your older dog wants to have a little play and when they have had enough and need a bit of peace and quiet. And they deserve to be able to have peace in their own home, they after all were there first, it's up to you to control the situation. It's just like being at a family gathering, you wouldn't stand there and let your toddler jump all over grandma or grandpa, you wouldn't allow then to pull their hair, smack them in the head, scream in their ears or swing on their arms and legs, no you'd be absolutely horrified if they were doing that, well that will be exactly what's happening in your home between your old dog and your new pup. That's why rules of respect need to be put into place and you need to make sure those rules are being heeded to. Of course puppies are cute but they need to learn that your old dog is not like they are, it's our job to play with the pup ourselves, wear the little fella out so he'll leave your old dog alone. Give him a few extra toys to play with too, buy him some new exciting ones that will keep him amused for hours. Well that's what we have always done on the occasion we have had a puppy join the family anyway because I think it's very important to do that. You always need to think about both sides.

Amber and Awesome

There were times when Amber did have a little play with Awesome, well it was more that she would feel him whizzing around and try and grab hold of him as he went by. I think the ecstatic running was what attracted her. She sensed some excitement in the air and wanted to be part of it, even if it was only in a very small way. She managed to catch him a few times too, usually when he was ready for settling and began slowing down, she would never have been able to catch him on his first dozen or so laps around the lounge room. Usually he ran with a toy in his mouth, ran real fast too like there was another dog running after him, there never was, it was just Awesome being a silly puppy but he was amusing himself greatly. Perhaps he was pretending that there actually was somebody on his tail to make the game more interesting. Amber would sense his speed reducing and knew it would be a good time to strike. She would lie in wait, tuck herself in amongst the clothes horses or in between the coffee table and couch and just wait for Awesome to go by and even though she may have done the exact same thing the day before and the one before that he still got the shock of his life when she grabbed hold of him. I think that too is a puppy thing, puppies don't tend to keep hold of things for very long, I've seen it a few times with babies, it's like each day is completely new to them. So Amber would pounce and Awesome would jump out of his skin then begin to play with her, like all puppies they don't stay startled for very long. He would regain his composure quite quickly and either walk in tight circles with her granny gnawing on the side of his shoulder or he would flip himself onto his back and move across the floor like that, stretched out and squirming around with little Amber pushing her face into him. No matter what she did he simply let her do it, he was wonderful with her, let her have free reign, never snapped, never lashed out, just stood or lay there enjoying himself. I think he was happy she was giving him some of her attention, he liked that she was playing with him. I too liked seeing them there together, playing in the only way a little old blind dog can play, on her terms and in her own way. Amber would occasionally play with her other siblings too and it always started with her lying in wait in one of her hidey spots. Just standing there waiting for some unsuspecting soul to go innocently wandering by and then she'd pounce. I thought she was pretty clever actually, keenly using her ears like that, listening for them coming, knowing that if she'd raced out too soon the sibling she was trying to scare would have seen her way before they got to her and merely thought she was just meandering about and of course if she held back too long they would have had no idea she'd shot out behind them, they'd have already passed by, now their minds would be on other things, on what was going on in front of them, sure they'd have heard her clunking out but not thought anything of it. No, in order to have full effect, the effect Amber wanted, she needed to clunk out at the perfect moment and over and over again I'd witness her doing it and thought she was pretty marvellous for being able to achieve that, such was her skill she didn't miss a beat. But The Divine One wasn't the only blind pug I've shared my life with who has done this when playing, Arthur used to do it too, did it when he was playing with Horton. I just think blind pugs are very clever little beings and seem to give a whole lot of situations a whole lot of thought in order to have the greatest impact. They work with what they do have, they don't seem to dwell on the things they have lost and in that I salute them. And due to that I am in awe.

I bet you think I am going to tell you that in the last year or so of Amber's life that she did end up quietening down a lot, but I can't tell you that because it would be a lie. She was still as feisty as all hell but she was no longer up to the prolonged periods of bossiness physically, she just didn't have it in her strength wise to keep it up. And of course due to who she was she didn't know it was the case, she was still trying to go at it with full force, but I knew she wasn't up to it so I'd be monitoring her with an extra keen eye. Watching and waiting for the right time to step in. I did still let her do what she wanted to do as I felt she was happy doing it. It was what kept her going some days. I'd see her clunking off and go after her, keep an eye on the proceedings, sometimes she would just clunk over and woof at somebody to get out of a bed she wanted to get in and if they didn't move, which 99% of the time they didn't, then she'd just get in next to them and go to sleep, but those little back legs of hers needed help lifting up at times so I would do that for her. She could get in bed by herself in that slow unsteady fashion of hers but then her little back legs would sometimes be hanging out, it was like she was a little too tired to drag them in so that's where I came in. I'd ever so gently move them into a positon I knew would be comfortable for her. Couldn't leave them hanging out getting cold and you have to be extra careful how you lift a very old dogs legs too, you can't go moving them the wrong way or being the slightest bit rough. Sometimes it'd be like I was positioning fragile glass, well that's the way I was handling those little divine legs anyway, treated them like they were the most delicate things in the world. Sometimes Amber wasn't even aware I was moving them, she didn't wake up, just carried on sleeping and I'd pause and watch her for a few moments before quietly backing away. Like all old dogs she slept most of the day away but when she woke up she'd sometimes feel like being feisty again. I guess she felt revived now so was ready to have a little burst. Sometimes I'd have to pick her up and carry her off to another part of the room and she'd be in my arms little mouth open, telling me off and trying to tell everybody else off in the process, her head would be trying to look back and I knew she couldn't see so it was more her way of telling me that she'd not finished doing what she wanted to do, she was telling me with the toss of her head and her growly bark that she wanted to be taken back to the spot in the lounge room I had just picked her up from. But I knew I couldn't do that, I knew it could well be the end of her if I did. Her breathing was heavy. She needed to be taken off so she could quieten down. Get her breath back. Get her heart beating at its normal pace instead of racing. So I took no notice of her demands, just carried on walking, carried on doing what was best for her. I'd pop her down in an area nobody else was in and she would spin around fast searching for some opponent but once she realised they were no longer there she would disengage, de-puff, go back to being her normal little self again. I'd wait for her to fully calm down and then I'd pop a treat into her mouth and leave her alone to eat it. She'd happily chomp away and forget all about what had annoyed her in the first place. She'd slowly eat her treat in peace then come join me and her siblings in the kitchen, and the little girl who clunked over to us was very different to the one I had just carried away. She happily stood by my feet with the others while I was getting dinner ready, she'd woof and climb up the side of my leg in order to get some extra food. I'd roll a bit of food into a ball and pop it into her mouth and she'd climb down off my runners, eat it and as soon as she'd done so I'd be able to feel her there climbing up again. So I played the dinner game with her, fed her extra little bits because the look on her face when I did so was the best thing ever and what I was giving her was mainly coming out of her own bowl. We were already hand feeding The Divine One all her meals at this point because she found eating out of a bowl by herself too hard. Feeding her little bits while I was getting everybody else's dinner ready was no big deal and she'd have already eaten half of her meal by the time I was ready to put the rest of the bowls down. So I'd sit her on my knee and hand feed her the remainder of her dinner, then say "All gone now" so she knew it was over. I mean you had to say it every time or she'd keep looking round for more. Once I'd said those vital words she knew it was time to get down. So I'd kiss her little old head, lower her to the ground and watch her clunk off to see if any of her siblings had left anything for her in their bowls, they never did but she was happy to go check each bowl regardless and when she got to the last one I knew it'd be ok to go round and collect all the bowls.

Nemo and Amber

CHAPTER EIGHTEEN

Strokes

I am not an expert on strokes in dogs by any means and nor do I claim to be but I have over the years had four dogs who have suffered from a stroke and so although I can't tell you how it is for all dogs who've had a stroke I can share with you my experiences with my four dogs and what I learnt from going through the process with them so that's what I am going to do here. And the reason I'm talking about strokes in the first place is because The Divine One was one of our dogs who suffered a stroke and we believe she also had a mini stroke as well. Arthur, Ruben and April are our other pugs that had strokes. I guess you'd now be wondering what similarities these four dogs had to cause them to have a stroke in the first place, well if I was reading this right now that's where my mind would be going so I'll answer that question for you. The thing they had in common was that they were all elderly dogs, Amber, Ruben and April were in their mid-teens. Arthur was a little bit younger. He was around the age of ten, so I guess it may have had something to do with his genetic makeup or maybe it did not. It's the same with human beings you will have cases where strokes happen in younger people. But the common factor I had with my dogs was age. Strokes in both dogs and humans are more common amongst the elderly. Strokes are also often related to heart disease which again is more common amongst elderly souls. I found out that strokes happen less frequently in pets than they do in people and that a stroke is more common if your elderly dog is dealing with other health issues. I've also been told that fifty percent of canine strokes have no specific underlying cause, they just happen, the same way they can just happen in people. Some people believe that dogs can't actually have a stroke. I was told this by somebody in rescue about a decade or so before all of this happened with Amber, Ruben, Arthur and April. Not sure why they thought this but clearly it's not the case. They can and they do. I've witnessed it up close. Anything with a brain has the potential to suffer from a stroke. Strokes occur when the brain is deprived of blood and oxygen causing brain cells to die. How severe a stroke is depends on how long the brain goes without blood flow and the effect a stroke will have on the body depends on the part of the brain that has been affected by the stroke. A neurologist told me once that we have come a long way in understanding the human brain but we still don't know everything about it, that we are still leaning. He was a top neurologist in his field too and if he admitted to such a thing then it must be true. What he said did surprise me though because I thought in this day and age with all our medical advances that we knew it all, and I guess we know a heck of a lot more than we did a hundred years ago but I suppose when it comes to the human brain we are still learning. And if we are still learning about the human brain then I'd say there would be a heck of a lot more that we don't know about the canine brain. I did learn that for both us and dogs strokes are classified as ischemic or haemorrhagic. If the stroke is ischemic that means a part of the brain isn't receiving a proper supply of blood which damages the brain tissues. If the stroke is haemorrhagic it means a vessel in the brain begins to bleed and that bleeding causes swelling and pressure on the brain. How well a dog bounces back from a stroke will depend on the part of the brain that has received the damage, how his body works after a stroke will too depend on the part of the brain that has been most affected, the length of time the brain was deprived of blood and oxygen and the time it took for medical help to be administrated. All of these things factor in to how a dog is going to be after having a stroke. I personally think brains are incredibly sensitive instruments. Before living through these periods I never really gave the brain much thought and I guess that's generally how it is if something is working properly. You don't tend to think about it because there is no need to really, but then you come face to face with a problem and suddenly you'll want to know everything you can about it. Before I began looking into strokes I didn't even know there was such a thing as a spinal stroke but there is and it occurs in both dogs and cats but is a lot more common in larger breeds of dogs then it is in little ones. We have never dealt with a spinal stroke here on the farm and fingers crossed we never will, but if we did we would do everything possible for the dog in question.

There are steps you need to take if you think your dog has suffered from a stroke with the first one being get to a vet as quickly as possible, this is vital, I cannot stress this point enough. Get in your car and drive to your vet. Keeping your dog calm during this time is very important also and as hard as it may be you'll need to keep yourself calm too because you freaking out is not going to help the situation at all. It'll only make your dog worse because they will be picking up on your emotions, even in the state they are in they will still be able to sense things from you and you need to let them know that you "Have this" and that you are "In control", they will have no control over themselves or what is happening inside their body at this point so it's vital that you show strength. Falling apart is not an option for you right now, do it later on if you must but for now your job is to be an asset to your dog so that's what you need to do. Your dog will be having trouble supporting him or herself so they will need some form of cushioning for protection. Cushioning for them to lie on and also cushioning for their heads. Ours had no control over their heads or bodies, their world was spinning. We use a basket for vet travels when dealing with something like this. We line the bottom of the basket with a soft blanket and also have a bit of cushioning between the side of the basket and their heads to prevent them banging their head. They become like new born babies when they've had a stroke, not able to support their heads properly. If you don't have a suitable basket simply put a blanket on the floor of the car, don't have your dog on the seat, you don't want them falling off during the drive. Also I would not suggest holding your dog in your arms, I know if something was going on in my body that I didn't fully understand the last thing I would want is for somebody to be holding me in any form of restraint. I also think it's the same thing with seizures, a seizing dog needs freedom of movement not restriction. Also some dogs can be in pain after suffering from a stroke, the pain is sharp and sudden and a lot of the time it will disappear after a few minutes but that's just a guideline it's not always the case sometimes it can take a few hours for the pain to ease, holding your dog in your arms during this time could be painful for them. Pain is also another reason you want to be getting to a vet right away. Your dog will need medical care just like you would need medical care if you had suffered a stroke. Your veterinarian will perform a full physical examination and could also recommend blood work or x-rays to rule out other underlying problems that have signs that are similar to a stroke. Even though this will be a very worrying and emotional time for you, you need to really listen to what your vet has to say. Keep yourself calm and take everything he is telling you in. Be guided by that but also know your own mind. The one thing I really would like people to understand is that a dog doesn't necessarily need to be put to sleep if they have suffered a stroke. I know a lot of folks think it's automatically the case but it is not. Of this I know for sure. It saddens me greatly to think of dogs being put to sleep because their owners thought that this was the end, and yes there will be times when it may well be the end, but not always. I feel really sorry for dogs that if given proper treatment and time to recover may have gone on to live a few more years. Strokes are a huge thing for the body to deal with, the body needs adequate time to recover, allow your dog that recovery time. I'm not going to lie to you your dog is not going to look great after suffering from a stroke and that can be hard to see, but how they look in the early days is not how they are always going to look and be. Don't rush to end a life that may not need ending. I've always seen improvement; mine have always recovered quite well so I've not as yet had to make that decision. But of course if appropriate time had been given and there was not the slightest sign of improvement then I would be once again going to see my vet, getting his opinion and making a quality of life decision and I would not shy away from doing that. But I would have done everything possible to give the dog the best chance of recovery first. You have to know deep down in your heart that you have done everything in your power to give your dog a chance it's only then that you can walk away with peace of mind. No corners cut, no refusal to put the work in or give the care that is needed to get them through this, just did everything you possibly could. Yes you will walk away with great sadness and the path of grief is going to be hard but you will at least have no guilt and believe me that's what you will need in order to heal. Anything other than doing everything possible for your canine son or daughter will bring guilt and guilt stifles the grieving process and the grieving process, I know from much experience, is hard enough as it is.

There are some common signs that your dog has had or is having a stroke but they are not going to be identical in every single dog, they will quite often vary, they did with us. And you'll have some dogs that won't show any signs at all that they are about to have a stroke, it'll come out of the blue, no tell-tale signs whatsoever which is exactly what happened with two of our pugs. I didn't notice anything out of the ordinary with either one of them, nothing different about them on the day or days leading up to the stroke. Sure they can't tell you if they are feeling a bit off but there are ways, if you know your dog that you can tell if something isn't quite right and I never noticed anything with two of the pugs until the stroke itself occurred. Both went from seeming normal to severely impaired very quickly. With the others one had a seizure about a week before the stroke and the other one vomited a few hours before having her stroke. And note was made of these incidents, it always is, but again I didn't know these things were going to be followed by a stroke because vomiting and seizures happen for other reasons too. Also strokes can cause dogs to lose vison but our pugs were already blind or almost blind so it wasn't the case with them because you can't lose what you don't have in the first place and the one that did have a little bit of vision left, she didn't lose any more. And nor did them being blind have anything to do with why they had a stroke it was just a coincidence really. Some of the common signs of a stroke are loss of balance, falling over, rolling to one side, pacing, circling, head tilting, unusual movements of the eyes like a rotary movement, impaired vision, abnormal facial expressions, there could also be vomiting and loss of bladder and bowel control. Your dog may collapse, even lose consciousness altogether. One or all of their limbs become weak. And it's hard because the onset of other conditions can mimic a stroke, another reason why it's so important to go see your vet so he can tell what's going on, he'll be able to rule other things out so you'll know exactly what you are dealing with. Brain tumours and middle ear infections can cause some of the same symptoms as a stroke. I saw it in Ruben and thought he had suffered another stroke and was so relieved to hear our vet saying it was his ear this time. Ruben was the first one my pugs to have a stroke so when Amber, Arthur and April had theirs I had an idea of what was going on because I'd seen it before. April actually suffered a stroke when I was almost at the end of this chapter and was recovering while I was writing the rest of the book so this chapter was once quite different to how you are reading it today. Because it was so close to being finished I decided to leave it how it was and add a bit on the end about April. But when I came back to do the first edit I looked at it and decided to rewrite the entire thing putting April in from the start. It seemed the right thing to do. She after all was sitting beside me in a cot with her little head on the side while I wrote the remainder of this book. I was taking care of her and writing tiny bits here and there whenever she was sleeping, then as soon as she woke up I'd go take care of her, carry her outside for a wee, hand feed her, that sort of thing and that's the reason this book was not ready for publication when I promised it would be. But my writing has always been done around the pugs and I knew The Divine One wouldn't have any issues with her book being late. I knew she would want me to be taking care of her siblings, putting their needs first like I always do. I knew she'd fully understand because I had done the same thing with her over all the years she was with me. Many a chapter in a book got shoved to the side while I rocked Amber in my arms. It's just what good Mum's do and I learnt from the very best.

Ruben, Amber, Lilly Rain, Emily and Arthur

When Ruben had his stroke it was quite scary because I didn't know what was going on. I remember it was a wintery Sunday afternoon and I was writing the first of the Grace Farm books at the time. That day I was sitting in the middle of the bed surrounded by big pillows and gentle sleeping pugs. Ruben was by my feet and I noticed him start to stand up, well try to stand up but sink down again pretty quickly. I thought he wanted to be taken outside for a wee but was comfortable and warm so had decided against it. It wasn't unusual for him to do that kind of thing so I didn't think anything of it. I watched on for a few moments just in case he changed his mind and wanted me to take him outside after all but he seemed to be sleeping so I carried on typing. An hour or so later when the time came for me to pack up my computer and take the pugs for their afternoon walk it was then that I noticed there was something wrong with Ruben. He was unable to stand, couldn't support himself at all, balance completely gone and his head was slightly tilted to the side. Because the stroke affects your dog's brain it interferes with their ability to stay upright but being unfamiliar with strokes I didn't know that at the time, if I did I would have known exactly what was going on and acted sooner and I do feel bad about my ignorance. I now believe Ruben suffered a stroke when I first saw him attempting to stand. I believe what had taken place in his body had caused some pain which made him jerk upright and I felt really bad for not investigating further at the time. But he didn't make any noise, no crying out, no sound at all, just raised his body up and sank back down again and because it had started to rain I figured he'd heard the raindrops on the roof and decided to stay put for now, hold his bladder a little bit longer so he wouldn't get wet, but of course I now know that was not the case at all. Ruben was taken to our vet and to be honest hearing the word stroke was unnerving, we'd not walked down this particular path before so we were inexperienced, we didn't know what to expect and that was probably the hardest part, the not knowing, the unknown can be worrying. Especially seeing Ruben the way he was now. He didn't look too good at all and of course he wouldn't would he, nobody looks their best after having a stroke. But how they look at the start and how they'll look months down the track can be very different but again we didn't know that. I remember watching our vets face trying to gage from his reaction how bad he thought Ruben was. He'd no doubt dealt with a lot more incapacitated dogs then we have. He's seen the ones that were carried in in all sorts of conditions and he'd also have a pretty good idea of what their chances of recovery were and in knowing this I was watching his expressions as he was examining my old blessing. As I watched on I starting thinking that there are always going to be cases that will surprise you. You hear about it in humans and animals too, there's always going to be situations where predictions were not good, doctors not expecting patients to live and months later seeing them walk out of hospital on their own. I've seen such things happening here on the farm too and I don't know if they are miracles that have taken place or if it's the will of the dog or if it's that this particular soul has a super resistant body. I'm probably going with all three because I've seen cases where a dog's will, their incredible drive, simply wouldn't allow them to give up or give in and you are just blown away from seeing what they go on to achieve. With Ruben I did have some peace of mind because he received medical assistance right away. I knew by doing that we had given him the best chance possible of a good recovery and so you cling to that and do a whole lot of praying while you are leaning over that slumbering body and a dog that's had a stroke will do a whole lot of sleeping during the recovery time. And that's a good thing because sleep aids the body's healing. We always pen unwell pugs off in an area where they can rest without interface from the other dogs, think of it this way would you want to be to in amongst a whole lot of people if you'd suffered a stroke, no you would want to be left alone to heal in peace and quiet and it's vital that you give this to your dogs as well. The penning off is very important for other reasons too because some dogs will have a go at a dog that is incapacitated. It's how it is in the wild and it can happen in your home so you do what needs to be done in order to keep the little soul safe, protect the one who's had a stroke and this is even more important to do when you are not at home. Don't think just because your dogs have lived together for years that things can't happen. I was told of a lady who's 13 year old dog suffered a stroke and was attacked by one of her others dogs, she was even at home at the time it occurred, she'd gone outside to do something and was only gone a little while she said but when she walked back into the house there was blood everywhere and her pug was dead. I just couldn't understand why she didn't think to protect her pug, to me it's basic common sense but I suppose she didn't think she needed to and her pug paid the price. So please take precautions, not just with a dog that's had a stroke but with any dog that is unwell because it's far better to be safe than sorry.

Nemo, Amber, Casey and Ruben (Brian and Lilly Rain at the back)

When our pugs first had their strokes they became totally bedridden, all four of them did. It was a case of round the clock monitored care. You will have to do everything for them because at this point they won't be able to do anything themselves. None of our pugs could stand unaided, couldn't hold themselves upright on their own, we had to hold them up while they had a wee, you have to become their limbs while they recover, well you become everything for them really because that's what they are going to need. One look and I could see they'd need my help in every single area and that's fine I'm used to being the eyes and ears for some of the pugs we have on the farm and with a stroke you have to step up even more. We hand fed each one of our pugs for quite some time after they'd had their strokes, sometimes it was David who did the feeding other times it was me, it all depended on who was that particular pug's favourite person. You know who they respond to most so one steps forward while the other steps back, no hard feelings, just doing whatever it takes to get food into that hungry little mouth. I fed Amber and Ruben. We both took turns of feeding Arthur and April. You have to help them eat because at this stage their heads can be a little wonky, some more so then others and they have no control over that so it's up to you to get that all important nutritious food into them. None of ours had any trouble eating the food once it was in their mouths, no trouble swallowing and no loss of appetite with any of them either, in fact some seemed even hungrier than they usually were. Always hungry, always such good little eaters, which by the way is great at a time like this because if they refuse food you know you're in trouble. But ours ate everything they were offered and knew exactly when it was dinner time too, little wonky heads shot up and began trying to look around as soon as they heard or smelt food on its way. Each one knew when it was treat time as well. We often give a treat as an incentive to hurry up and have a wee, especially at night and we'd be carrying out the little one who'd had a stroke and you'd be holding them up to have a wee and as soon as they had done so their little wobbly head would be sniffing the air for the treat they knew was coming their way and because of how they were Dave and I would often grab two treats from the jar before walking outside because we were both just so proud of how our little ones were doing. Also I must mention here that if your pug is being finicky about food then you should go ahead and give them anything they want because at times like this it's vital they eat something, later on when they have healed somewhat, when they are further along in their recovery you can go back to their regular food and again this is not just the case with a stroke it's the case with any dog that isn't feeling well, food rules change in our house at times like this and really it's no big deal, we all like being fussed over, we all enjoy having something fun or special to eat when we are not feeling well and it's the same for our dogs. But mainly it's done due to getting a sick pug to eat because they need to keep their strength up.

Amber being hand fed in her cot

Although the onset of the strokes was a little different with each pug the one thing they did have in common was the time we began seeing those first signs of recovery. Each pug started showing improvement on day four, one took a little longer but it was around four days for the others. That's not being their normal self but certainly showing signs of improvement. That's when they will start to try and stand up, even be able to hold themselves upright unaided for a little while, legs actually supporting their bodies more now and once they've mastered that they will start moving around a bit, walking a few steps, still unsteady, still needing you to be there with hands either side of their bodies to catch them but certainly doing better, like a little corner has been turned. We found it was baby steps when recovering from a stroke. The strokes hit fast but recovering does take time and they are going to need some special looking after in the weeks and months to come but they will be showing signs of improving all the time. With our pugs we found their will was quite strong, strong in every one of them, each one wanting to do more and as soon as their bodies were up to it they'd be doing it, well trying to do it anyway. It's a case of monitoring your pug because they will let you know what they are capable of and each one differed slightly in that area too. But as soon as they let us know they were up for it we would let them try and always be right beside them should they need us. I remember with Arthur it was raining hard the day he let me know he'd like to try and support his own body. I had carried him outside like I had been doing for the past few days. I put him under the back veranda, on the grass but completely sheltered from the elements. I didn't want him getting even the slightest drop of rain on him. I remember him standing there swaying a bit, I was crouched down ready to support his body. Hold him up while he had a wee like I had been doing. A few of the other pugs had come outside with us but very quickly disappeared back inside the house and I was glad they had done that because I didn't want them accidently knocking Arthur over on his first good day. They gathered around the two of us, sniffing my hands, sniffing at their little blind brother's face, seeing if he was ok, seeing if perhaps I had another treat in my hands for them. Arthur was fine and I had no treats left, they'd already been given out when a squat or leg lift had taken place so I watched them shuffle up the ramp and shoot inside the house again. Arthur was unsteady but happy enough to not have me holding onto him this time so I took a step back. I was actually standing behind him because where some will topple to the side, The Divine One being one of them, Arthur used to fall backwards. If he was going to fall I knew it wouldn't be to the left or right always backwards with him so I'd positioned myself behind him so that I could catch him before he hit the ground, not that he would have hurt himself, simply gone backwards and been sitting down, but I didn't want him sitting on the wet ground. I watched him swaying for a few moments, sort of teetering but not at all worried or unhappy I could tell that by his face. He was just glad to be outside after days of being in bed. He was sniffing the air as he was wobbling, he could smell the rain and was enjoying it. I too love the smell of rain and so we stood there together for a little while. I was giving him a bit of time to strengthen his legs, he'd had a few days without walking, there would have been a bit of weakness there. Arthur had spinal issues, he'd had major back surgery so was a special little soul due to that and I was always mindful of his condition. But I was watching him and he seemed to be liking standing there with his little head slightly tilted and then on shaky legs he lowered his body down to the squatting position and had a wee. Then just like that he stood back up again all the while keeping his balance and I was so proud of him in that moment. Due to his back Arthur always squatted down to wee, lifted his leg in the early days of his arrival on the farm but then his back went and he needed surgery and well that was the end of him being able to cock his leg, it was always a lean down to wee, pretty much like a male horse does when they are urinating and as Arthur aged he began fully squatting down like female dogs do. But he had done it on his own today. Still in a weakened state but managed it regardless, got his body back up into the standing positon and I gave him a few more moments of air sniffing before carrying him inside. So that's how it was for Arthur, one stroke, a good steady recovery period then back to being how he was before the stroke, never any other issues with him besides what was going on with his back but such a thing was expected as Arthur aged and we were aware of it but it didn't have anything to do with the stroke.

One thing I did find unusual was that Amber and Arthur had their strokes within a week of one another and I couldn't for the life of me figure out why that was and that's because there was absolutely no connection there at all. I gave it a real lot of thought trying to work out what had taken place in the days and weeks leading up to the strokes and came up with nothing and that's because there was nothing to come up with, no link whatsoever. A stroke is not something one can catch from somebody else. It's not like the common cold or a case of gastro being passed from one pug to another. It was just something that happened and so we now had two pugs recovering from their strokes at the same time. We had Amber in a cot and I set Arthur up by the window on a few layers of blankets and he seemed happy enough with that. I also had a rolled up blanket against him as he was still leaning to one side, the rollup gave him some support, something to lean against, helped prop him up. I didn't put him by the window so he could see out because he was blind but he did like feeling the warmth of the sun through the window that's why I put him there. He was sleeping most of his days away and the blanket area was big enough for some of the other pugs to wander over and join him if they wanted to which a few did on occasion but mainly they just left him to his own devises. If they had become a nuisance to him I would have had to pen Arthur off, and I did always put him in a pen if I wasn't home, but while I was wandering around doing housework he was fine on the blanket and the others more or less left him alone. They occasionally went over for a sniff or a little lick of his face then be off doing their usual thing again, following me round the house. I'd go over and pick Arthur up as soon as I noticed he was stirring then carry him outside so he could have a wee and on the way back inside I would hold him up near the water bowl so he could also have a drink. Arthur was always a big drinker and would sometimes be standing there for the longest time lapping at the water. The fact that I was holding him up didn't seem to bother him at all. Some won't drink if something is amiss but not little Arthur, nothing put him off. He was thirsty he was getting his fill and didn't care if somebody had to help him do it. When he indicated to me that he'd had enough I'd dry his chin and carry him back to his blanket for some more rest. After a few days Arthur began woofing for me when he needed something, woof to let me know when he needed to go outside and woof if he was thirsty or hungry. Arthur was very good at letting me know his needs whereas Amber at this stage in her recovery was asleep in the cot not saying a word. She would more often than not wee and poo in the cot and that was ok she was doing the very best she could do at the time so I'd come by and lift her up, slide the wet towels out from underneath her and slide two clean towels where the wet ones had been and sometimes she wouldn't even wake up while I was doing it. I'd use three towels and sometimes it wasn't just the towels that needed changing the blankets needed changing too. But she was resting and healing so I'd smile down at her and tell her what a great job she was doing of that. Sometimes when I was changing her bedding I would pause, holding her in my arms, just to feel close to her for a little while. I'd talk to her as well, sing to her too, kiss her little ears, walk over to the door or window so she could hear the sounds of the farm. Let her know everything was still here waiting for her when she returned, give her something to keep fighting for, the other pugs would be running around on the floorboards sounding like they were tap dancing. A few would be over by the window, glued to the window like they were most days so I'd walk over and slide the door open and they'd all fly out onto the deck. Sometimes I'd carry Amber out there for a bit. Give her a break from being in the cot because she was eating all her meals in the cot as well, basically she was in that cot 24 hours a day but because she wasn't able to do anything but lay there the cot was the best place for her. She never ever missed a meal, she'd be asleep and I'd be going about the business of feeding the other pugs and her bowl would be lined up on the bench with everybody else's. So I'd fill it then put it to one side figuring she could have it the next time she woke up, but she must have heard all the commotion because her head would come up as I was putting everybody else's bowls down. She was never once late eating. I'd go sit by her cot and hand feed her small mouthfuls until it was all gone and she ate at the same speed she always ate at, the stroke didn't seem to affect her little mouth or jaw action and if I wasn't going fast enough she would soon let me know. Yes her bark was weak but she was trying to woof anyway and because I was so close I could hear it and be rolling another small ball of food to pop into that little mouth. Over the course of a week her bark became stronger and stronger.

I'd give Amber's underside a sponge bath once a day just to keep her feeling and smelling nice and fresh, some days she'd need two sponge baths, then back in the cot she would go. I don't think she was bored in the cot because she was mostly sleeping but in knowing how much she loved hearing the birds settling into the trees of an evening I'd carry her outside because I thought it'd be lovely for her to hear it now too. Arthur was in a position where he could sometimes walk unaided, not up to walking around the farm by any means, but able to take a few slow steps at a time, able to go get a drink by himself when he wanted one, able get off his blanket and come out on the deck to join us if he wanted to. If he was sleeping he'd sleep but if the vibration of the pugs rushing through the door caused him to raise his head he'd slowly saunter out and have a bit of time on the deck with us. Amber always stayed in my arms. Whether I was sitting, standing or walking I always kept her in my arms. Each night just before dark I would slowly walk from one end of the veranda to the other and Amber would just lay in my embrace with her front paws dangling over my arm. She was giving a few contented signs so I continued carrying her around, back and forth we would go, slow steady steps, walking from one end of the deck to the other and back again. I walked that path quite a few times each evening giving The Divine One chance to smell the different smells that came floating by and they can be slightly different depending on where you are on the deck. Ruben was barking near the plant pots. Amber and I would side step him as we went by, with the pugs that were following on behind us doing the same thing we had just done. None of us disturbed him. Ruben had suffered his stroke a year before and was now doing great. I watched him woofing and tapping that one back paw of his and smiled then leant down and kissed Ambers little grey forehead, whispered in her ear that her time would come. I looked around the deck and out into the paddock, concentrated on what was happening around me, listened to the happy woofs, the snuffly noises, the pitter pattering of many paws, began counting my blessing, watched the pugs coming and going, enjoyed the moment and was thankful for it. These lovely old darlings and this little farmhouse made me happy. Sure I had some sick pugs but I had so much to be grateful for as well and I was deeply grateful. If things had turned out differently some of these pugs may not have been with me today and yet here they were meandering round my feet. Yes Amber was in the midst of another battle but being in my arms she would have been picking up on everything I was feeling and I believe the joy I held inside would have benefited her. Everybody benefits from good vibes and happy feelings when they are healing. A calm contented positive environment is a must I believe. My eye was drawn back to Ruben again because he had just started weeing on the side of the doorframe with most of the wee going inside the house. He mistook it for a veranda post and that was ok, no big deal, just a quick clean up once I put Amber back down.

There was a time during Amber's recovery period when I was extremely worried about her. I'd be peeping over the cot wondering if she was going to recover. There was even a day where David and I both felt she may not. The day before she started showing improvement we really thought we were going to lose her and as she lay motionless in the little pink cot Dave and I were standing down the bottom of the paddock, out of Amber's earshot, in hushed tones discussing where we were going to bury her and we decided that she was going to go next to Billy. I remember looking down at her before walking out the door. I'd set Amber up in the cot on a thick blanket and underneath the back end of her body was a pretty pink and purple patterned towel, well it was more pink and lilac really and I could see parts of it peeping out from underneath her tail as I paused to caress her ears. I'd pause to make sure she was ok and I'd pause to let her know that we were going outside for a little while but wouldn't be gone too long, just long enough to give her siblings time to have a wee. Amber didn't respond to me, she was sleeping or not sleeping maybe just resting her little eyes but I always talked to her to let her know what was happening. I figured if she was still in there but just not able to respond that she would have appreciated knowing what was going on. Amber loved to walk and I thought how hard it would have been for her listening to us walking out the door, she no doubt could hear the frenzied pitter pattering, hear the clip of paws on the metal strip, hear the excitable woofs getting softer and softer as we all walked further and further away from the house. I felt sad that she couldn't be with us but knew she was better off where she was. If I put her in a pram and brought her with us what happiness could it possibly bring her, absolutely none at this point I thought, if I did it it would have been more for me than her so I left her where she was. In the pram she would have been disturbed from sleep, jostled about on uneven ground, a thing you really don't want to be doing to a pug that's in recovery. As we walked David and I started discussing Amber in detail. We didn't want her to hear our concerns or that we thought this may be the end for her because we never ever talk about things like that in front of our pugs just in case they have other ideas and want to keep on fighting which is exactly what Amber did because the next morning she got up and began walking down the road to recovery, literally, after not doing so well she started to turn the corner, started ever so slowly doing things herself. It began with her standing up, attempting to support her own body when being carried outside for a wee and went on from there. I think the reason it took Amber longer to respond was due to the fact that she was such a delicate little flower to begin with so needed more time. But recovering from a stroke isn't a race, it is a case of each pug doing the very best they can each day and so you help them through and give each one the recovery time they need. Seeing Amber how she was right after the stroke I thought she would never again be climbing my legs like a kitten then a few months later she began doing it again. As soon as she came good and as soon as her balance was better she went right back to tugging on my socks for food and it was the most wonderful feeling in the whole wide world. Amber recovered from that stroke pretty well. Once she was able to walk she began outwalking the other two pugs that had suffered from strokes but then again walking was her favourite thing. At times you'd look at her and couldn't even tell that she'd had a stroke and I was grateful for that.

Some dogs are always going to have mild wobbling or a head tilt after a stroke, some only slight, some more defined and others over time will eventually have their heads go back to their normal position. But if they do retain the head tilt we have found they are able to regain their sense of balance so walking isn't a problem. Our vet told us a remaining head tilt isn't really an issue that a dog can live just fine like that and after experiencing it in our own home we now know he's right. One thing I have noticed though is that when they are overdoing things the head tilt does become a little more prominent so that's when I'll go rein the little blessing in, make them hop in a bed and get some rest or carry them on the walk to prevent them from exerting themselves even more. I do this a lot with April as she really does like giving the dogs next door a good woofing at and she'll run back and forth along the fence when doing it. I let her go for a little while, don't want to ruin her fun because the fact that she's had a stroke and can still run as well as she does is a wonderful thing. But I do always stand watching on and the first sign of wavering I'll scoop her up and carry her, if I didn't she would just keep on running and woofing until she fell over, she has no idea how tired she can get until she's completely worn herself out. Her mind is only on the woof and the fun whereas my mind is on her not overdoing things. She's done so well since her stroke the last thing I want is to lose her now. Circling is another thing that differs in dogs that have had strokes. Some people believe that all dogs circle after having a stroke because in their eyes that is the true definition of a stroke but we found it's not always the case. Ruben was by far our worst circler, some didn't circle at all and one did a little bit but not for very long, nowhere near as long as Ruben did. With Ruben he was walking in circles for quite some time. I would carry him outside and put him in an area that was free of trees. Put him in the middle of a paddock so he could have a bit of a walk around, get some strength back into his legs but not be banging into anything. Ruben only had one eye and he was blind in that eye and I couldn't have him circling into trees or fence posts injuring himself. Even if he could see he wouldn't have been able to avoid walking into something because his reactions were slow, his responses dull, they were there but they were dull. Also he didn't have a real lot of control over where his body was taking him at this point. To Ruben himself he probably wouldn't have been able to tell the difference. To him I think it would have been like he was walking in a straight line but he wasn't so I'd put him down in a big open space then draw the other pugs away so they too weren't getting in his way. All of us would stand on the sidelines watching Ruben and rushing to his aide when he needed help. I didn't let him do too much on any given day. It was always just a little wander around whenever I carried him outside for a wee. But the funny thing was that he could still cock his leg, couldn't walk in a straight line and was still very wobbly but when lifting his leg he was always in perfect control, perfect form and then he would lower his leg again and go back to circling. It was like he was using everything he had in him to control that leg lift and because he couldn't see he was lifting his leg in mid-air, never against anything because there was nothing close for him to cock his leg against. Although he did wee on my leg a few times when I went over to help him but that was fine he had done it a few times over the years he had been living with us anyway. Mistook David's or my leg for a tree or fence post, we'd be standing around talking waiting for the pugs to have a wee then one of us would feel wetness on our leg and look down and there would be little blind Ruben John Comer with his leg cocked weeing with all his might. And we'd both just laugh, regardless of who had been mistaken for a tree we both laughed our heads off about it. We actually thought Ruben was pretty clever, he could sense when something was near and if it happened to be our legs so be it. That's just life with blind dogs. Ruben could lift those back legs of his quite high too, raised them up a lot higher than some of the other male pugs did, it was like he was always aiming for the sky so it wouldn't only be the bottom of your pant leg that was wet it'd be wet from just around your knee all the way down. The stroke did alter how high he could lift his leg for a little while, in the early days he would only be lifting it ever so slightly off the ground but over the following months he began lifting it higher and higher until he was able to lift it to the height he used to do. I'd put him down and he'd start slowly circling then pause and up would come his skinny little back leg and he'd wee and sometimes wee and wee and wee because he'd been holding his bladder and was glad to be outside setting it free. At first Rubens circles were very tight, not much more than a dog turning around on the spot but over time those circles became bigger and bigger. Then it got to a stage where he'd start off circling then be off walking in a line, only a short line and the line was never entirely straight, more pulling to one side but it was a line never the less and then he'd go back to walking a circle again. As time went by the breaking off to walk in a line became more and more frequent until that's all he was doing. Circling completely gone but still slightly walking off course but happy never the less to be sniffing and weeing and enjoying being outside with us all.

After our first stroke occurred I did try and find out if there was perhaps something I could have done other than what I was already doing that would prevent or delay a stroke from taking place and was told that unfortunately there is no way to prevent a stroke from happening but keeping your dogs as healthy as you possibly can will make a stroke less likely. Time and time again I heard how regular veterinary check-ups were important because your vet can pick up on all sorts of things and early detection and treatment of underlying diseases can reduce your dog's risk of suffering from a stroke. Also teeth are important, keeping your dogs teeth in the best condition possible is vital as it's not just the mouth that is affected by rotting teeth bad teeth can have an effect on the entire body. Our pugs are all well known to our vet, he is very familiar with each little blessing and that is a really nice feeling to have. Also dealing with the strokes did start me wondering what the percentage of strokes was in canines but I guess I'll never have an answer to that question because I reckon there are a lot of strokes happening that aren't diagnosed and a lot of mini strokes that could even go undetected and that could be because the signs are very subtle or that they are thought to be associated with something else. It'll usually take an MRI to get a definitive diagnosis. When Ruben first had his stroke I contacted my friend Stephen Dale because he had personal experience with a stroke. I was interested to know what a stroke feels like from the inside. Outside I could clearly see how the stroke had affected Ruben but I had no way of knowing what would have been going on inside of him but Stephen did and he answered my questions, helped me know how Ruben would be feeling. I asked about pain levels and Stephen told me he had a lot of pain in his joints and it was handy knowing that because it helped me help not just Ruben but the other pugs too. All of our pugs went on to live for quite a while after their strokes and I think that was due to a number of things. One being they are given excellent care and nutrition on a daily basis. Two because the strokes may not have been as bad as they could have been and again I believe that is due to good looking after, well in most cases it would be but again there are always going to be times when something is going to go wrong in their bodies even though you are doing everything right and that's all to do with how the body is aging, also genetics, bloodlines and breeding come into it too and those things are taken out of our hands because we take in older dogs, we don't breed ourselves. And the third thing is that each pug that had a stroke was taken to see our vet right away. They received professional treatment without delay. Time is vital when you are dealing with a stroke, you must act quickly, you have to get them the care they need as fast as you possibly can because it will make a huge difference in the recovery time. The quicker you get them the help they need the lesser the effect the stroke has on their body. If left untreated the problem can worsen in a short period of time. The longer treatment is put off the greater the chance for permanent neurological damage. I found out that long-term prognosis is good in dogs that are treated early and given the supportive care they need. But that's just basic common sense isn't it because the longer you wait before being seen for an acute medical condition the worst it can get.

CHAPTER NINETEEN

Changing With The Times

I have shared my life with a lot of old dogs and where it's true that they do age somewhat differently there are some common similarities that they will have. It's just that they can come on at different stages in their life, it has a lot to do with how they have lived their lives, the care they've been given and naturally genetics has something to do with it as well. There are some things that most of my pugs will get as they grow older and then there are things that only one or two will get. It's like human beings, not all of us are going to age the same or get the exact same illnesses either. Yes my pugs will all slow down, they will all show signs of joint deterioration, body stiffness, a degree of back leg weakness, they will get tired and some of their senses will lessen or be lost altogether. And you need to keep an eye on their teeth as this is very important, rotten teeth and gum disease is not good for their mouth but if left untreated it can also lead to other things going on inside the body. Also cancer is more common amongst the elderly but if they do get cancer not all of them are going to get the exact same type although we have found some types are more common. And for little old pugs incontinence is very common. Amber suffered from incontinence in the latter part of her life and we worked with that, we didn't alter her life just because she was no longer as good as she used to be at controlling her bladder. If they could hold on they would hold on, you know that to be the truth, you can see it on their faces and in their eyes and so we never punish any of our pugs for something that is now beyond their control. We know they are doing the very best they can do with the changes that due to age are happening within their bodies. We would never make them go and sleep in another room or god forbid be so cruel as to kick them outside. We know their life would be shortened if we did that but not only that it'd break their little hearts too and we won't ever do that to them, our pugs will never be cast outside for any reason. We just assess each situation as it presents itself and work out the best way to help. With Amber she was used to sleeping on our bed, she had been doing it since a few months after she arrived on the farm and now she was incontinent we were going to let her keep doing what she loved. We didn't want to hurt her feelings by making her go sleep somewhere else. We wanted her with us as much as she wanted to be with us. We weren't going to ban her from sleeping on the bed just because she was old and incontinent. We wouldn't penalize her for something that wasn't her fault, couldn't have her in a bed on the floor wondering what she'd done wrong because the truth of the matter was that she'd done nothing wrong, her body had changed that's all and so her routine of care now needed to change as well. But due to how her body was tinkle trousers or a nappy were out of the question, yes they are great for incontinent dogs but they weren't the answer for Amber. I wouldn't have minded The Divine One wearing tinkle trousers to be honest because I knew how well they worked for Horton but I knew that due to how Amber's back and back legs were they wouldn't have worked. It would have made movement difficult for her. It may have been ok if she wasn't the type of pug who loved to walk, if she was more the type that didn't move around much we may have considered them but Amber was a walker, unless she was asleep she was rarely still. And it was important to keep those little legs of hers going because that was helping her in so many ways. Movement was keeping her joints flexible and Amber had quite the appetite on her as well so walking the amount she did was helping her get a good amount of food in her dinner bowl, she didn't know it but we did, if she had known I reckon she would have tried to run a marathon every day. Even at sixteen years old Amber loved to walk, sure her step was slower and more unsteady than it had once been but it wasn't enough to stop her from going where she wanted to go or sniffing what she wanted to sniff, it just took her a little bit longer to get there is all. But she was out there having a ball and I was watching on knowing the fun she was having was beneficial to her overall health, aided her greatly, mind, body and soul all benefitted.

Amber, Casey and Ava

Day time is a little easier when you have an incontinent dog, you just take them out for a lot more wee breaks of course you'll still have accidents in the house and little leaks in beds but they'll be less if you are giving them more frequent opportunities to relieve their bladders. And every one of us enjoyed those extra trips outdoors, not just the little incontinent soul but they all loved going out for more frequent sniffs. As for night-time, well, once we became aware of Amber's situation we decided to set things up differently for her on our bed so that on the nights she did have an accident it could be quickly sorted out. No more middle of the night bedroom light flashing on and mad dashing around grabbing fresh sheets and blankets from another room while trying not to disturb little old pugs that lay sleeping in their beds. At that time we had a lot of pugs sleeping on the bed with us, nine I believe it was back then, so we'd have to disturb each of them as well. Wake them all up and put them on the floor and we didn't like doing that, some of them were in real deep sleeps and because we never wake them up fast it can take a bit of time and all the while the first few you lifted down will be looking up at you wondering what the heck is going on and woofing because they don't want to be on the ground they want to be up on the bed sleeping. One of us would remake the bed while the other took Amber outside to see if they could get a bit more wee out of her in the hope of preventing another accident later on, but it was no good she'd already emptied her bladder and was now ready to go back to sleep, she just had to wait for the bed to be remade. It can tug on your heartstrings when you see them like this because Amber had been so good at holding her bladder and also very good at letting us know when she needed to wee. Just a little woof to wake us up so she could be carried outside but now she was no longer able to do that all the time, yes she would still bark for us when she needed us but she sometimes couldn't hold it in until we reached the grass, you could tell she much preferred going outside, the bed was not her first option, but she couldn't help what was going on in her body, no elderly being can. So we tried to help by taking her out for even more wee breaks, especially from late afternoon onwards, we were just trying to give her as many opportunities as possible to relieve herself so her bladder had nothing much in it when we climbed into bed. But old age causes bladder weakness, it's just one of those things that happens to the body as it ages, we did have Amber checked out by our vet though, you have to really just to make sure there is nothing else going on besides merely growing older. Bladder infections can cause excessive weeing so we had to get her looked at and cleared. Sometimes it was a little bit of leakage other times a huge gush and she was still most times letting us know she needed be taken outside and we'd be carrying her out and all of a sudden her little back legs would come up and she'd wee mid-air, didn't make it all the way out to the grass, simply could not hold on any longer. As soon as we felt those little back legs of hers come up we'd put her down on the ground wherever we were standing. Sometimes she'd wee in the house, a lot of times it was on the deck or one of the ramps. And if we moved fast enough she could still go on her special weeing tree, it all depended on how long she could hold it in for and how fast we were at waking up when we heard her growly woof. We became quite the experts David and I. Experts at waking up fast and being out the door at lightning speed. You have no idea how fast you can go from being sound asleep to wide awake and moving until your little girl needs you. Although I did run into the wall a few times and I heard David toppling in the hall when trying to find the light switch, but both of us made sure Amber was always safe and after a few months of doing it your body simply just kicks in, learns to react when you need it to react. Your night time mad wee dashes through the house with Amber become your new normal. I guess all parents with new born babies know this to be the truth. Our babies are old but it's the same level of needing you to take care of them and whenever your babies need you you spring into action day or night, do whatever has to be done in order to keep their life running smoothly. The older Amber got she wouldn't even wake up when she needed to wee, she'd sleep through the entire ordeal only waking up after she had gone. The motion of weeing was what woke her and she'd do her growly woofs to let us know what had gone on. After a while we realised this was not just a few accidents kind of thing but the way Amber was always going to be from now on so we set the bed up accordingly, altered her little nest to accommodate the changes in her body. We put a protective sheet over the mattress. Its interior held up to 2.5 litres of water over 8 hours so I knew we were good. Now whenever she did have an accident it was just a case of one of us wiping her down with a warm hand towel then drying her off while the other one gave her nest a complete change. We had the towels, blankets and a spare protective sheet sitting next to our bed for easy access. It could all be done quite quickly then and we'd all be back to sleep in no time. Amber would be clean, couldn't have her smelling of urine that wouldn't have been nice for her, her nest would be fresh and dry and her old bedding would be in the washing machine ready to be set off first thing in the morning. It all worked out pretty well and it was really handy that The Divine One was the type of dog she was because once Amber was down she was down, she wasn't one of these dogs that walks all over the bed at night time, she got put into her nest, given her medicine and that was it, she settled down to sleep. Not a peep out of her unless she needed us and sometimes she could go until the early hours of the morning before her growly woof could be heard, other times she'd be calling out for us an hour or so after lights out. Not every night was exactly the same so you just have to go with the flow. But one thing that was the same was that you could rely on Amber to stay put. She may wake up and move positions but not beds, never beds, she knew her nest was hers and so would stand and turn around to get more comfortable then lie back down and fall asleep. So really it was only like we had to secure the one area on the bed, the area in-between our two pillows. That was The Divine One's spot, that's where she'd been sleeping for years so that's the spot we layered with protection. I don't know what we would have done if she'd been the type to wander around, I guess we would have had to give it some more thought and come to a solution where our bed could be protected and Amber remain happy.

One thing we did do, well one thing we have always done, not just for Amber but for all our elderly pugs is to make sure the house is sitting at a good temperature and it's especially important during the winter months because you will find that pugs wee more if they are cold and of course that's a double whammy when you have a pug that is incontinent. We always make sure the temperature is right for the pugs to be comfortable. Of course little fluctuations aren't too bad, the pugs are still ok but if you vary too much that's when they'll start to feel it so we always keep the inside of the house at a good temperature all throughout the year. It can be hard to do at times, in the depth of winter or the heat of summer it can be especially hard. But we still do our best and it's a case of consistent monitoring, I find that I actually monitor the temperature as much as I monitor the pugs. The pugs night time bedding is constantly changing throughout the year too. Cotton sheets in summer and thick blankets in winter. But then again there are no set seasons anymore they all seem to be blending more and more with each passing year so you can be forever changing bedding to suit, and of course underneath Amber's bedding there would always be a mattress protector. But The Divine One wasn't aware that anything was different, she drifted off to sleep in the middle of her Mum and Dad like she had been doing for many years. I find that you can always work around things if you want to, there is always a way of keeping them happy and the bed dry. And keeping your dog happy is a very important thing to be doing, especially for delicate elderly dogs, you don't want them clocking out because they think you no longer love them or that they have done something wrong. We take care of the needs of elderly relatives and it is no different for our dogs. Sure it's extra laundry, the washing machine gets a bit of an extra workout but who cares about that. Amber was happy, her world had not been disturbed, she still felt loved and contented. She got to put her little old head down beside us every night to me and David that was very important.

When Amber developed bladder stones her pattern of urination changed again and it was different to being incontinent and it was different to showing the signs of having a bladder infection although to be honest at the start that's exactly what I thought it may have been, a bladder infection, and you have to get on top of those pretty fast because they can turn nasty in no time and also they can make your dog feel very unwell. I remember walking down a street a few years back and seeing a pug in a yard and of course I was instantly drawn. This little pug was sitting by the corner of house looking quite sad, I got her to come over to me and she didn't look too well, there was something about her eyes. I was bending down stroking her ears when a lady came out of the house with a few pugs on her heel. We got to talking and after a while being curious I asked her why the pug I was first patting wasn't allowed in the house like the other pugs were and she started going on about frequent weeing and that until she stopped doing it she had to stay outside. I found out the pugs name was Emily and I had an Emily at home so told the lady that. I asked how long her Emily had been outside for and the lady said a few days. I asked if she'd taken Emily to see a vet and she said no and I just couldn't hold my tongue. I told her that if the weeing in the house was new and sudden and out of character for the pug that it probably meant there was something else going on here. And she said no she's just being a very naughty girl and I said no she isn't and although I could have completely lost it I tried to remain calm in order to help the pug. I knew calling the owner all the names I had going round and round in my head would have made the situation hostile and she would not have listened to what I had to say. So I took a deep breath before I continued. I told her the pug didn't look well to me, that I noticed it as soon as she came close, I also told my experiences with bladder infections and left hoping she listened and did the right thing and got that poor little pug some help. That bladder infection wasn't going to heal up on its own and leaving her outside day and night was the worst thing she could have done. Imagine being unwell and cold and alone. My heart broke for that little girl it really did. I went home and hugged my Emily close. Days later

I still couldn't get the other Emily out of my mind so decided to go by the house again. I couldn't see her in the yard anywhere so hopefully she had been taken to a vet, was on some form of antibiotics and once again back inside the house where she belonged.

But on closer observation I noticed that when Amber was weeing or trying to wee only a drop or two was coming out at a time, she seemed to be constantly in the act of trying to relieve her bladder. Continually pressing down and that was different to being incontinent because that just leaked out without her even being aware of it, just unexpected little leakages that she had no control over. She never once tried to push the wee out the way she was doing now. I knew there was something going on with her but I didn't know what. I am always watching what's going on with all the pugs and yes there are quite a few to keep track of but I still manage to do it, I've always been very good at picking up on something not being right with somebody. So I began paying special attention to Amber's wee but there was no blood or cloudiness there. Another thing Amber was doing was laying differently to how she would normally lay.

She'd be in her nest but couldn't lie in her normal position for very long, kept getting up and repositioning herself trying to get comfortable. She lay tilting her body more to one side. Amber was giving me all these signs, constant little giveaways so I knew something wasn't right. She couldn't tell me with words but observation was letting me know. You pick up on so many things when you are constantly observing. The constant act of pressing down trying to empty her bladder and next to nothing coming out told me there was something stopping her from weeing. I'd never dealt with bladder stones before so it was new to me. I was in the kitchen one night and Amber and some of the other pugs were with me while I was cooking tea, the rest of the pugs were outside with David helping him feed the sheep and horses. I noticed Amber squatting beside me and instinctively reached for a serviette and placed it over the wet patch to absorb the urine. Then I gently picked the serviette up and studied it closely. I noticed there were a few stones on the surface of the napkin, three little stones and one slightly larger one, all glistening pale stones. Bladder stones I thought to myself and went off to show David. At last we had an answer to what was wrong with Amber and I was pretty happy about that. Not happy that she had them but happy that we now knew what was going on. I put the stones into a small plastic container so we could show our vet, it's best when you can actually show them rather than just describe them, sometimes you have no choice but to describe things and so you do your absolute best to do that but showing them is always better and because Amber had gone indoors and not in the middle of a paddock it was easy for me to collect the stones. The next morning Amber and the little plastic container went to see our vet and of course he knew right away what was going on, he examined her, gently pressed around and felt she had a lot more stones still in there so surgery was booked for the following day. We brought Amber home with us that night, sure he could have kept her there overnight but we wanted her to sleep at home because we knew she would be happiest there and our vet said he could see no reason why she couldn't do that. It meant David had to be up extra early in the morning in order to drop Amber off before work but we would rather do that so she could sleep in her own bed. I was nervous about the surgery due to The Divine One's age and also because she was such a delicate little soul health wise, but there are times when you have to go ahead and put them under anesthetic, when there is no other option available to you and this was one of those times. We couldn't leave her in that uncomfortable state, clearly she was in pain, there was a lot of pressure being put on her bladder and we had to free her of that. Having a vet you trust is vital, I knew Amber was in safe hands. Didn't stop me from constantly looking at the clock and worrying though, but that's just what us mothers do at times like this isn't it. I cannot rest and be normal until I know they are safe and well. And the hours always pass by so slowly when you are waiting for news. I kept looking at Ruben walking around the place, he was the exact same age as Amber but he was very different to how The Divine One was. If it had been Ruben who was being operated on that day I wouldn't have been as worried, yes concerned but I would know that he could have handled things better due to being in better health. But our vet was right Amber did have more stones in there, a heck of a lot of them actually, I got him to save them for me so I could have a look. There were eight stones that were the size of peas, quite a few slightly smaller stones and a whole lot of gravely sand like stones, crystals. And like our vet said any one of those stones could have become stuck in the urinary track and caused a whole lot of trouble for Amber. That's why you have to get them removed. At times like this you weigh up the cost of putting your pug under anesthetic and the danger of what could happen to them if you don't.

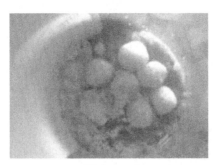

"The stones"

Amber was already passing some of those stones and at any time any one of those stones could have totally blocked the urinary tract. If that happened we would have been in real trouble real fast. A complete obstruction can be life threatening and requires immediate emergency treatment. We didn't want that, we didn't want Amber being rushed off in the middle of the night to be operated on by a vet who we didn't know or trust. Also if an obstruction is not relieved the bladder can rupture spilling urine into the abdomen and yes I fully believe that would have been the end of Amber. She would never have survived it. I studied those stones closely, poor little sweetheart must have been feeling so unwell, those stones would have been putting a heck of a lot of pressure on her dear old body no wonder she couldn't lay in her normal position. Little soul would have been in such pain and discomfort. I'm just glad I was observant enough to see what was going on. I'm also really glad the first sign had been those few smaller stones, if she had tried to pass one of the bigger ones and we were not aware of what was going on we would have lost her. Amber was very groggy when we picked her up and it did take her a little bit longer to recover and we knew it would do, she was an older dog after all, old dogs just like old people take a bit longer to come good after surgery, you just have to give them the extra care they need until they are feeling like themselves again. So we kept her quiet and gave her all the time in the world to come good. Her first day home Amber slept for eleven hours straight. I kept going over and checking on her making sure she was ok, checking she was still breathing and she always was, so I'd stand there for a few moments watching that beautiful tiny body of hers rise and fall in deep exhausted slumber. I figured she would need all her bedding changed as soon as she woke up because I felt sure she would have let her bladder go while she was still groggy and not even known she was doing it. But to my surprise her bedding was completely dry when she finally lifted her head. She woofed for me to carry her outside and I shot over to her at lightning speed, so happy was I to see those little eyes of hers open. I checked her stitches as I was carrying her out and they were looking good. I actually checked Amber's stitches every day when I carried her outside, always making sure there was no infection happening and there never was, everything always looked clean and neat, no signs of swelling or redness anywhere.

Throughout this ordeal Amber's appetite was still very good. We were told to keep her fluids up so her meals were pretty sloppy but she'd get them down no worries then sleep most of the day away. She actually slept ninety percent of the time the first week after her surgery, but never once had an accident in her bed. She was tired but still very much communicating with me when she wanted or needed something and I was ever ready to go over and help her. After she got what she needed it was back to full on sleeping again looking more like a field mouse then she normally did. The rest was doing her good, it was the best thing she could do in order to heal. I put her in a pen on her own so she wouldn't be disturbed by any of the other pugs. They could see her but they couldn't get to her, she could rest quietly and comfortably, no constant interruptions, rest is so important when one is healing. Sleeping helps the body do its job of repairing itself, it was like all Amber's energy was going into helping her heal, she had little left for anything else. It can be hard when they are used to living in a pack though because they want to be around their family while they heal and so pens are handy things to have, we use them a lot here for all sorts of reasons. I set a pen up in the lounge room for Amber and made a little nest in the middle of it, that way she could hear her siblings walking by and she was able to get a bit of afternoon sun on her head as well and she seemed to really like that. The other pugs kept going over and checking on her, peering through the bars at their snoozing little sister. The Divine One would have been well aware of them being there, she was just far too exhausted to offer up any form of acknowledgement, but just knowing they were near would have brought her a great deal of comfort. She was with them but she was safe from being trodden on, pawed at or even laid next too. Sure none of her siblings would have thought they were doing any harm, they would have been doing what they always did, but a heavy thud against Ambers side would have hurt her and all the sibling would have been doing was simply getting in bed next to their sister but when you are recovering from surgery things like that will cause pain. I used the biggest pen we had because I knew there would be a few little legs going through the bars trying to touch her and the last thing Amber needed was constant tapping on her little old head. I watched on as the pugs went over to check the new setup out, watched the blind pugs sniffing at the bars, watched a few of the sighted pugs reaching in trying to connect with Amber, saw them swipe and swipe then pull their legs back out again because they couldn't reach her. Ava Lindy Lou even tried to break her sister out of jail, day after day she kept chewing on the bars in order to make a hole. She didn't realise Amber was in there for her own safety. Ava Lindy Lou was used to her blind siblings going into pens to eat their meals but they always came right back out again as soon as the meal was over. But Amber was very rarely out of her pen and Ava Lindy Lou couldn't understand what was going on, why she was in there for longer than normal and in her own little way was trying to rectify the situation by freeing her. I actually thought it was a very sweet thing for her to do. It touched my heart that she loved her little old sister so much that she was trying to help her escape. I went over, picked Ava Lindy Lou up and gave her a snuggle, tickled her tummy the way she likes me to do, smothered her face and ears with kisses too, just trying to get her mind off Amber because if she was trying to break her out clearly seeing her in the pen all the time must have been upsetting for her.

A few of the pugs went and lay down beside the pen, especially in the afternoon they went and laid there and shared the sun with Amber. And I believe she would have liked hearing them snoring beside her, the fact that they were near would have been reassuring and such things help the healing process I think. Nobody wants to be without their loved ones when they are not feeling well. As time went on and Amber became more and more alert she began sniffing the air for her brothers and sisters before putting her head down to sleep, it was like she felt she could rest more easily if she knew they were nearby. After a few days she even began woofing for them so I got a few of their beds and brought them over and put them beside her pen that way they were separate yet together, well as together as they could be during her healing time anyway. It was the same with me when I was recovering from surgery, I liked knowing all the pugs were there, loved hearing the pitter pattering of their paws on the floorboards. I couldn't have them up on the bed jumping all over my stitches but I sure did gain comfort from knowing they were nearby and I reckon Amber would have felt the exact same way. Each day she was a little less tired than she had been the previous day and on each trip outside she began walking around a little bit more too. I always carried her out but then I'd put her down and let her have a sniff and a quiet wander around, the others pugs were all coming out with us now too. Earlier in the week when I'd taken Amber outside it had just been the two of us because I couldn't risk her being knocked so I gave her a few days to come good before allowing everybody else to join us. Around day three or four I did start bringing Ava Lindy Lou out with me and Amber and that seemed to make her really happy and leave the bars on the pen alone too. Ava Lindy Lou is a quiet gentle little girl I knew she wouldn't go rushing at Amber.

Ava and Amber

The first time she came out she went over and sniffed Amber's entire body and that was it they went off sniffing the ground together, after that Ava Lindy Lou made sure she was ready to shoot out the door with me and Amber whenever we were going outside. She'd hear Amber woof, watch me walk over and pick her up and be waiting beside the door ready to fly through it as soon as I slid it open. I think it was on day seven or eight that I let the rest of the pugs come with us and when that happened I noticed Amber began walking around a little bit more. She'd had a few days of rest and she had all her siblings with her now, she seemed happier to be off sniffing within the group. They were all feeding off each other like they normally did and that was encouraging her to walk a tiny bit more then she had been doing and I didn't have a problem with her doing that. Just stood close making sure she wasn't overdoing things, she was pretty good though, only walked until she'd had enough then she'd stop and sit down, wait for me to go pick her up. Sometimes she was already up on her feet and walking again by the time I got there though, especially if I was doing something for one of the other pugs. I always had her in view, always knew what she was up to and each day she walked that little bit more then she had done the day before. I remember the day Amber made it all the way out of the house on her own. I was off helping Ruben when out of the corner of my eye I saw in the distance this lovely little frame slowly walking over to the horses. Amber was only taking tiny steps, just taking her time and slowly sniffing the ground as she went and my heart skipped a beat when I saw her. She had been fast asleep when the rest of us left the house but knowing she would soon be waking up I had left the back door open for her. The reason I knew The Divine One would soon be waking up was because I'd stood over her watching for a few moments before taking the other pugs outside and Amber had been doing her little twitching face thing, a thing she did when she was coming out of a deep sleep. I knew she'd more than likely wake up before we got back and wanted to give her the option of coming out to join us if she wanted to, which is exactly what happened. I wasn't there to see her wake up but I knew she would have twitched more and more until her little eyes finally sprang open. She would have then paused and listened for us, sniffed the air for us too and on sensing we were not in the room would have left her nest in search of us all. First she would have checked every room in the house and when that didn't bring her face to face with somebody she would have headed for the back door and was probably very glad I had left it open for her. I think her first intention was to come find us but then as she was coming down the ramp she must have smelt the horses on the wind so decided she may like to go over to the fence and say hello. They had already moved on by the time she got there though but that didn't bother her, she couldn't see them anyway and their scent had been left behind and she was happy enough with that. A week after her surgery The Divine One was back to barking at the birds every night. Not her usual going nuts bark, just little woofs every time they chirped, no running just standing there woofing, simply enjoying herself and then she'd slowly walk back inside. For a delicate elderly dog Amber actually did very well with the surgery and recovery and I think that was due to a good vet and the care she was given when she got home. It was lovely seeing her slowly getting back to her normal self again, well she was better than her normal self wasn't she because now she didn't have all those painful stones in her bladder, life was a lot more comfortable for her now. She was also back to being able to lay in her nest in her usual position as well. Amber actually ended up having two surgeries for bladder stones. After the first surgery we had made alterations to her diet in the hope of her never having to deal with bladder stones again. But they came back regardless. And I did wonder if it was due to Amber never being much of a drinker, sure that couldn't have been the only thing to cause them but it wouldn't have helped. I was pretty disappointed that she was going through all of this for a second time, sad that my little blessing had to have another operation. The second surgery came eighteen months after the first one and she was even older this time so I was once again back to worrying. But I also once again knew the surgery needed to be done and because I'd dealt with it before I knew the signs well so booked the surgery right away. Booked her in so fast I didn't even make note of the date until I was wandering around the farm worrying how she was doing. I took out my phone, checking in case I had missed the call telling me how the surgery had gone. I looked down at the screen and there it was in big lettering "Friday the 13th" I think with only thinking about Amber my mind hadn't been on dates, only days. I am not overly superstitious but I guess I must be just superstitious enough because finding out it was Friday the 13th did make me pause in the middle of the paddock and call the vet right away. They seemed to be taking forever to answer the phone and all the while so many thoughts were going through my head. What if they were not answering because something was wrong with Amber, in my mind I visualised vets and vet nurses rushing around trying to help my little girl. But the reality of the situation was that it was Friday, a very busy day at our vet surgery. When they finally answered the phone I tried to sound as calm as I could, don't know how convincing I was but I took a deep breath and tried to make my voice sound light and carefree even though light and carefree was the complete opposite of how I was feeling in that moment. The vet nurse sounded even more flustered then I was which again told me they were very busy that day. I am usually contacted when the surgery is over, hearing my voice on the line they probably thought I was just being an over anxious mother. And I was. I really, really was, so I was very happy to hear that Amber was in recovery and all had gone well. And not just well but "Beautifully" was what they told me. They also told me that Amber only had the one stone this time and I thought that was odd, from the way she was behaving I felt sure she would have had more, perhaps even the same amount she'd had last time but when they told me the size of that stone I knew why there was only one, it was a whopper and there wouldn't have been any room left in her bladder for any other stones. I once again reminded them to keep the stone for me so I could have a look then hung up the phone. When

I eventually saw the stone I couldn't believe how big it was, how a dog of that size could have had a stone so big. It measured 34 mm.

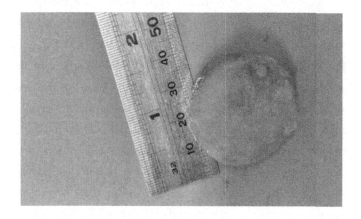

In the latter part of Amber's life she started sleeping in longer and longer and I was used to this happening with older dogs. I had a lady write to me once worried sick because her old dog slept most of the day away and I told her that this was a perfectly natural thing for elderly dogs to do, absolutely nothing wrong with it. Some will sleep longer than others but all will sleep longer than they did in their younger years. As long as they are eating, drinking and having regular little walks it's ok for them to sleep as long as they like, it's all up to the dogs really as they know how they feel, if they are tired let them rest, you can't keep waking them up fearing something is wrong which is what this lady was doing. Old dogs need to be able to enjoy their retirement. But I did tell her that if she felt something wasn't quite right that she should take her dog to see a vet because I am all about gut instincts and that it's better to be safe than sorry. I never heard back from her so I guess I must have given her peace of mind or she did take her dog to the vet and got things sorted out.

With Amber I always let her sleep for as long as she liked and sometimes she'd sleep for ten or more hours straight, if she had days were she was really sleeping in then I'd keep monitoring her. Kept going and checking on her and she was always fine, just in a deep deep sleep so I'd tiptoe from the room and carry on with what I was doing but always with one ear waiting for her call. I knew she'd begin woofing as soon as she woke up. Woof to tell me she was awake, woof to say she needed to have a wee so I could take her outside, at times woofing just to make sure I was there. She'd sense me entering the room, but sometimes she'd still be tired so wouldn't fully open up her eyes, just sniffed the air with her head up, feel my hand caressing her ears and forehead and lay there like that for a little while enjoying the moment. No rush to move off right away, just taking her time coming round and she needed that bit of extra time to come round otherwise she was unsteady on her feet, all dogs need to wake up on their own and in their own time, they cannot be rushed or woken with a start, it's not good for them at any age and especially not good for them as they get older. It's the same with old folks, grandma and grandpa can no longer wake up and spring out of bed like they did in their youth. They need to be given a bit of time and Amber did too so I'd be pottering around folding laundry or in the kitchen getting breakfast ready just waiting for that all important growly little woof that signified The Divine One's day was ready to begin. I'd race in to see how awake she was, was she still coming round or was she already standing up because she desperately needed to wee, each morning was different, each morning a quick observation was done and acted upon. If she was standing then I'd quickly take her outside so she could do her business. If awake but eyes closed I'd go sit beside her, massage her ears and talk to her. And if she was awake with eyes open then I'd rush to the fridge and grab a handful of blueberries, 8 or so small blueberries was normally the go. I'd lie on the bed beside Amber squashing them and popping them into her mouth while she came round.

By the time she'd eaten the last one she was more alert, a lot more alert then she had been when I first walked into the bedroom so I'd carry her out to her special weeing tree and she'd potter around on legs that yes were a little unsteady due to age but a lot more steady then they would have been if I'd just scooped her up and rushed her outside while she was still coming round. Amber would walk up the ramp on her own but these days I was now back to lifting her over the metal strip on the glass sliding door, just like I used to do when she first came to live with us. Only now I was doing it due to age, at over sixteen years old she would sometimes not lift one of her back legs up quite high enough to clear the strip, one would occasionally get caught so I'd always be right there to lift her up and over, pop her gently down on the other side and watch her clunking off towards the kitchen ready for breakfast. Although there was the odd occasion when I was off helping somebody else and misjudged the amount of time it took Amber to get from the tree to the back door, some mornings she was a little bit too fast for me and I'd have to go jumping over the other pugs like an Olympic hurdler in order to get to Amber before she attempted to go inside on her own. Her speed in the mornings was food driven, she'd gone all night without something to eat and a few squashed down blueberries were a very nice appetizer but now she wanted the real thing and her speed when she started heading up to the house was an indicator of that. At that point we were hand feeding The Divine One all her meals as well because she was having trouble eating by herself. It's not uncommon to hand feed old dogs, we've done it with a few over the years because you do whatever you need to do in order to get that all important nutrition inside them. It's no use if they are constantly dropping it and smushing it into the floor when trying to pick it up again, some need hand feeding because of lack of teeth, some lack of strength, some because they can't see properly or because they now want to lay down when they eat and trying to eat out of a bowl while laying down is quite an impossible thing to do. So either David or myself will sit beside them, roll food into bite sized balls and pop it into little mouths, we have found that rolling the food makes it easier for them to keep hold of, it's normally me who feeds them but if David gets home from work in time he likes to join in on the hand feeding too because it's a lovely time of being with your son or daughter. A special time of talking to them as they eat, a time of togetherness until the bowl is empty and their tummy is full. We have cots that we use for lots of different reasons and hand feeding a pug that is now at a point where they are finding it hard to eat on their own is one of those reasons. It's handy because it means you can sit level with them, be level with their head, you can fully see what's going on and are more able to get that ball of food into their mouths properly if you are sitting level with them. David made the cots himself so they sit at the perfect height. Store bought cots sat too low for our needs. It's all about making things easier on the pug and getting that food into their hungry little mouths as fast and efficiently as possible. Although you do have to make sure they swallow before giving them another ball, can't have them gulping fast in a hungry feeding frenzy and choking or dropping what's already in their mouth because they've opened up again ready for more. You have to time it just right otherwise it defeats the purpose. And it's different with each dog because they all have their own way and style of eating. Their own speed too and it has to do with a number of things, one of them being which side of their mouth they've got the most teeth on so you need to be mindful of putting the food on their best side in order to help them chew. The dog that needs hand feeding is always fed last because you can't be sitting there all blissful and happy feeding a pug in a cot when you have a pile of hungry pugs going nuts on the floor, its fairer if you put all the other bowls down first then pick up the last bowl and quietly walk over and pull out a kitchen chair. I have the cot ready and waiting next to the chair and off we'll go. The pug in the cot is happy and the other pugs are all happy too because they'll be already eating their dinner, they now have no interest in what's going on anywhere else. The pug in the cot eventually gets used to being the last one to eat, they can see or hear what's going on, see or hear Mummy racing round with multiple bowls in her hands and know that one will soon be coming their way and that I'm not going to get to them any faster if they are screaming their little old heads off, after a few days of doing that due to being new to cot feeding they begin to realise the best thing they can do is merely wait quietly, oh and get their little old mouths ready to open and chew once I get there.

Amber and Ava

There was a time when I was hand feeding two dogs at once, did it for quite a while when we had two little blessings that began needing help at exactly the same time. Well no I think Lumen was already being hand fed when Lilly Rain joined her and it was fine when David was there to help out but he was more often than not at work when the pugs were being fed so I used to do it by myself, me sitting on a chair in the middle with a cot at either side. Again I'd get things set up beforehand as that always helps. When it's just you and a pile of hungry pugs you need to set everything up first in order to make things quicker and smoother. And most times that's exactly what happens but you are always going to get times when you aim for smooth sailing but things start falling apart. It was funny though because we have wheels on our cots, Dave put them on to make things easier, but when Ava Lindy Lou entered the house she developed a habit of jumping up trying to peep through the bars seeing what was going on up there. I think she felt she was missing out on something so her little face would peep in from time to time making sure that didn't happen. She did it on and off throughout the day too but mainly at meal times because it was food she was after. I'd put the cot in place only to see it being pushed across the room a few moments later. She'd push it around like a pram but due to the wheels was never able to push it completely over. The speed at which she ran at those cots and the force she had behind her she could have easily toppled a cot that was made to stand still. Ava Lindy Lou isn't a big or overly heavy pug but at meals times she would get very excited making her force strong. And once the cot was moving she just went with it, little hind legs walking along with whoever was in the cot simply looking down watching what she was doing. I'd be in the kitchen getting things ready and hear Ava Lindy Lou woofing for her dinner, some nights she was quiet but if she was very hungry her woof matched that. I always knew how famished she was by her volume and the force at which she'd make those cots move. I'd glance up and see Lumen in her little pink cot being pushed into the middle of the lounge room and have to go retrieve her, bring her back and put her in position again. Lumen wasn't bothered that she'd been moved, it was all the same to her, she didn't care where she got pushed to just sat there enjoying the new view until I went and rescued her. And when she was once again where I needed her to be it'd be back to racing round with bowls full of food, then jumping on the chair and pulling the cots closer. It was two bowls on the kitchen table when I was feeding two at once with both hands going like the clappers rolling two lots of food into bite sized balls and popping it into hungry little mouths. You'd think it'd be hard hand feeding two little souls at exactly the same time but it's really not, once you work out how they eat and the speed at which they can actually finish a mouthful it can be a pretty easy thing to do. You feed one and while they are chewing you turn and feed the other one and by the time you turn back again there will be a little empty mouth waiting to be filled, totally relying on you to not miss a beat, get it right, get the right food in the right mouth and also remember who eats in what way. And you can go on like that for months on end and then things will change again so you just work things differently to compensate. Hand feeding Lumen and Lilly Rain together was a lovely time in my life and years later when you look back on it, just like I am doing right now in writing this, well you are so glad you had the opportunity to experience such a beautiful special thing.

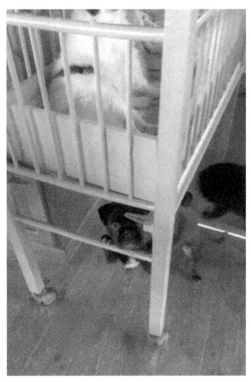

Ava pushing the cot

CHAPTER TWENTY

This Is Not The End

I do not think this life we are living now is "It". I believe when we die we move on to another place a place where all those we love will be waiting to greet us. My personal belief is that this place is called heaven and that one day I am going to see my Mum and Grandparents again and I am also going to be reunited with every dog I have been blessed enough to share my life with. Other people have different views on where it is they will eventually pass over to, but a large majority of people do believe there is life after death, something else out there. And of course some believe that all we have is the one life we are living right now and when we die there is absolutely nothing, totally nothingness everything goes black, no loved ones waiting, no memories of the life you have lived, just total darkness and who knows they may be right but none of us will actually know the truth until we die. I have a deep belief that I will simply close my eyes in this world and open them up in heaven and that within a few moments of that happening a whole pile of furry little four legged blessings will come bounding towards me, followed close behind by some very special souls with two legs. These beliefs keep me going and they also make it a little easier when I lose those I love because I know one day I'm going to see them again, that we'll all be together for eternity. The faith I have brings me a lot of comfort and when I'm saying my goodbyes I always whisper in their little ears that me and Daddy will see them again one day. I tell them that we'll be coming to where they are going and to be happy and enjoy themselves until we get there. I also explain that there will be a lot of family members waiting to greet them on the other side, some they have lived with and some they will be meeting for the very first time. And since my Mum passed away I will also walk over to my favourite photo of her and ask her to look after the little soul who has just left my side. I'll say "I can't do anything more for them now Mum so can you please love them and take care of them for me until I get there" I find it lessens the sting of loss for me, it's like my babies have gone from my arms straight into my Mum's arms and Mum was a beautiful nurturer, the very best, she is who I learnt this instinct from. Of course I am still totally heartbroken by my losses but since Mum passed I now feel like I have somebody up there that I am sending them to, somebody who understood how much these little blessings of mine mean to me and in that there is a feeling of peace. With Amber the loss was hard but I also knew how well she had done to reach the age she did and so on one hand you are grieving terribly but on the other you are proud of what she accomplished and thankful you got to have her with you as long as you did. I do think when one passes from old age there is a feeling of closure, of being able to celebrate a life well lived. It's like the life has gone its full course and now it's time for them to leave their earthly body behind and in that there is some comfort. Comfort when it happens with our canine family members and comfort with humans beings as well. A life that is cut short, well there is a whole lot of pain in that and there's added pain too because you are not left with just mourning their loss you are also mourning the loss of years they should have been granted and that can make things tough, it plays on your mind a fair bit. So with The Divine One although her loss was enormous I at least had the joy of knowing she had reached a brilliant age and her ending was a good one too so there's that, she simply died of old age, a thing that is not granted to everyone. She died peacefully in her sleep as well and again not all losses go so smoothly. For me I felt things couldn't have gone better, if you have to lose them and of course you do at some point because nobody lives forever, then this is the very best way to go, at home surrounded by all those who love you the most. It's like movies I've watched, more often than not they are country folk so what's happening is taking place on a farm. You'll see grandma or grandpa with their old withered faces falling asleep in a big comfy bed under a layer of warm blankets then never waking up. And those who loved them and lived with them, because of course the entire family all live together in the same house because the best movies have their characters doing that, are heartbroken but they are also more accepting of it because old people do die. And the family they leave behind go on to share stories of their life which is exactly what David and I do here. We can be crying over missing them one moment then be laughing at something adorably cute they did the next and The Divine One left us with a whole lot of wonderful memories to be laughing and smiling about for the rest of our lives.

I remember Amber's final day so clearly in my mind, I was writing on the bed and a lot of the pugs were up there with me like they always are. Amber became quite restless about hallway through my writing session. She'd already had her carrot juice and blueberries before settling down so I knew she wasn't hungry. I figured she must have needed to go out for a wee so out we went. I left one or two of the pugs on the bed sleeping and took everybody else outside for a wander around. When you live in a pack nobody ever wee's alone and that includes David and me. Amber was fine milling about, she had a wee and so did the others then we all came back inside. As I walked by the kitchen bench I paused beside the nummy jar, which is our name for the treat jar and fed Amber a few treats. I gave the others a treat too but Amber was in my arms so I was able to sneak her a few extra treats without anybody else noticing. After that we all got back on the bed and I began typing. Amber settled down to sleep for a little while but was soon up on her feet again. Not ill just unable to settle, I checked her out and couldn't see anything wrong with her but she still wasn't settling so I knew there had to be something going on. I called David at work and told him what was happening. It was August, the last month of winter, still cold and miserable and we were all pretty much sick of the cold dreary days by then. We talked about taking her to see our vet and I said no let's give her a little more time to see if she settles before calling him. I didn't want to rush her out on a cold wet night if there was no reason to. An hour later I called David again and said that I think we should get our vet to check her out just to be on the safe side. So Dave left work early and off to the vet we went. Our vet said he wasn't happy with her breathing but couldn't find anything else going on. Her breathing had been more or less normal all afternoon but now she was panting a little bit. He gave her a couple of injections, just doing all he could to give her the best shot possible of coming good but she was 16 and a half years old and our vet said that we may have to face the fact that Amber was coming to the end of her life. He said she'll either "Come good" or "She won't" and you may think that is being rather blunt, but we know our vet well and he knows we appreciate honesty. No need to sugar coat things we are not children. So home we came with our little girl stopping for a treat like we always did and Amber ate her beef patty and part of David's too then slept most of the way home. I remember holding her in one arm and rubbing her back with my free hand, put my hand underneath her fluffy pink coat and gently caressed her little old back. As soon as we got home we fed the pugs their dinner. Amber wasn't that fussed about eating but that's because that little tummy of hers was already full of beef patty, her treat food, why would she be interested in normal home food when you have a tummy full of meaty goodness. The fact that she attempted to shove down a few mouthfuls at all really did surprise us. We did our normal nightly routine with the pugs, dinner, wee's, them sleeping while we watched a bit of TV then a final night time wee and all tucked up nice and warm and the lights turned off. Amber wasn't much different to how she had been before seeing the vet, no better and definitely no worse. Although she did settle down nicely to sleep while we watched TV so something our vet gave her was at least allowing her to do that and she had a full tummy too so that always helps. I remember looking at her tiny face before the bedroom light was turned off, she was just there in her little nest doing her field mouse pose, breathing ok and sleeping soundly and that was the last time I saw my little daughter alive. Amber passed away at three o'clock in the morning. David was with her, I was sleeping, I do so wish he had woken me up so that I could have been with her but he said he didn't know she was going, it just happened. The main thing was that The Divine One had one of us with her as she took her final breath, well she had all her family with her she didn't pass away alone, it was just that only one member of her family was awake at the time she left us. Dave said he had woken up and was lying beside Amber stroking her shoulder when she slowly and very gently took a final breath. She was nearest to his pillow and he had been checking on her whenever he woke up, we both had and she always had her little head down gently snoring away. Of course I was hoping that Amber was going to wake up in the morning, have what our vet gave her be able to give her a few more months with us but you always hope for that don't you. You are always going to want to have more time with those you love the most. And really if anybody could pull a rabbit out of a hat it would have been The Divine One, after all we had seen her to do it a lot over the years, just not this time. I guess our vet had a fair idea what the outcome would be though because he had seen Amber an awful lot over the time she was with us, seen her in all sorts of conditions and never said what he said before. Me, well, in that moment looking across at my tiny girl I just wanted more time. Loss is sad, well it's more than sad it's absolutely heartbreaking but they have a right to get old and die, they are allowed to. Everybody leaves you until you leave them and it is alright, it's how it goes, does it hurt, absolutely yes, is it sad, heck yes, but that is how life is and how life is always going to be, nobody escapes death. Amber had a right to die of old age and I had to be brave enough to let her, to be ok about it and be thankful for being able to be her mother so that's what I chose to do. I wanted to honour her life and the time we had together. In life sometimes you just have to be grateful for what you've been given and leave it at that and I was incredibly thankful for the time I had been granted with Amber, well extra time really because nobody thought she was going to live as long as she did. Also I decided I was not going to let The Divine One's passing be all about sadness, that was a choice I made very early on so every time I cried about losing her I would then make myself think of a happy time we shared, go with the tears because they are healing but walk away from that chair with a smile on my face after thinking of a beautiful memory and as time went on I found that easier and easier to do. And I think the way she left us helped with that. Amber's exit was a beautiful way to go. She left this world gently and quietly, put her little old head down next to her Daddy in that same spot she had been sleeping in for the past seven and a half years. Laying down in your own bed, or in Amber's case her little nest, closing your eyes and drifting off into a peaceful slumber is the most perfect way to go I'd say. She closed her beautiful old eyes here on the farm, a place that she loved, and went to live in heaven. She went from a place of love to a place of love and you can't ask for better than that can you. No pain, no suffering, no worry, just her little old heart saying I have had enough. I've been beating for a very long time and I would like to rest. And really would you want them here in a body that was old and worn or would you want them in a new body running around heaven until you got there, once I saw it in black and white like this it made it all that bit easier to cope with. And for me there was no agonising over if I was going to keep on rescuing this time, with Horton there was but it didn't happen with Amber nor has it happened any time since and I think that's because I'd reasoned everything out in my mind all those years ago, I knew if I didn't stop back then I wasn't ever going to stop at all, well not until I am too old to do this anymore.

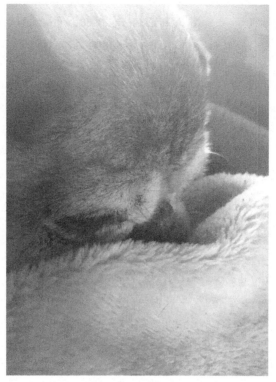

"Kissed by an Angel"

I do think Amber's body was in the early stages of shutting down when I noticed her acting unsettled that afternoon. Of course I didn't know exactly what was going on at the time but knowing what we know now that's clearly what was happening and if we hadn't taken her to the vet she still would have passed away, maybe not at that exact hour, could have been earlier could have been later but she was going no matter what we did to try and make it otherwise. I am glad we did take her to the vet though, we did at least try to see if there was something to be done. The Divine One's loss was an enormous one for us but her death wasn't just felt by David and I it was felt by people all over the world. It had a ripple effect throughout the pug community, we got some beautiful letters from people who loved and cherished Amber just as much as we did. Some of them were grieving so deeply for our special girl and wanted to know exactly what happened. So I talked about dogs dying due to just being very old, they have completely used their bodies up, it is no longer serving them anymore and so they move on to what comes next, they leave in a very peaceful way and that's how it was for The Divine One. I told them David was awake, gently stroking our daughter then her little old heart gave one last pump and she took one last breath and she was gone. It was quiet and peaceful and a beautiful way to leave this earth. The Divine One was a lovely little sweetheart who deserved a lovely departure and that's exactly what she got. I told people to try and be happy because Amber had a beautiful ending after very good innings and we, her parents, were grateful for it, grateful in every single way possible.

Another thing that helped with Amber's death was that I started thinking about her arrival in heaven and what that would have been like. I was walking the pugs round the farm about a week or so after Amber's death and suddenly my mind went back to a funeral I had attended in my youth. At that stage I hadn't attended a whole lot of funerals but I'd seen enough to know this one was different. It was the funeral of a pastor's wife, a mother of four who had died of cancer. I was around ten years old at the time but it stuck in my mind because all the other funerals I'd attended were sad ones, full of people wailing and crying, all of them the same and then suddenly here was this pastors wife being given a completely different send off. There was singing and dancing and smiling everywhere I looked. Even the immediate family were smiling. They were pleased because she was now living in heaven, people were happy for her, genuinely happy, not faking it. I know because I was watching them closely, concentrating on their faces and there wasn't even one sneaky tear trickling down the side of a cheek because they knew she was now in a wonderful place. And I guess part of the happiness would have been because she was no longer in pain. Mum knew this lady well. She'd seen the struggle up close. Never any complaining but her body showed signs of great illness. I'm not sure why my mind took me back to that place. I'd certainly not thought about it for many years yet here it was forefront in my mind as clearly as if it'd only occurred yesterday. I thought about that funeral some more as I watched the pugs milling about then my mind was once again on Amber. I doubted very much The Divine One would be up there full of sadness. I didn't see her moping around in some gloomy place with her head hanging low. No I saw her running over beautiful flower covered fields, in bright light and much colour. I felt her heart would be full of joy. I do think death is harder for us who are left behind. We are the ones who feel the pain of loss, we are the ones who are grieving, the ones who have left us have moved on to a beautiful place. I imagined The Divine One's arrival in heaven to have been a happy one. As soon as she got there I pictured her being totally surrounded by the siblings she knew and lived with, completely enveloped by them all and when those joyous greetings and times of high excitement finally settled down I imagined Amber going off to meet her other siblings, the ones she'd never met but knew she was related to because they all had the same Grace Farm Mum and Dad. I pictured their introductions to be full of excitement and enthusiasm, much chattering being done because they'd each have so many stories to tell about their time here with us. I smiled as

I walked along because I knew what a lovely experience that would have been for all of them. I also imagined Amber from time to time sitting on a cloud looking down on us all and with that sassy attitude of hers telling some of the inhabitants of heaven exactly what was going on down here.

I have since thought about the pastor's wife's funeral, since losing many loved ones of my own I can now see why that ladies family and friends were behaving like they did that day. Amber wasn't in pain when she passed, but what if somebody you loved was and then suddenly they weren't, in the blink of an eye they were healed, pain and suffering instantly taken away, well you'd be happy about that wouldn't you. I know I sure would be, of course I'd miss them terribly but I would feel peaceful that they were in a much better place, living a better life than the one they had been living in their final stages down here. So I decided to come at things from this place with Amber. Death doesn't always have to be sad. If heaven is such a magnificent place and I believe it is then why should we be sad when somebody we love goes there? Especially when they go there after living a very long life like Amber did. I felt she wouldn't want me feeling sad all the time and I don't just think it's the case with Amber I think it's what all our dogs would want for us. When people talked to me about Amber's passing and how sad they were I would share these thoughts with them. I think at the start it was a bit hard for them to take in because it wasn't what they were used to hearing but I shared my views anyway because I truly felt this was what Amber would want for everybody who loved her. She had a beautiful life but it was time to go, physical bodies don't last forever, they are not meant to, but souls do. So I carried on in the belief that The Divine One was happy where she was now residing, those were the things I was bringing to people's attention. I was going to honour her in a way I felt was right. Don't get me wrong I am not and nor will I ever be in a place where I can be rejoicing when I loose somebody I love because I miss them and want them here with me. But I then got to thinking is such a thing selfish of me? Did Amber not deserve to die of old age and go on to claim her prize of living in that truly glorious place? Well I think she did and those thoughts made me take on a different view of things and it was those things that I was going to focus on now.

Because David had to leave early for work we decided that we'd bury Amber when he got home and I was happy with that because it meant I got to be with her for a little bit longer. I moved her from the bedroom to the lounge room because that's the most central place in the house, that's where I would be spending most of that day, I'd be able to see her as I was coming and going and because we are open plan I could see her whenever I was in the kitchen too. I remember going over and stroking Amber's little old head quite a few times during the day and sometimes I'd lean down and kiss her ears or head as I walked by. She was wearing her pink stripped coat, the one I thought looked a bit like bacon, I remember thinking to myself that she had died wearing a coat that wasn't exactly a favourite. I remember standing and looking at her a lot too, long lingering gazes at the tiny body and perfect face, I wanted my mind to store that little face forever because I knew once she was in the ground she would be gone. Gone from me being able to hold her in my arms, gone from my sight too and yes there were hundreds of photos on my computer, photos I knew I'd be looking at for the rest of my life but they were not the real thing, the physical thing, they were just images. I knew that as soon as we buried The Divine One that those images would be all I had left so I lingered and I kissed and I talked to her. Being winter it was dark by the time David got home so Amber was buried by porchlight with a torch for a bit of extra light when needed, we buried her beside Billy like we had talked about doing. He was a lovely pug and I knew she would be happy being next to him. It was a cold night so I left the rest of the pugs in the house. It was only me and Dave out there. They weren't happy about not being with us, a few kept pawing at the door and the others were woofing trying to remind us that they were locked inside, I think they may have thought the door had been closed by accident but it wasn't. David lowered our little angel into the ground and positioned her then he looked up at me, shovel ready to add dirt. I think he paused in case I was going to say a few words. I shone the torch over the pink bacon coat and studied The Divine One's little old body making sure she was alright. I like them to look like they are comfortable, little legs positioned right, silly I know but it's important to me to do this. I had a bracelet on. Well it wasn't a bracelet really merely a string of leather with one small silver pug charm hanging from it. I meant to buy more charms to add but never got around to it and the little pug looked kind of lonely sitting on the kitchen table so one day I grabbed some leather from my sewing box and tied it to my wrist, the little silver pug was no longer alone I thought to myself as I headed out the door. I said to David that I wanted to tie the pug charm to Amber's coat so that she would have something of mine in there with her. He said "But you love that charm" and I said "Yeah but I love Amber more" he said he would buy me another one exactly like it so that me and Amber could be wearing the same thing. And he kept his promise too, but getting an identical one was harder than he thought because the place he got the first one from was no longer stocking them. About thirteen months after we lost Amber he came across one on eBay and bought it for me right away. Made me smile holding it in my hands, it was very special to me because I knew my little love had the exact same thing with her, it was a bit of a connection and when we lose the ones we love any kind of connection is a wonderful thing to have, it brings comfort. The scissors were inside the house and I didn't want to let the dogs out so I held out my arm to David and he broke the leather, it didn't take much because that leather had been on my wrist for quite some time and was pretty worn and thin. I looped the leather through the neck of Ambers coat and secured it. I made sure the little silver charm was sitting with its head facing the open paddock the same way Ambers little face was. We always burry them with a good view, David did it with Lilly the first pug we buried on the farm and we've been doing it with everybody since. It just seems nicer to have them facing the green hills and trees, have them looking out over the paddocks they've been wandering around every day they've been living here. The pugs inside the house were becoming really antsy by this time. David and I could hear them carrying on but we weren't for rushing, you can't, we were taking our time, we stood around talking about Amber. We were saying how blessed we felt that she came and stayed with us for seven and a half years, she didn't come and leave in less than a year or within a few years like we've had happen before. No The Divine One was with us for a long time and we were both really happy with that outcome, well more than just happy we were overjoyed. I looked down at my darling and said "Well done little mouse, very well done" both of us felt that Amber had given us everything she had in that little body of hers. She deserved a rest. We were both sad but we also had a peace about it. We talked about that and a few other things and then David started to fill in Ambers grave and as he did all the pugs broke free from the house, came flying out the door, ran along the deck, down the ramp and came racing towards us, little corkscrew tails wagging like crazy, going completely ballistic jumping up and greeting us. Some of them were screaming too, screamed when the door first opened and screamed even more when they reached our side, they all seemed incredibly pleased with themselves for being able to escape. But we knew it wasn't all of them that had done this, we knew it was all Ava Lindy Lou's doing, she was the one who'd broken everybody out. Being able to slide the glass door open was one of her tricks and thinking back I'm amazed it took her as long as it did to make the escape. But maybe she wasn't in the right spot to open the door, maybe some of the other pugs had been blocking her way, she had to be in the right position to pull this stunt off and I guess as soon as she was able to she let everybody out. It was nice seeing them all come flying out towards us, the image made me smile through my tears, perhaps they wanted to say goodbye to their sister too. And we would have let them do that later on but I suppose they wanted to be with us right now, doing everything as a family like we normally would do. They had no idea I was protecting them from the cold. But I don't think they got too cold that night, they were keeping themselves warm by dancing around. We started laughing at them and we were especially laughing at Ava Lindy Lou because she looked like she was incredibly proud of herself the way she came skimming across the deck. Fast, giddy with excitement, looked like her little paws were barely touching the ground. She was the last pug to make it outside because to slide the door across she had to push on the other side so the pugs that were standing at the part of the door that was opening got to race out first.

After Amber's grave was secured we all went inside and did our normal nightly routine but it didn't seem quite right with The Divine One not being there with us, it never does, it takes some time to get used to them no longer being by your side. Later that night I crept outside by myself and stood beside Amber's grave talking to her, thanking her for everything she had given me, the joy she brought to my life, told her over and over her how much she had blessed me. I believe she already knew but I just wanted to go out and tell her again. I stood there in the cold, hands shoved deep inside my pockets, coat collar pulled up as high as I could get it, after a while my nose and cheeks felt like ice but I didn't care I wanted to be out there with my little girl. I stared up at the stars and thought about our life together. I knew Amber was not in the ground by my feet, well her earthly body was yes but I knew that she was up there now just beyond the stars. I guess that's why I had my head tilted up looking at the night sky as images of our time together went racing through my head. I thanked Amber for so many things that night and not just that night but all throughout the day as I passed by her tiny body. I had spent the last seven and a half years thanking her too, I'm the kind of person who if I feel something I have to say it so I was often whispering words of gratitude into those little ears of hers. I was grateful to Amber for a whole lot of things. She entered my life when I was the most broken I have ever been. It was like this little old scuffed up paw reached out to me and brought me back from a very sad and heartbreaking place. People said I saved her but the reality was that she saved me. Yes, I was in a state with the loss of Horton but who knows what kind of worse state I would have been in if it wasn't for Amber. I thought she needed me and in a way she did, but as it happened I needed The Divine One a whole lot more. She helped me heal, I believe a lot faster than I would have done without her. The pugs that lived with Horton, well, I had their routine down pat. I could care for them without even thinking about what I was doing because I was so used to doing it, but with Amber everything was new. I had to figure out why she walked the way she did and I had to work out how best to help her, how best to build her strength and body up. She needed a lot of time and thought put into her and I was the one who had to do it. I was now her mum. She needed me to be there for her so that's what I did. I grieved for Horton, took care of my other pugs and worked on helping Amber heal and feel safe in her new home. She became a big priority. It had to be that way because it would have been unfair of me to bring an old pug into my home and not give her the love and attention she deserved. I wouldn't have been being true to myself if I had made her wait until I was feeling better before taking care of all her needs. Amber is special to me for a whole lot of reasons and the precise time she entered my life is just one of them. Eyes fixated on the stars I thanked Amber for her outpouring of love and I thanked her for putting her trust in me when she first got here. I thanked her for the laughs, of which there were so many. I thanked her for battling on when she could well have given up. I told her that she taught me something huge by doing that. I also talked about the happiness I felt at being able to be her mother. The wind was now starting up making an already cold night even colder but I stood there regardless. I talked to Amber about those character traits of hers that I loved so much, her many little unique mannerisms. I mentioned her facial expressions too. With The Divine One there was nothing but total and complete happiness from the moment I first glanced at her photo. My heart was bursting with gratitude towards this little soul. I also thought about how she'd ended up coming to live with us. Being in that pound and almost blind would have been awful for her, she would have been terrified, wouldn't have known what she'd done wrong to have landed in such a place and of course the answer to that question is she'd done nothing "Absolutely nothing at all" but she didn't know that. I truly believe that Amber had always been divine, been divine since birth, but clearly her divineness wasn't recognised by her previous owners. If it had been they wouldn't have put her in the pound. I used to think about the people who dumped this little old girl, nine years old and tiny, she had a bad back and was almost fully blind and yet somebody still thought dropping her off at the pound was an ok thing to do. One thing I am very happy about was that Amber could walk. Yes her back was bad but she was at least still able to walk. And I'm glad because if she couldn't I think she would never have made it out of that pound, she would have been simply put to sleep because pounds overflow and an old dog that couldn't walk in their eyes would have no chance of ever getting a home. I thanked Amber for everything one more time before going back inside the house. David was in the kitchen making a cup of tea, he asked where I'd been, I think he thought I'd gone down to check on the horses. "Just talking to Amber Blossom Bug" I replied then went and stood by the fire for the longest time trying to get some warmth back into my body. I had the pugs doing circles around my feet then running into the kitchen to see what David was up to. I think they were hoping some type of food was going to accompany that cup of tea. It didn't but they didn't seem all that disappointed merely kept scurrying from one parent to the other in an excitable manner. I watched as they came and went and felt blessed. Felt deeply appreciative of my little family. Thankful that I was living the life I am, grateful that I got to care for all these little blessings. I had just lost one who was so special to me and I knew it was going to take a long time to recover from that loss, get used to going about my days without her by my side, but I had a feeling that she was always going to be with me, part of me, a little face peeping over my shoulder watching everything I was doing for the rest of my life.

As I come to the end of this chapter it's been three years since we lost Amber and she does cross my mind an awful lot and I knew she would and when she does I smile on remembering her and all that she was and it is a nice place to be in. I will be forever grateful that when I saw her little face I chose to act, because how different and lesser would my life have been if I'd simply turned and walked away from the computer that day. I'm glad that in amongst everything else I was feeling at the time that I chose to follow my heart because in doing so it lead me to one of the most special beautiful loves and one of the most meaningful relationships I have ever had in my life. My time with Amber was precious and wonderful and joyous. I'd do it all over again if I could, in a heartbeat I would and I wouldn't say that this time I'll take my time and savour every moment because I feel that I did this the first time round. I feel I do this with all of my pugs, it's a lesson I learnt many years ago, they are only with you for a short amount of time, it pays to live in the moment, to stop and enjoy each second they are by your side. I began slowly, very slowly, writing this book a couple of months after I lost Amber and instead of being sad I found myself really looking forward to the project because I knew I was beginning to tell the story of a winner. A complete and utter little champion because that is exactly what The Divine One was. Amber won, "SHE WON" she wasn't well at times, she suffered from things and yet she still went on to reach this remarkable age. A heck of a lot of dogs don't make it to 16 and a half and yet this little blessing did. I'm not saying I never had any sad days, sure I had sad days, this was no light-hearted project for me. I knew I would not be getting off scot free. I knew I'd be feeling every single emotion under the sun, feeling them deeply too but I was still more full of joy and anticipation than I was anything else. On the hard days of missing her I didn't engage. I'd go off and do something else because I didn't want to be bringing those feelings into her story, didn't want the sadness I was experiencing in that moment reflected in these pages. So me and the pugs would go off and I'd do some chores around the farm then come back a day or two later and start typing again. I guess to some it would look like I wasn't hurting because I wasn't talking about that, but I wanted to keep Amber's story uplifting as a way of honouring her and all that she was because the biggest part of The Divine One's life here was inspiring and I enjoyed reliving those moments again as I was typing. That's why I'd stop and clap. I just had to give Amber a much deserved round of applause, there were many, many days when I was so terribly proud of her that my hands were off the keyboard and in the air before I even realised what I was doing. I'd be thinking to myself "You little beauty, you little star, look at what you did, look at all you achieved darling, look at how fantastic you were" and really about 95% of this book was like that, written with a heart full to the brim of love and pride. Certainly Amber did a lot more than either David or I expected her too and that's what I was excited to tell everybody about. A lot of the time while I was writing memories kept coming to me, things I hadn't thought about in years, things I had almost forgotten about, in a way it was like I had this little pug angel on my shoulder constantly whispering into my ear saying "Remember to tell them this or don't forget to tell them that" and when I told you I reckon Amber was up there clapping her little paws together with glee. I remember the day I told David I was going to give Amber an entire book. He said "Ok" then he asked how many pages I thought her book was going to be, just making conversation I think because how long a book is or isn't is neither here nor there to him, he just does what I call de-dyslexifying the books before they get sent off to the other proof readers. He is the only person I trust to do this and if it wasn't for my husband I don't think I would have the confidence to put any of my books out there. Anyway I had Nemo on my knee when he asked the question. I was happily massaging his shoulders and looked up and said "175 pages" in a rather matter of fact way. At that Dave's mouth crinkled into a smile. He said "Oh so not 174 or 176 pages, definitely 175" I think he was teasing me a little because of the way I was being so precise. I don't know what made me pull that figure out of thin air but I think Amber's little ears heard what I said and she had other ideas. Not so long ago I was telling somebody this story and their response was that there was no way you could fit a personality as big as the one Amber had into just 175 pages. They then asked me how long the book was and when I told them they said "Well now that's more like it".

Over the last few years I have often wondered what Amber's previous family would have thought about her living to 16 and a half, of course we will never know the exact path that lead her to the pound in the first place but if they did think she was old at nine you wonder what they would have thought about her living to the wonderful age she did. Yes she had a few health issues, issues that would flare up from time to time throughout her life. But with some tender loving care, a routine of wellness that couldn't be strayed from and a good vet she went on to live a very long life and I bet they never expected she'd be able to do that. Or maybe they wouldn't care that she did, perhaps they weren't the kind of people who wanted to take care of an old dog, but I tell you what they really missed out on a fantastic experience here because Amber was an amazing little being and I'm glad it was us who got to have her with us each day of those seven and a half years, she blessed us in every single way possible. She was a one in a million pug, an incredible soul. And we got her, we got to be the ones who had her blessing us in all the ways that she did and grateful doesn't even come close to describing how I feel about that. When I finished writing this book I sat and clapped then spun round and round in my office chair and clapped some more, I clapped for The Divine One and how wonderful she was, I applauded the length of time we were granted with her, I clapped because I was so blessed to have had it. The Divine One was feisty and she was spirited, she was smart and she was courageous, she was sweet and she was serene, she was beauty and grace, she was everything rolled up into a little ball of loveliness and this is exactly how I am going to remember Amber. I am always going to smile and thank god and be grateful upon every remembrance of her. Because God bless my little Divine One, God bless her.

CHAPTER TWENTY ONE

A Glimpse Of Heaven

A Glimpse of Heaven was a piece I wrote when informing everybody that we had lost Amber. I had great empathy for those who were about to find out that The Divine One was gone. I knew exactly how Amber's aunties and uncles would be feeling and my heart went out to them. They loved her very deeply so I knew I was about to shatter a whole lot of hearts and you never want to be doing that do you. I had tears in my eyes at the thought of people reading our news. But I also knew that we would all be united in our grief and would be a comfort to one another. I actually really love A Glimpse of Heaven. I haven't read it for a long time but rereading it again now makes me proud. I'm so glad I wrote it, as hard as it was to write at the time I am glad I persevered because it means a lot to me. It is exactly what I think heaven is like, how I envision it and it's exactly what I imagine happening when one of our loved ones leaves our side. I felt it was therapeutic for me and I know it helped other people too because they wrote and told me so. It seemed to find its way to people who needed it the most and I was grateful for that. Some said they felt it was like one of their canine family members who had passed away was speaking directly to them. A Glimpse of Heaven has been shared many times over the years, it has been passed on to folks who needed it the most and I am grateful for that too. The thought of bringing even a slither of contentment to a broken heart does make me happy. People seemed to benefit from it for a lot of different reasons. It spoke to them in the ways they needed it to. I believe an animal's arrival in heaven to be a very beautiful experience. No matter what age the animal is or how they passed I firmly believe that they cross over to the most wonderful place and when they do there is much rejoicing being done and many arms spread wide open to welcome them. I read a poem many years ago about old dogs being made to sit outside heaven because they weren't allowed through the pearly gates. They were dogs that had been abandoned on earth. Well this poem made me sad but it also made me angry and I was so disappointed because I do not think for one second this kind of thing would be happening. Why would God ban innocent pure hearted animal's access to a place he created for them, especially after the way they had been treated on earth? He would know how much those little hearts would be hurting, that they would have felt a huge amount of rejection during their lives. So why would he make them go through it all over again and the answer to that is he would not. I believe this poem was written by somebody wanting to give a nod to all the rescuers out there because it went on to say that the dogs eventually got to go inside when escorted by their rescuer. And yes I am very grateful for all those people in the world who rescue and look after unwanted animals, I have the highest regard for them because I know how hard they work and how much they love the animals in their care. But I also believe that none of them would want those animals waiting outside heaven until they got there, no they'd want them to be inside enjoying themselves, being healed and feeling loved. No true rescuer would consider themselves more important than the dogs. I think the poem fell short in capturing a true rescuers heart because if you truly love animals then you would want the very best for them and being denied access to heaven for any length of time is definitely not that. I cannot imagine anything more heartbreaking than a dog that's been rejected in life being rejected by heaven. To me it would be a double dose of rejection. Rejection and abandonment on earth and rejection once they pass away and I do not believe God would ever allow that to happen so I wrote things a different way, the way I firmly believe it is. I think there will be a whole lot of animals waiting to greet any rescuer who passes over but they will be doing it from inside the pearly gates. And when those huge gates are flung open to reveal that all too familiar face a whole lot of animals will stop what they are doing and come running from all over the place because that to me is a proper and more fitting greeting for an animal rescuer. I also wanted to talk about how it was for puppies that enter heaven, for those little souls whose lives ended before they even had time to begin. I imagine babies of any species will be given the most glorious welcome once they get to heaven and much attention will be given, there will be lines full of souls wanting to play ball or sing a nursery rhyme. People thanked me for giving them a picture of heaven and what it would be like for the dogs they had lost. Some said it was Amber herself who had given me this gift of words, that she had guided me through it. And they could be right because it was written on one of the saddest days of my life and yet it was written with such speed and clarity, it simply flowed, so perhaps there was a tiny pug angel sitting on my shoulder with her little tongue peeping out as she whispered in my ear. I chose the most beautiful photo of Amber to go with A Glimpse of Heaven. A photo of her little face smiling, it was what I considered a really gorgeous photo of her. It was a quick shot taken of Amber on the grass with her siblings, she was looking up at me and her mouth was slightly open, like she was smiling for the camera. I was feeding them all a treat on a glorious sunny day, a very happy time to take a photo, a perfect moment of joy really and all of that was captured so well on that little face of hers. So when I was looking for a photo to go with the post I knew there was no more perfect one than this.

A GLIMPSE OF HEAVEN

This will be my last post because you see I am living in heaven now and it is the most beautiful place you ever saw and the wonderful thing is that I can see it so very clearly now since my sight has been restored. I can see acres and acres of rich green grass and hills that go on for miles and miles. There are trees and lakes and I can hear a light breeze rustling through the leaves and the water in every lake is sparkling. There are flowers of every colour and description and rainbows too and I can see them all with my own little eyes. And I gaze at everything in wonder. Colours are more beautiful than I ever remember them being.

There are animals everywhere, all types of animals up here, lovely big animals lay beside tiny little animals and nobody gets stepped on or hurt in any way at all. This morning I spent an hour sleeping with my head resting on a big lions paw and it was so soft and comfortable and he licked my little face when I woke up. There are birds flying through the air chirping happily but they are not the only animal noises I can hear. All the animals are making their own unique joyful sounds, they all blend in so beautifully together it's like they are being conducted, they sound like a symphony orchestra, everybody is having a little sing, I may even join in with them myself later on.

Oh and there are no old abandoned dogs sitting waiting by the gate, waiting to be allowed in. Somebody down there on earth once said that's how it is but I'm telling you they got it very wrong because it isn't like that at all, no, the gates are immediately flung open for all of God's creatures. And the dogs and cats who were dropped off at the pound by their owners, who were dragged down the middle of the pens by their collars and never seen again well there is a very special welcome up here for them. Trumpets play and all the animals rush to the gates to welcome the little heroes in, they are hoisted up and carried on shoulders and much cheering and clapping can be heard. And the loudest clappers and cheerers are the dogs who were bought as puppies and lived in the family home their entire lives, they can't help but be loud because they know how lucky they were and how unfair life has been to these other dogs. And a huge fuss is also made of the dogs that were given up by their owners because they became old and were no longer considered beautiful or were considered too hard to look after, well lines are formed and they are given a hero's welcome and salute. Because everybody here knows the heartache they felt when they were given up on, they all know how hard it was at times for them to settle into new homes and allow their hearts to heal, but they did it, they adjusted and that is why such a fuss is made and that is why they are considered heroes. And when puppies arrive here nursery rhymes are played and squeaky toys are sought and little soft balls thrown and those little baby faces are smothered in kisses.

But what I think is really wonderful is seeing those dogs that were ill come limping and staggering towards the gate, some have limbs missing, some have growths still attached. But they come and they come ever so slowly towards the gate, some pause and wait for others to catch up, and then two or more frail bodies carry on along the path together, as they grow nearer soft music starts playing and two huge doors begin to open up and a bright light shines. There is a line on the ground and as they step over that line growths disappear and limbs reappear, steps are quickened and again a huge round of applause starts up, thunderous cheering and clapping and howls of support.

And there is little sixteen and a half year old me, The Divine One, standing in amongst it all. I like heaven. I think I'm going to be happy living up here. I've already met some of my brothers and sisters that I didn't get to live with there on earth. I recognised them immediately because they had an aura of specialness around them, a specialness of love that only our parents can give and we are drawn to each other because of it. Other dogs are the same here, they too have found their family members by being drawn to their own unique aura.

And one day I know my Mummy and Daddy are going to join us all up here and we will live together forever, it may be this afternoon that they come or it could be tomorrow, time is so different here in heaven than it is down there on earth. I know for me it won't be long but for them it will be. And while they are waiting to be reunited with us all, while they are down there living all the years they've been granted I know they will be spending their days taking in other dogs and looking after them. Lonely old dogs who found themselves being abandoned just like I did. Mummy and Daddy took me in when I was nine years old and I had the most wonderful life with them. Seven and a half lovely years of being loved and wanted and so well cared for, I even slept on their bed. And I am happy that they will be giving some other needy soul that same kind of deep love and tender care that they have given me. I know it won't be a puppy I know they will honour my life by adopting an oldie and giving it a chance, the same chance they gave me when I needed it the most. I know one day soon another dog will be wearing my coat, sleeping in my bed and eating from my bowl and I am ok with that, in fact it's how I want it to be. I am here, I am safe, there is no more they can do for me now but they can help one of my elderly canine brethren and I'm happy and very proud of them for doing that. It does not mean they love me any less, it does not mean the other dog is going to take my place in their heart because I know I will always have a special place there. But their hearts are big enough to let another old dog in. There's plenty of room for all of us in those two huge caring hearts and I see no reason at all why another dog shouldn't benefit from them.

So as my last post draws to an end I want to thank you all for following my posts and becoming my Face Book family. I treasure each and every one of my special Aunties and Uncles. I also want to remind all of you that life is so short and it's even shorter for us in the animal kingdom. I encourage all of you folks to be kind to people and even kinder still to the animals of this world. Have a soft heart towards us because we really need it. And seeing as I see myself as a bit of a champion for the oldies, I ask you to think about me The Divine One and make your next family member a senior, please don't leave us sitting in the pound just because our faces have turned grey and we walk a little slower then we used to. Please take us home and love us and give us the care we deserve. That's about all I have to say for now so I'll end by saying take care of yourself and when you find yourself on the other side of the clouds why not look me up. I'll more than likely be running across the hilltops with my friends or rolling in the long lush green grass, or seeing as I was blind for over half my life there on earth I could be standing around gazing at all the beautiful colourful things up here or I could even be sleeping once again on that lions huge paw but please feel free to wake me up because I'll be more than happy to give you a tour around this incredible place.

I love you all,

The Divine One

xxxx

Thanks for everything Mummy and Daddy I had the most wonderful time living with everybody at Grace Farm.

"Da End"

ABOUT THE AUTHOR

Andrea Comer is an Australian author with a talent for being able to tell a story as though you are actually standing right beside her seeing exactly what she is seeing. She has the ability to take you onto Grace Farm with her, making you feel that you are part of her magical life, caring for and loving her beloved animals. Andrea's books have been read and loved by people all over the world. Her first book The Joy of Horton was published in 2016 and she has gone on to write more books since then and is still writing. Andrea was born in the United Kingdom and migrated to Australia when she was six years old. From a very young age she became aware of the way animals were treated in this world and vowed that one day she would create a place where elderly animals could live out their natural lifespan without knowing fear, feeling pain or enduring suffering. Andrea lives with her husband and a cloud of elderly pugs, sheep and horses. Her days are spent taking care of her large four legged family, but sometimes in the late afternoon when the pugs are sleeping she has time to write.

Books by this author

The Joy of Horton	ISBN 978-0-9953904-0-9
The Divine One	ISBN 978-0-9953904-5-4
Grace Farm - Senior Pug Sanctuary	ISBN 978-0-9953904-1-6
Grace Farm - Always and Forever	ISBN 978-0-9953904-3-0

Made in the USA
Las Vegas, NV
05 November 2022